TOM LAWSON is Professor of History at Northumbria University. He is the author of *Debates on the Holocaust* and *The Church of England and the Holocaust: Christianity, Memory and Nazism*.

THE LAST MAN
A British Genocide in Tasmania

Tom Lawson

BLOOMSBURY ACADEMIC
LONDON • NEW YORK • OXFORD • NEW DELHI • SYDNEY

BLOOMSBURY ACADEMIC
Bloomsbury Publishing Plc
50 Bedford Square, London, WC1B 3DP, UK
1385 Broadway, New York, NY 10018, USA
29 Earlsfort Terrace, Dublin 2, Ireland

BLOOMSBURY, BLOOMSBURY ACADEMIC and the Diana logo
are trademarks of Bloomsbury Publishing Plc

First published in Great Britain 2014 by I. B. Tauris
This paperback edition published in 2021

Copyright © Tom Lawson, 2014

Tom Lawson has asserted his right under the Copyright,
Designs and Patents Act, 1988, to be identified as Author of this work.

For legal purposes the Acknowledgements on p. xi constitute
an extension of this copyright page.

All rights reserved. No part of this publication may be reproduced or
transmitted in any form or by any means, electronic or mechanical,
including photocopying, recording, or any information storage or retrieval
system, without prior permission in writing from the publishers.

Bloomsbury Publishing Plc does not have any control over, or responsibility for,
any third-party websites referred to or in this book. All internet addresses given
in this book were correct at the time of going to press. The author and publisher
regret any inconvenience caused if addresses have changed or sites have
ceased to exist, but can accept no responsibility for any such changes.

A catalogue record for this book is available from the British Library.

A catalog record for this book is available from the Library of Congress.

ISBN: HB: 978 1 7807 6626 3
PB: 978 1 3502 2791 0

Typeset by Tetragon, London

To find out more about our authors and books visit
www.bloomsbury.com and sign up for our newsletters.

For Arthur and Florence

in memory of Doug Robinson

CONTENTS

LIST OF PLATES	IX
ACKNOWLEDGEMENTS TO THE 2014 EDITION	XI
PREFACE TO THE PAPERBACK EDITION	XV
INTRODUCTION *From Thinking about Britain and the Holocaust to Writing about Genocide in the British World*	XXI
ONE *Defining Terms*	1
TWO *Genocide in Van Diemen's Land*	29
THREE *Ethnic Cleansing*	69
FOUR *Cultural Genocide*	91
FIVE *'We have exterminated the race in Van Diemen's Land': Genocide in British Culture*	127
SIX *Coming to Terms with the Past?*	173
CONCLUSION *A British Genocide in Tasmania*	203
NOTES	211
BIBLIOGRAPHY	245
INDEX	259

LIST OF PLATES

1. Gov. Arthur's Proclamation to the Tasmanian Peoples, 1830. © Peabody Museum
2. *My Harvest Home* by John Glover © Tasmanian Museum & Art Gallery
3. *A Corrobery of Natives in Mills Plains* by John Glover © Art Gallery of South Australia
4. *Mount Wellington and Hobart Town from Kangaroo Point* by John Glover © National Gallery of Australia
5. Truganini Necklace from Exeter Museum (courtesy of the Royal Albert Memorial Museum and Exeter City Council)
6. George Augustus Robinson's grave (author's photo)
7. *Natives at a Corrobory*, under the wild woods of the Country [River Jordan below Brighton, Tasmania], ca. 1835 / John Glover © Mitchell Library. State Library of NSW – ML 154
8. *The Conciliation* by Benjamin Duterreau © Tasmanian Museum & Art Gallery

ACKNOWLEDGEMENTS TO THE 2014 EDITION

I am writing these acknowledgements on Flinders Island, as part of an ongoing research project into how the events described in this book are remembered. It is extraordinarily beautiful and utterly peaceful. It has certainly aided my understanding of the subject. While it is a wonderfully tranquil, indeed serene, place, I also feel rather uneasy here. I am as far from home as I have ever been. My mobile phone does not work and the place where I am staying has no internet connection. I feel somehow displaced and disconnected – too far away from the places and people I love. In some senses, I am, I guess, afraid. While this is a very modern, and utterly self-indulgent, form of fear, I feel it nonetheless. I wonder how far some of the violence that is described in this book was born of a much more profound fear, a sense of disconnection and displacement in a world in which the physical and temporal distances from home were so much greater.

The peace of Flinders Island also enables me to reflect on the various debts I have accumulated in the research and writing of this book. It was entirely written while I was at the University of Winchester, an institution I leave next month, after 11 years. I owe many people there a great deal. It has been a privilege to work with and for Kris Spelman Miller over the past four years, and her support for me and for this project has been crucial. I am similarly grateful to Liz Stuart. In the History department there have been difficult times, but Mark Allen and Colin Haydon have always provided friendly counsel. As did Neil Murphy, in whose office the title of this book was first articulated. Thanks also to Neil Messer and Jo Pearson, who helped me in drafting the application that secured a British Academy Mid-Career

Fellowship in support of this project. I was very proud of this award, and my thanks go to the British Academy for the faith shown in me.

As you will read in the book itself, this project really began with an edited collection titled *The Memory of the Holocaust in Australia*. I am especially grateful to my co-editor on that book, James Jordan. Not only is James a great colleague in all that we do together but he is also a good friend. I would not have made my first long trip to Australia without James and as such would probably never have embarked on this research at all. It was also with James that I met for the first time a group of people in Australia who have been incredibly warm and welcoming on each of my subsequent visits, and whose friendship it has been a pleasure and a privilege to enjoy. Suzanne Rutland, Konrad Kwiet, Mariela Sztrum and in particular Avril Alba have sustained me with their company on numerous occasions – on every one of which I have laughed more than anyone can reasonably expect to. I am especially grateful to Avril, who has become a good friend. Our apparently unending culinary tour of Sydney has been great fun.

Ann Curthoys and John Docker have also both offered good company and critical support. Dirk Moses and Damien Short equally provided crucial advice at important moments, as has Donald Bloxham. I am also very grateful to scholars whom I have never met, but without whom this project would have been impossible. I am thinking here especially of Lyndall Ryan and Henry Reynolds.

Many thanks to all of the people who have shown me round archives, and who have taken the time and trouble to discuss the project with me and locate records for it. Len Pole at Saffron Walden and Tony Eccles at the Royal Albert Memorial Museum in Exeter were especially helpful. Thanks also to Margaret Clegg at the Natural History Museum and to the University of Edinburgh for providing important material and perspectives for the chapter on the return of human remains. Thanks also to Patrick Scarff who worked as a research assistant at the very outset.

I am very grateful to the anonymous referees for their critical appraisal of the original manuscript – it is much better for that process.

Acknowledgements to the 2014 edition

At I.B.Tauris Jo Godfrey has been supportive throughout and Alex Middleton has been a genuinely brilliant copy-editor. Thanks also to my dad for reading through the manuscript. As ever any remaining mistakes are all mine.

Thanks to Tony Kushner and all the rest of the Cavaliers, and to Simon Payling, whose company has made watching Arsenal more pleasurable than it might have been over the last few years.

And finally, to my family – no amount of thanks is enough. My wife, Elisa, has provided the space for me to write this book, and has brought up our children while I did so. Thank you, my love. Thanks also to all of those people who help Elisa with the children, especially when I am away, particularly her mum, Arlene Robinson, my mum, Linda Lawson, Judith Payling, Richard Levett and Vic Nicholas.

This book is dedicated to my children, Arthur and Florence. I am sorry that I have been away so much and so often over the last few years, and that I have been so grumpy when I have been at home but have been working. I love you both with all of my heart and I hope you will be pleased to see your names at the front of this book. Perhaps one day you will read it.

The book is also dedicated to the memory of my father-in-law, Doug Robinson. Doug died after a short but incredibly brutal illness at the beginning of 2011. He is greatly missed. It is a source of enduring sadness for me that Arthur and Florence will not have the privilege of knowing him as they grow up. For my part, I will make every effort to ensure that they remember him as he was: their wonderful granddad.

PREFACE TO THE PAPERBACK EDITION

This book was first published in 2014, which especially after the tumultuous events of 2020 feels like a very long time ago. While I hope the book has stood the test of time, it is clear that in some important ways the context in which it might be read has changed a good deal. First, the historiography of Aboriginal Tasmanian dispossession and destruction is rather more voluminous than it was; and second (and much more importantly) public engagement with the history of violence in the British empire has been transformed (at least superficially) by the Black Lives Matter protests of the summer of 2020.

The death of George Floyd at the hands of an American policeman sparked worldwide protests for racial justice under the umbrella of the Black Lives Matter movement. In Britain one consequence of the protests was to turn attention to the past and particularly public spaces in which the past was commemorated. In Bristol the statue of local benefactor and philanthropist (and more importantly slave trader) Edward Colston was pulled down by a crowd. The presence of his statue had long been controversial, out of step with a modern multi-racial city. Its removal sparked a noisy if not very enlightening debate about the presence of especially slavery in public narratives about the past in Britain. In Australia protests similarly led people to public spaces of commemoration, for example crowds gathering in Hyde Park in Sydney where there are several statues commemorating figures directly implicated in Aboriginal dispossession.

What is at stake in these debates is not the past itself, but our society's relationship with the past. In public in Britain at least they are a continuation of the Brexit culture wars, where imperial nostalgia accompanied an ultimately victorious campaign to the leave the European Union. That nostalgia sought to celebrate the British past and especially its martial glories – including the construction of empire.

The Last Man

The protestors who pulled down Edward Colston's statue rejected that nostalgia because it obscured the victims of those glories, and in the case of empire especially – the enslaved. The rights and wrongs of that debate are not our concern here – but it is notable that within them it is slavery that has become the totemic crime of empire. When the National Trust reviewed its properties for example it is those with links to the slave trade that were most prominent.[1] When the Mayor of London announced a commission to investigate the diversity of London's memorial landscape – the statues of slave owners were the first to be removed. There are many reasons for this, not least the sheer scale of the contribution that the slave trade made to the British economy and its modernisation. But of course more troublingly, slavery is comparatively safe terrain for a debate about the sins of the British past because apologists can immediately point to slavery's abolition as somehow compensation for the original sin of exploitation and murder. This is the most woolly of thinking but it remains prominent in public debates – see for example the logic inherent in this sentence: 'While some Britons traded slaves and ran slave plantations from the early 1600s, a penitent British parliament decided to abolish first the slave trade in 1807, and then slavery throughout the British Empire in 1833.'[2]

Despite the wishes of some commentators, the violence of empire is not washed away by the abolition of either the slave trade or slavery itself. This is not just morally true (self-evidently bringing a crime to an end is not moral compensation for committing it in the first instance) but it is true in historical terms too, because the violence of empire was not confined to slavery. The dispossession, murder, deportation and cultural destruction of Indigenous Tasmania described in this book almost wholly took place *after* abolition. Indeed some of the protagonists in the violence you will read about here campaigned to bring slavery to an end. George Arthur, Lieutenant-Governor of Van Diemen's Land throughout the period of the most intense campaigns against the Indigenous community, whom Nick Brodie has recently argued deliberately sought Tasmanian Aborigines wholesale destruction, was a committed abolitionist during his tenure as Superintendent of British Honduras.[3]

Even when the violence of empire is at the forefront of public consciousness and debate then, the form of imperial violence investigated in this book – genocide – remains obscured. While

Preface to the Paperback Edition

the destruction of peoples is commonly (most notably through Holocaust Memorial Day) identified as the ultimate transgression in modern Britain, its perpetration is not assumed to be part of British history. I am writing this preface as the public inquiry into the building of a Holocaust memorial next to the Houses of Parliament meets. The proposed memorial is to be built in Victoria Gardens. In 2007 the Royal Parks authority rejected Victoria Gardens as a proposed site for a memorial to the victims of slavery, but if the planning application is approved it will instead house a Holocaust memorial and learning centre from 2021. In our contemporary memory Olympics the Holocaust trumps all, and in this example clearly replaces even slavery in London's memorial landscape (although the Holocaust memorial will stand next to the memorial to the abolitionist Thomas Fowell Buxton whom you will also read about in this book). What is certain is that if built the Holocaust memorial and learning centre will make no mention of the genocides exported by the Mother of parliaments it stands next to. While genocide will be an acknowledged part of the British story in the memorial, and the degree to which our society has been enriched by Holocaust survivors for example will be brought to public attention, the destruction of peoples will be presented as something external to that British story.

And yet as this book argues such a view is historically illiterate. Genocide is a part of the story of the British empire and what is more its traces can be found in Britain today – not much more buried than the links to slavers and slavery that 2020 has brought to the fore. Edward Colston's statue in Bristol was not far from the grave of George Augustus Robinson, whom is commemorated in Bath Abbey Cemetery as the 'Pacificator of Tasmanian Aborigines'. Robinson was the central settler figure in the removal of the Indigenous Tasmanian population in the 1830s and you will read much about him in the pages that follow – but he remains an oddity and is not well known in Britain at all.

But perhaps more importantly for the contemporary debate about how we live with the violence of the British past, Robinson's grave is just one example of the ghosts and echoes of genocide in Tasmania that are set within the British landscape or which have been displayed in British museums. More of those links have become evident to me since the book was published. Rebe Taylor's brilliant *Into the Heart of Tasmania* demonstrates some of those through her investigation of the work and life of Ernest Westlake and the lives and deaths of Indigenous Tasmanians that he encountered at the beginning of the twentieth-century – these include Westlake's store of Aboriginal stone tools at Sandy Balls Camping park in Dorset.[4]

Taylor's book is one of a number that have sought to emphasise Indigenous Tasmanians agency in the shaping of their history that have been published since *The Last Man* was completed. Others include Murray Johnson and Ian McFarlane's *Van Diemen's Land* and Leonie Stevens history of the Aboriginal community at Wybalenna on Flinders Island *'Me Write Myself'* and most recently Cassandra Pybus brilliant study of *Truganini*.[5] All of these works, but especially Taylor's, have challenged me to think about the central idea around which this work revolves, that the destruction of the Tasmanian Aboriginal population, its culture and its communities was a case of genocide, carried out by British men, shaped by British ideologies and then incorporated into British identity.

The idea that what the British unleashed on Van Diemen's Land was genocide is controversial, as is the application of the concept to Australian history more broadly.[6] It is particularly difficult in relation to Tasmania because of the pernicious myth of Indigenous Tasmanian's extinction at British hands. This narrative alleges that *all* Indigenous Tasmanians were destroyed and was used to deny the existence of an enduring Tasmanian Aboriginal community throughout much of the 20th century. The concept of genocide, the idea of extermination as it were, has often become confused with the idea of extinction and as such it is possible to argue that the identification of genocide is just another way of targeting Indigenous Tasmanians and of denying their voices in the telling of their history. Certainly other books written about colonial violence in Tasmania have eschewed the concept precisely for this reason and in order to highlight that Indigenous Tasmanians were not just the passive victims of British might. Nicholas Clements *The Black War* is an example of this tradition of historical investigation published since this book was first written.[7] And reviewers of this book have repeated the mistake when criticising it for attempting to say something more general about the British empire. For example Bernard Porter argued

Preface to the Paperback Edition

that in other colonies where 'the indigenes were powerful enough to resist' no genocide occurred.[8]

The idea that genocide suggests only the passivity and surrender of the victims is a misreading of the concept in the first instance, and I remain convinced of its conceptual utility in this case. Nick Brodie has gone even further than myself and argued that genocide was not just the product of the logic of British colonial policies but the avowed intention of policy makers on the ground in Tasmania. Readers will need to make up their own mind, but to my mind it is only the historical (as opposed to purely legal) concept of genocide that captures the extent of the destruction that the British wrought in Van Diemen's Land.

I hope that *The Last Man* will be read in the context of our contemporary angst about who we are in Britain and how we tell or national story. Our history contains much of which contemporary Britons might be proud, but it contains many dark corners or chapters which we equally need to confront because those dark pasts shaped our present too. And the story told here is one of those. It is a story of destruction and dispossession, but it is also an account of how Britain mastered that past and came to tell itself an ultimately rather comforting story about its export of violence to the other side of the world.

As I have said I am writing this preface at the end of 2020. The future is at this point radically uncertain. We are, in the North of England, it appears still in the grip of the Covid 19 pandemic and are struggling to face up to the challenges that this poses. As Universities have discovered, our institutions are going to have to change quite profoundly in order to overcome these difficulties. But if the future is uncertain, so is the past. What are the stories we are going to tell ourselves about our country? *The Last Man* is just one of those stories and an account of the ways in which it has survived (and not) into the present. How we deal with stories like these, like how we deal with the legacies of slavery, is a fundamental question about who we want to be. For my part, I want to live in a country that can confront its past in all of its manifold complexity. *The Last Man* is in essence an account of how not to do that.

Morpeth, October 2020

Notes

1. Sally Anne Huxtable, Corinne Fowler, Christi Kefalas, Emma Slocombe (eds), *Interim Report on the Connections between Colonialism and Properties now in the Care of the National Trust, Including Links with Historic Slavery* (National Trust, 2020)
2. Nigel Biggar, 'Cambridge is lost in a cloud of leftist virtue signalling', *The Times*, 3 May 2019.
3. Nick Brodie, *The Vandemonian War: the secret history of Britain's Tasmanian invasion* (Richmond, Hardie Grant, 2017).
4. Rebe Taylor, *Into the Heart of Tasmania: A search for human antiquity* (Carlton, Melbourne University Press, 2017), pp. 14-15.
5. Murray Johnson and Ian McFarlane, *Van Diemen's Land: An Aboriginal History* (Sydney, UNSW Press, 2015); Leonie Stevens, *'Me Write Myself': The Free Aboriginal Inhabitants of Van Diemen's Land at Wybalenna 1832-47* (Clayton, Monash University Press, 2015); Cassandra Pybus, *Truganini: Journey through the apocalypse* (Sydney, Allen & Unwin, 2020).
6. Lyndall Ryan and Philip Dwyer, 'Reflections on genocide and settler-colonial violence', *History Australia* (Vol. 13, No. 3, 2016), pp. 335-350.
7. Nicholas Clements, *The Black War: Fear, Sex and Resistance in Tasmania* (St Lucia, QLD; University of Queensland Press, 2014)
8. Bernard Porter, 'How Bad are we?', *London Review of Books* (Vol. 36, No. 15, 31 July 2014).

INTRODUCTION

From Thinking about Britain and the Holocaust to Writing about Genocide in the British World

This book is the product of an intellectual journey that began not in thinking about Australian or Tasmanian history, or even the history of the British Empire, but with the history of the Holocaust and its contexts. I am primarily a Holocaust historian – I have written and edited several books in Holocaust studies, and much of my teaching is concerned with the destruction of Europe's Jews and its legacies. How I got from there to thinking about the role of genocide in the British Empire requires at least some explanation, especially because without it, it might be assumed that I am suggesting some broad equivalence between these two very different histories. I am not, but it would be disingenuous not to admit that it was thinking about the Holocaust that brought me to the study of an instance of genocide in the British Empire.

My foremost concern in Holocaust studies has been with the 'bystanders'. Questions about how Britain responded to the Holocaust were the first that I tried to answer, both in terms of specific institutional and intellectual responses to Nazi anti-Jewish policies, and in terms of imaginings and memories of the genocide of the Jews that abounded in postwar Britain. And it was one of the central questions of the study of the 'bystanders' that ultimately led me to this book. It is often proposed that one of the reasons that the outside world had such difficulty in responding to the Holocaust was that the Nazis' genocidal policies were beyond the imagination, that the notion of racial extermination was so alien to external observers that, to put it crudely, they simply could not believe that the reports emanating from German-dominated Europe were true. As I grew more and more aware of the monotonous regularity of racial violence, especially in the modern world, and indeed the destructiveness of the British Empire, it seemed to me that this assertion was not quite historically literate. As such, one of the motivations for my researching Tasmania in the first instance was to be able to place the history of British reactions to the genocide of the Jews more squarely within the context of responses to mass violence and genocide across a much wider chronology.

Added to this, in recent years in particular I have been concerned that a preoccupation with the memory of the Holocaust in contemporary Britain has become counterproductive. It has not become, as many campaigners for greater awareness of the Holocaust assumed it would, a prompt to self-reflection about the past, but instead a terrain in which some British national myths – of eternal tolerance, of the country as a haven for the persecuted, for example – are being further reinforced.[1] Instead of undermining the stable rituals of historical memory, Holocaust memorialisation has itself become ritualised and, rather than challenging, safe. Indeed in many ways it appears that Holocaust memorialisation is being fed more and more into ideas of British national pride, and is being used as an example of the inherent dangers of any alternative to our liberal-democratic selves. This was particularly so with the egregious invocations of the Holocaust in justification of some of Britain's military adventures at the beginning of the twenty-first century.[2]

These concerns did not lead me to think specifically about genocide in the British world until a first encounter with Australian history, which in many ways transformed my academic life. Again, this came through the lens of Holocaust studies. In 2008 I put together a collection titled *The Memory of the Holocaust in Australia* with my friend and colleague James Jordan. In that book we made no pretensions to

Introduction

be experts in Australian history, but used it instead to explore questions surrounding the global memories of the Holocaust in a specific and unfamiliar context.³

What our book lacked, however, was enough reflection on one of the particular contexts for Holocaust memories in Australia – the interaction (or otherwise) between the memory of the Nazi genocides and the genocides of indigenous Australians in the nineteenth century and into the twentieth.⁴ I felt this absence particularly acutely when we launched the book at the Sydney Jewish Museum and I witnessed for the first time the acknowledgement of Aboriginal dispossession that precedes all public events in Australia. It was while reflecting on our failure to do justice to that context – to explore fully how memories of the Holocaust interacted with memories of colonial genocide – that it began to occur to me (although the connection may have been entirely obvious to others) that this might have implications for my understanding of British history, and British Holocaust memories. Although Australia represented a specific site of genocide, it was a part of the British world, and as such genocide in Australia meant that such an atrocity was part of British history too. This is especially true when one considers genocide in Tasmania, which took place almost exclusively under direct *British* rule, and was committed by *British* colonists and settlers who were working either for the *British* Crown or for *British* companies, and who moved between Britain and the Antipodes. As such it occurred to me that the idea of racial violence and even extermination might be rather closer to home than either studies of the Holocaust and its contexts or the rituals of modern memory implied.

At first these observations led me to plan a book on Britain and genocide in the modern world – which would have begun by looking at genocide inside the British Empire, which in turn would begin with Tasmania. *The Last Man* is the product of the research for what I planned to be the first chapter of the Britain-and-genocide project. As the research developed it became increasingly clear that the interactions between genocide in Tasmania and British history were so intricate, multi-layered and long-standing that that case alone demanded a specific book. What follows considers the role of the British state in the genocidal destruction of indigenous Tasmanians.[5] It goes on to consider the echoes of that destruction in British culture, right up to the present day.

But the profound links that I write about in this book between the British past and the history of genocide are difficult to discern in our present. This is true when you observe both historical investigations of genocide in British Australia, and more general interactions with the idea of genocide (which usually means the Holocaust) in British culture. While the allegation that genocide occurred in Australia has caused and continues to cause paroxysms in Australian academia and politics, such 'History Wars' have been observed with detachment in Britain, as if it were very little to do with 'us' somehow. That the issue of genocide in Australian history has been so politically charged there is precisely because it has mattered so much – raising existential questions about Australian identity about what it means to be Australian. Yet somehow the existence or otherwise of genocide in the British world seems to cause no such angst within Britain itself. Indeed, as will be discussed later in this volume, that the idea of genocide in Tasmania can be discussed glibly by modern-day apologists for empire is evidence of how little the question of colonial genocide seems to matter in Britain today.

In Australia, too, scholarly debates about genocide often deliberately avoid detailed consideration of their implications for the British centre of the former Empire. Consider Henry Reynolds's *An Indelible Stain?* as an example. The title of Reynolds's investigation of the role of genocide in Australian history is taken from the text of a famous despatch sent by the Secretary of State for the Colonies in London,[6] George Murray, to the lieutenant governor of Van Diemen's Land, now Tasmania, George Arthur, in 1830. In it Murray demanded to know what was happening to the peoples of the island, ending with the following warning: that the 'extinction' of the indigenous population of Van Diemen's Land would leave 'an indelible stain' upon the

Introduction

reputation of the British government.[7] Reynolds takes up Murray's challenge, stating that

> the question that Murray's words still confronts us with is whether our history has left an indelible stain upon the character and reputation of *Australian* governments – colonial, State and federal – and upon the colonists themselves and their Australian-born descendants.[8]

Yet George Murray had not himself been that interested in the moral implications of genocide for the colony, but for the metropole. The 'indelible stain' that Murray feared was, it is worth repeating, upon the reputation of the *British* government.

Thus this book asks the questions of Britain and the British past that Reynolds sought to ask of Australia – considering both the role that the British government played in the development of genocide in Tasmania and the wider role that genocide in Tasmania itself has played in British culture. In doing so, I hope it will fill a historiographical gap by considering in depth a case study of genocide in the British Empire.

But why Tasmania? The story of genocide there is well worn, much more so than, for example, genocide in Queensland or indeed the 'continuing genocide' faced by indigenous peoples in contemporary Australia.[9] Much of the story I tell here will be very familiar at least to Australian readers. Surely the job of the historian should be to tread less well-worn paths to the past? In mitigation I would argue that while the history of genocide in Tasmania is well established, the role of the British government and the echoes of colonial genocide in British culture are not. Furthermore, this is a book for the present as well as the past, and it would be much easier for Britain to avoid confronting genocidal collisions with indigenous peoples in the 1850s and 1860s, because they occurred after the Australian colonies had become self-governing. Although the British state may bear much responsibility for the structural inequalities in the relations between white settlers and peoples in the colonies they established, it has

The Last Man

recourse to an explanation for genocide as the sins of the errant sons of Britain rather than their metropolitan parents. This is not the case for Tasmania, where (notwithstanding the vagaries of colonial administration) Van Diemen's Land was under the direct rule of the Crown during almost the entire period in which the indigenous population was rapidly declining.

What is more, the sheer fact that the story of genocide in Tasmania has been so well worn in Britain from the 1820s onwards is itself of crucial importance. The 'Black War' between colonists and the indigenous peoples of Van Diemen's Land, and the idea that the latter had been exterminated, was culturally significant in Britain during the nineteenth century and has remained so since, albeit somewhat less prominently. Indeed this book seeks to demonstrate that this is a genocide that has become part of British identity. As such understanding how it is that identity-building in Britain has incorporated genocide is crucial in order to uncover the degree to which Britain is itself a post-genocidal state and society. This is therefore not a book about Tasmania but about Britain. While in the process of writing it I have learnt much about Tasmanian history, my aim has been to learn about the *British* genocidal past.

But as I have already said there is little or no acknowledgement within a wider memorial culture today that Britain has such a genocidal past, or that Britain is in effect a post-genocidal state. Indeed there is an overwhelming tendency to represent genocide as a crime committed only by others. Self-evidently the genocidaires of the Holocaust were, for example, the enemies of Britain, and liberal democracy is often represented as the alternative to genocidal regimes. Perhaps the best example here is the Imperial War Museum in London, a place in which British military success is remembered and celebrated. Yet at the same time it also contains an exhibition about the Holocaust. It is difficult to avoid the impression that the Holocaust exhibition exists in this context to present a worked-through example of the alternative to British liberal democracy. Such an impression is further embedded by the accompanying 'Crimes against Humanity' exhibition, which

Introduction

sets the Holocaust in the context of the history of genocide. Yet within that history there is no mention of Britain's imperial crimes (although there is engagement with the crimes of, for example, the *German Empire in South West Africa*).

In contemporary British culture then, genocide can be made use of in the celebration of being British. This book is a warning against that tendency – it seeks to demonstrate how genocide is part of British history rather than suggest that British history simply offers alternatives to genocide. It is therefore a book that has a live political purpose, which asks that Britain confront the implications of its genocidal past, rather than continuing to wallow in a genocidal past in Europe. This is not in any way to fall prey to the temptation to say that the Holocaust is not part of British history – its entanglements with Britain are many and profound. Instead it is to say that an understanding of the Holocaust has allowed us to see more clearly the moral imperatives of genocide, and as such it behoves us to ask awkward as well as comforting questions of our national past too. In a world in which politicians and others often suggest that we should turn to Britain's imperial past for our historical narratives, this book serves as a reminder that some of the most cherished national assumptions about that past – about our liberal selves – disguise a darker history, which failed absolutely to recognise and cherish the diversity of mankind.

ONE

Defining Terms

The earliest traces of the inhabitants of the island that we call Tasmania are some 40,000 years old. At least 8,000 years ago the island was cut off from continental Australia by the flooding of the Bass Strait. Remarkably, indigenous Tasmanians in the nineteenth century reported that their ancestors had walked across the land before the flooding – suggesting a folk memory or legend that had endured for more than 300 generations.[1]

In the very latter stages of this deep history, in 1642, the Dutch explorer Abel Tasman named the island, which was known to its inhabitants as 'Trouwunna', 'Van Diemen's Land'.[2] The next Western visitor to the island arrived in 1772, beginning a flurry of activity that ended in the creation of a permanent British settlement in 1803 and 1804. In the meantime British men from New South Wales had begun an informal colonisation of the island, which included starting relationships with indigenous women. When the British formally established their base, there were several thousand indigenous people on the island in as many as nine different nations. When the colony was awarded self-government by the British just 53 years later, there were officially just 17 of those inhabitants or their descendants still alive, although many more lived beyond the official gaze. Nonetheless, Tasmania had witnessed a calamitous population decline, one that had been the direct result of the British presence on the island – indigenous peoples had been the victims of settler violence and imported disease, before the relatively few survivors were rounded up and deported from the island. These survivors were settled on Flinders Island in the Bass Strait between Tasmania and continental Australia. There, unable to leave, the population were subjected to a crude campaign to transform them into 'Europeans' who cultivated the land and worshipped the Christian God. This new settlement witnessed a further, disastrous population decline. When one of the few survivors, William Lanne,[3] died in 1869 it was declared in Britain that the 'Tasmanian race' stood on the edge of extinction. For he was 'the last man', survived only by two women, Mary Ann Arthur and Truganini. Mary Ann died in 1871 and Truganini in 1876. After the latter's death, it was universally declared that the Tasmanian population had been entirely wiped out.

Claims of total destruction completely ignored a mixed-race community concentrated on Tasmania's outlying islands, and a number of mixed-race children living in white-settler homes. The former was the product of the original informal colonisation of Tasmania. It would not only survive but flourish across the nineteenth and twentieth centuries to form the basis of the Tasmanian Aboriginal community today.[4] But if the destruction of their ancestors was not total, it was comprehensive. All original communities had been destroyed since the British invasion, and the population reduction was greater than 99 per cent. This was a British genocide, carried out on the other side of the world by British men, articulating British ideas, discussed in British newspapers and ultimately embedded in British history and remembered in British museums.

A BRITISH GENOCIDE

The British settlement had been established to forestall any French claims to the island in the midst of the Napoleonic wars. Van Diemen's Land was also a remarkably benevolent land. Its climate was much more temperate than that of its parent Australian colony, New South Wales. There were abundant supplies of game, which flourished in open pastureland close to the coastal areas, which were the first to be settled. There were equally abundant supplies of shellfish in the

Defining Terms

coastal waters. While at the time some imperial propaganda suggested that Tasmania had been a harsh, unforgiving land, which the colonists had to overcome, in fact what the first settlers discovered was a 'veritable Eden'.[5]

Little thought was given to the indigenous population that had in fact shaped much of that environment.[6] Both British and French expeditions to Van Diemen's Land before 1803 had experienced encounters with the inhabitants of the island – but comparatively little attention had been paid to them. They were certainly not seen as a barrier to colonisation. Those accompanying Captain Cook in 1777, or d'Entrecasteaux in 1792, had noted only that the population seemed to pose little threat; they were 'harmless and content; an extraordinary remnant of primitive innocence'.[7] François Péron, historian of the French explorer Nicolas Baudin's expedition to the island in 1802, had been repulsed by the 'savage hordes' he encountered, but had agreed with earlier observers that that they were not threatening.[8] No such extensive descriptions of the existing population were offered by the first British settlers, but if they considered these people at all,[9] the British assumed that they could recruit them in the process of developing the island – in the first instance as a penal colony. Indeed the first authorities in the British colony were instructed to treat the 'natives' with 'amity and kindness' in order that they too might share in the benefits of colonisation.[10]

Probably the most eloquent indication of how little impact indigenous populations had on the British mind or that of other European colonisers was the widespread belief that their land was vacant and thus ripe for possession. Of course, the British did not believe that the land was literally uninhabited. But, in a concept that became known as *Terra nullius* ('land that belongs to no one') by the end of the nineteenth century, the British and other European powers understood that continental Australia and Tasmania represented so-called 'wastelands'. As such, because indigenous Australians did not operate any formal laws of property, and indeed because they did not exploit natural resources through farming in a manner that the British could recognise, it was assumed the land was essentially empty. The British thus concluded that they could declare ownership of that land, and sovereignty over its peoples.[11]

In fact the nine nations in Tasmania had a complex relationship with their country. The land was managed to support the main sources of food (for example, grazing pasture was created by fire), and clans moved across the country according to where the food supply was most abundant at different times of the year. Movement across the land does not mean, however, that there was no sense of property: the clans (which made up a nation) had a clear understanding of the demarcation of their territory, although not the exclusive ownership of it. In the most comprehensive survey of indigenous communities and their social relations, Brian Plomley identified some 48 different clans at the time of the British invasion with specific territories, although Lyndall Ryan argues there may have been as many as 100.[12] It is difficult to be precise because all of these functioning communal units were destroyed by the British.

Because of that destruction, we simply cannot know exactly how large the existing population was in 1803, but the most recent speculations suggest that it could have been as high as 8,000, and that it was rising.[13] Certainly it massively outnumbered the original settlers and convicts, of whom there were just a few hundred spread across three main settlements.[14] Contact between the very small settler population and indigenous peoples was necessarily very limited – in effect the British mainly occupied a small enclave in the south-east corner of the island in the first months of occupation. Although we know that those nations located on the sites of settlement watched the British arrival carefully, much of the population on the rest of the island may have been oblivious to the British presence for some time.[15]

Although contact between the British and the inhabitants of Van Diemen's Land was limited at the beginning of the settlement, it was very quickly lethal. As Lyndall Ryan writes: 'from the outset the British in effect were trying to eliminate the Aborigines by killing the parents, abducting their children and transforming them into white people.'[16]

Defining Terms

The killing of indigenous people in defence of the expanding settlements and farmlands was tacitly accepted by the colonial authorities.[17] And although the documentary evidence is scarce, it appears that at least until 1808 the new colony was defined by violence between settlers and indigenous nations, especially over control of land that supported game such as kangaroo.[18] Those groups that inhabited the lands on which the towns of the new colony were established seem to have been devastated. According to Lyndall Ryan, 'The Mouheneenner clan, whose territory included Hobart, experienced massive population decline in this period.'[19]

After 1808, however, a period of calm and indeed coexistence seemed to descend on the colony. As the rate of colonial expansion stabilised, conflict between settlers and indigenous Tasmanians subsided. Indeed, it is possible to argue that between 1808 and 1820 a Creole society was created: a 'potent mix of cross-cultural, economic and sexual interaction'.[20] As well as the European–indigenous relationships in the seal-hunting communities, groups of islanders could for example be seen in the settlements looking for food. At the same time, more and more indigenous children were taken into white homes, and some were even sent to England to be educated. The practice of taking children suggests that any coexistence came with little respect for local culture, and indeed those who served as domestic servants were in effect being used in a form of slavery.[21]

By the end of 1819 the indigenous and colonial populations were roughly equal in size. Yet that parity meant that each population was 5,000 strong, and as such we should not underestimate the immediate demographic impact of colonisation. In the first 15 years of settlement, the indigenous population declined by more than 30 per cent. Indeed, in 1819 Governor William Sorell told of an enduringly violent relationship on the Tasmanian frontier, where attacking the island's peoples had become habitual. We can only speculate as to the numbers of casualties.[22]

After 1819, however, there is no doubt that colonial Van Diemen's Land was defined by violence. Massive population and territorial expansion in the 1820s not only increased settler attacks on indigenous peoples, but also drove the latter to resist settler expansion more actively. In the same report in which Sorell had referred to habitual violence on the frontier, he had predicted that expansion would lead to more attacks on settlers and their livestock, and he was right. During the 1820s and especially after 1824 Van Diemen's Land was the site of a war for control of the land. At some points during this 'Black War' (as it was known at the time), colonial authorities believed that indigenous violence jeopardised the very existence of the colony. It certainly threatened to derail any further development, as individual settlers claimed they were unable to defend the frontier without military assistance.[23]

From November 1823 onwards the indigenous population fought back with increasing success, and a spiral of violence ensued. Between the warring communities sat a colonial government instructed by London both to protect the original inhabitants of the island and to defend the colony from depredation. Such instructions were deliberately contradictory, and tell us a great deal about the priorities of the London government with regard to its Empire. Ultimately the security of its territorial settlements took precedence over the lives of the original owners of the land on which those settlements stood. As a consequence, the colonial government, then under Lieutenant Governor George Arthur, pursued a series of measures that by 1828 amounted to war with the indigenous population, after a declaration of martial law in the colony. The 'Black War', which saw both licensed and unlicensed forces pursuing indigenous populations, who themselves continued to attack settlers and their livestock, continued until the end of 1830. It ended with a spectacular show of strength from the colonial authorities when almost the entire settler population was militarised and attempted to confine the clans in a corner of the island. This action, known as 'the Line', was a miserable failure, in part because by then the number of indigenous Tasmanians was so small. It is not clear how many were killed directly at British hands during the conflict, with British weapons, but Lyndall Ryan can account for approximately 800 deaths on the Tasmanian frontier.[24] We can assume that much violence went unrecorded too. As James Boyce argues, the conflict was much better documented after it became formalised in 1828, but by then most indigenous Tasmanians were already dead.[25]

The decline in the island's original population was precipitous and by 1831 there were only a few hundred survivors. This had been matched by an equally steep increase in the British population. The survivors were for the most part collected together by George Augustus Robinson, who himself had emigrated to Hobart, the capital of the Tasmanian colony, at the beginning of the 1820s. Robinson was employed by the colonial government to 'conciliate' the antagonistic indigenous population from 1829. In that role Robinson, and a group of indigenous guides on whom he relied, eventually brought together the vast majority of the surviving members of the clans. He brokered their peace with the colonial government and eventually arranged for their removal en masse (you might call it deportation) to Flinders Island, which was separated from the north-west coast of mainland Tasmania by some 40 miles. There, in a settlement known to its inhabitants as Wybalenna, the population was beset by disease. Although it would be wrong to characterise the settlement as a place of decline, and descriptions of it as a concentration camp or gulag are unhelpful, it is impossible to escape the view that the efforts to transform and 'civilise' indigenous Tasmanians that were enacted there had calamitous consequences.[26] By 1847 there were just 47 people remaining in the community on Flinders Island. In little more than a generation the original population had been reduced by 99.5 per cent.

One of those surviving on Flinders Island was Truganini, a woman who had been with Robinson since he first took control of an 'Aboriginal establishment' on Bruny Island in 1829. Truganini and the other survivors were sent back to the Tasmanian mainland in 1847. She was the last of that community to die in 1876. At that point it was widely declared that the indigenous population of Tasmania had been wiped out. As I have said, such a claim ignored the existence of a mixed-heritage community both in Tasmania and on other islands in the Bass Strait, but it articulated a widespread sense of the superiority of the British. The Empire was, it was assumed, so powerful that it had swept an entire people out of existence.

The book that follows attempts to tell a version of the story of the violent dispossession and deportation that I have summarised here. However, its focus will not be the indigenous victims of the process, but the British forces which shaped it.

HISTORIES OF GENOCIDE IN TASMANIA

This book is certainly not the first history of genocide in Tasmania. In fact, histories that identify that indigenous Tasmanians were the victims of a deliberate campaign of extermination pre-date the working through of the concept of genocide by more than a century. Henry Melville, a Hobart newspaper proprietor, wrote of the 'war to the knife' between settlers and indigenous islanders in his *History of the Island of Van Diemen's Land* in 1835. Melville's tale of 'destruction' was specifically aimed at implicating the colonial government in a campaign that 'swept' 'populous tribes [...] from the face of the earth'.[27] John West's *History of Tasmania*, one of the foundational texts of Australian historiography, confronted the destruction of the indigenous population directly in the early 1850s – describing it baldly as an example of 'systematic massacre'.[28] West lamented the 'fate of the Aborigines', and described their 'tread[ing] [...] to the dust' as a calamity that ought to 'check exaltation' at the triumph of colonisation. His *History* was part of a campaign against the system of transporting convicts to Van Diemen's Land and as such alleged that genocide had been the result of Britain's export of her most depraved sons to wreak havoc in the New World.[29]

Both West and Melville wrote about the destruction of the indigenous population for an audience in Britain, in order to draw attention to the politics of colonisation. Later in the nineteenth century James Bonwick, who had been a schoolteacher in various parts of continental Australia, wrote the first history of the decline and destruction of the indigenous community, *The Last of the Tasmanians*, which was again directed at a British audience and again had a political purpose. Bonwick's account became the classic narrative of destruction in Tasmania, and was particularly influential in informing anthropological investigations of what was then understood to be the extinct Tasmanian population at the end of the nineteenth century. Bonwick's aim was to ensure that other indigenous peoples throughout the world were preserved.

In the aftermath of World War II, Tasmania was often identified as one of the sites of the newly recognised crime of genocide. The author of the idea of genocide, Raphael Lemkin, who was also largely responsible for its codification in international law, included the Tasmanian case in his projected history of the concept. Lemkin's account of genocide on the island was largely based on Bonwick's work. At a similar time Clive Turnbull identified the 'extermination of the Tasmanian Aborigines' as the key element in the colonisation of Van Diemen's Land, a microcosm of the relationship between conquerors and indigenous peoples throughout the history of European colonialism.[30] The idea that genocide in Tasmania was a kind of British 'Final Solution' also became embedded in critical histories of the British Empire in the postwar period – betraying the interaction between a perception of the murder of Europe's Jews and the understanding of colonial violence.[31]

Because Raphael Lemkin included it in his survey of genocide and because it was (outside Tasmania and Australia) almost universally assumed that the destruction of the indigenous population had been total, Tasmania is frequently included in general surveys of genocide in the modern world.[32] Yet Henry Reynolds has argued that this can often be the result of an almost reflex action, based on little understanding of the particularities of Tasmanian history. In particular, the insistence on the totality of extermination that is sometimes contained within these accounts is in some ways a perpetuation of colonial thinking about the nature of the indigenous community and its relationship with colonial authority. The idea that *all* of the original Tasmanians had been exterminated not only ignores the endurance of an indigenous community on the island, but subscribes to a racialised imagination that assumes that the children of mixed-race relationships in Tasmania were somehow rendered 'white' by the blood of their fathers. Moreover, the story of genocide itself – which often suggests that the helpless islanders were the passive victims of the all-powerful white settlers – is to perpetuate a colonial discourse that denies the possibility that indigenous communities were agents in their own history after the arrival of white Europeans.[33] Such a view ignores the fact that much of the violence was the result of indigenous efforts to defend their land.

As a consequence, the most recent accounts of genocide in Tasmania (although not all would accept the use of that term) have been contained within what might be described as post-colonial Australian histories. Scholars have particularly sought to draw attention to the survival of some indigenous Tasmanians – in part bringing historical narratives in line with the assertive contemporary politics of the Tasmanian Aboriginal community. In particular, such histories describe the active role played by the island's existing communities in the conflict with settlers in the first three decades of the colony. In such a formulation, depopulation has been recast as the consequence of war *between* settler and indigenous communities, of active competition for the land rather than the result of the British men of modernity sweeping the island clear of the passive and helpless indigenes. The most modern historiography rejects the passive-victim thesis as essentially patronising,[34] and asserts that indigenous peoples were the subjects rather than the objects of their own history.[35] In rejecting the idea of the total extermination of indigenous Tasmanians as itself a colonial myth, such history points to the living vibrancy of the Aboriginal Tasmanian community and hints at the complexity of deploying the term genocide too.

It is not only in the assertion of indigenous agency that such histories of colonial Van Diemen's Land present what might be called post-colonial narratives. In common with much 'new imperial' history, the contemporary historiography of Tasmania demonstrates that the Empire must be understood in the exchange between imperial authorities and the settler colonies or the societies they created. As such Van Diemen's Land was not a society somehow transplanted from Britain by pioneering settlers who tamed a harsh and unforgiving land, but the product of interaction between the settlers, the land and the peoples that they conquered.[36] This interaction included exchange with the existing population, and, as Lyndall Ryan has argued, histories that see only a destructive relationship between indigenous peoples and the British obscure the development of important Creole cultures that were the product of positive colonial encounters.[37]

Some of the most important recent histories have therefore been richly detailed local studies. These works set the story of population decline firmly in the communities and the landscape in which it occurred.[38] And of course the local contexts for the history of genocidal conflict between indigenous and settler societies have a real and essential political dimension in the contemporary relationship between 'white' and indigenous Tasmanians.[39] Yet one of the unintended consequences of this assertion of the importance of the local is that the metropolitan centre can be almost written out of the history of colonial Tasmania and its impacts on the island's original inhabitants. For James Boyce, for example, genocide was a consequence of the specific local Tasmanian culture and took place *despite* the metropolitan British.[40] For Lyndall Ryan genocide took place in a policy vacuum created by the British government's lack of engagement with Van Diemen's Land.[41]

Other histories, concerned more generally with indigenous dispossession in Australia, also tend to marginalise the metropolitan British. Henry Reynolds's re-examination of the legal basis of settlement, for example, and his assertion that British colonial authorities *did* recognise the land rights of existing peoples (both in Tasmania and throughout colonial Australia), played a crucial role in Australia's recent search for a more equitable settlement with indigenous communities.[42] But again the interpretative consequence of this for British history is to distance the British government especially from the violence on which colonial rule so often depended. Reynolds argued that the Colonial Office in Britain, and certainly evangelical reformers who sought to influence Downing Street, held assumptions about indigenous rights that were the diametric opposite of any will to exterminate that might have been seen in the colonies themselves. In such a thesis the British are portrayed as the (albeit hapless) protectors of the indigenous community from the ravages of the settlers.

In what is the most comprehensive history of the tragedy that the British unleashed in Tasmania, which rejects the label genocide, Reynolds suggests that although policy towards indigenous peoples was confused and contradictory the British government was essentially the source of restraint – that in their entreaties against violence the British held back settlers who from the mid 1820s wished to destroy the existing population, who were attacking them in a war for control of the land.[43] In doing so, Reynolds unwittingly found common cause with scholars engaged in a quite different historical and political project. Niall Ferguson, for example, wishes that his book *Empire* might rehabilitate the historical memory of British imperialism. Remarkably, he uses genocide in Tasmania as evidence in support of his case, arguing that the British attempted to prevent genocide there and succeeded in doing so on continental Australia. Ferguson describes 'one of the most shocking of all chapters in the history of the British Empire' in which 'the Aborigines in Van Diemen's Land were hunted down, confined and ultimately exterminated'. Perhaps most remarkable is the significance that Ferguson ascribes to genocide in Tasmania:

> All that can be said in mitigation is that, had Australia been an independent republic in the nineteenth century, like the United States, the genocide might have been on a continental scale rather than just a Tasmanian phenomenon [...] one of the peculiarities of the British Empire was the way that the imperial power at the centre endeavoured to restrain the generally far more ruthless impulses of the colonists on the periphery.[44]

Defining Terms

In such a formulation Britain is set free of the burden of genocide in its history. Colonialism and imperialism can be reclaimed as respectable political discourses. Genocide was carried out not by the British, but by colonists who had somehow betrayed their British heritage.

Such interpretations of the relationship between Britain and the violence in its colonies have long roots. The idea that colonial society was itself a kind of savage deviation from the noble traditions of British politics and culture was well established in the nineteenth century. Indeed the Colonial Office convinced itself that the devastating impact of colonial Van Diemen's Land on the indigenous population was a result of a rejection of the essential tenets of British rule. As a consequence, some of the first chroniclers of the destruction in Tasmania argued that the 'home authorities' could be 'exonerated' from any charges with relation to the treatment meted out against indigenous peoples by the settlers.[45] And even the most challenging histories of the colonial experience have long asserted that the devastating consequences of imperialism can be explained by the idea that colonial outriders were somehow set free from the control of metropolitan Britain.[46]

The story of genocide as a consequence of British actions has not therefore been comprehensively explored. It is not that historians haven't suggested that genocide in Tasmania is linked to British history – that would be absurd – they have just not fully worked through the implications of such arguments. John West's *History of Tasmania* played into that cultural separation of the savage settler from the respectable British. He excoriated the British practice of transporting convicts. But at the same time he linked violence against indigenous Tasmanians to wider currents in British history. West stated clearly that the British government was 'remiss and culpable. The crimes of individuals, without diminishing their guilt, must be traced to those general causes which are subject to the disposal of statesmen and legislators.'[47] In the post-colonial world several scholars, and indeed politicians, have loudly asserted British responsibility for genocide in Tasmania, but not gone on to explore the interactions between action and policy and the intentions of, for example, the British Colonial Office.[48] The then prime minister Paul Keating's efforts to reappraise Australian history and confront responsibility for the 'evils of colonialism' in the late 1980s and early 1990s transferred much of that responsibility to the 'imperial master'.[49] More recently, even those historians cited above as contributing to the sense of a gulf between genocide in Tasmania and British policy have referred obliquely to the wider links between violence and the centre of empire. Lyndall Ryan suggested that British colonial policy was the root of the destruction of Tasmania's indigenous community, but offered no detailed analysis of how the British government interacted with policy towards indigenous groups in Tasmania.[50] And Henry Reynolds also recognised that the original impulse for violence must be traced to Britain and the 'colonising venture' itself, again without fully exploring such an idea.[51]

What follows will attempt to flesh out that relationship between Britain and genocide in Tasmania. I will argue that genocide was the result of the British presence in Van Diemen's Land. This does not mean that the British government or its agents explicitly planned the physical destruction of indigenous Tasmanians. They did not. But genocide was the inevitable outcome of a set of British policies, however apparently benign they appeared to their authors. I will show that those policies – even those aimed at protection – ultimately envisaged no future whatsoever for the original peoples of the island. The specific policies that led to genocide may well have been made in Tasmania by the colonial authorities and the settlers, but they were approved by His Majesty's Government in London, reported in the British press and ultimately responded to the desires and demands of a British colonisation.

Furthermore, *The Last Man* will demonstrate that the links between Britain and genocide in Tasmania do not travel in only one direction. It is not just that the destruction of indigenous Tasmanians and their culture was the consequence of British politics, but that it had an impact on British politics and culture too. What follows will show that genocide in Tasmania has been a shadowed presence in Britain since

Defining Terms

the 1820s, which at times breaks the surface of public discourse right up to the present day. For example, the debates about the origins of mankind in the mid to late nineteenth century and those about the return of human remains stored in British museums to indigenous peoples across the world in the late twentieth century relied heavily on the idea of genocide in Tasmania and both demonstrate the links between genocide and the articulation of certain identities in Britain today.

ON GENOCIDE IN AUSTRALIA

The idea that what occurred in colonial Tasmania should be labelled genocide is, as seen earlier, contested. Henry Reynolds's investigation of the issue in Australian history concludes explicitly that the demographic disaster precipitated by the British in Tasmania did *not* amount to genocide. Focusing on the concept of intent, Reynolds argues that we can find no evidence that the British deliberately planned the wholesale destruction of indigenous Tasmanians and therefore that what occurred does not meet the definition enshrined in the 1948 UN convention, which codified genocide as 'acts committed with intent to destroy, in whole or in part, a national, ethnical, racial or religious group'. In part because the British in Tasmania so frequently employed the rhetoric of protection, Reynolds concluded that there was no 'intent' to destroy and thus no genocide.[52]

It is the apparent absence of an explicitly and generally murderous intent that has made the question of genocide in Australian history so controversial. Witness the reaction to the 1997 report *Bringing Them Home* by the 'National Inquiry into the Separation of Aboriginal and Torres Strait Islander Children from Their Families', which was commissioned to investigate the practice of forced removal of children from indigenous communities, especially those of mixed heritage, by Australian states up to the 1960s. It concluded that there was enough evidence to suggest that the purpose of removing children was the cultural eradication of those communities: 'when a child was forcibly removed that child's entire community lost, often permanently, its chance to perpetuate itself in that child. The Inquiry has concluded that this was a primary objective of forcible removals.' As a consequence, it devastatingly suggested, 'they amount to genocide.'[53]

Reaction to the report from the conservative right wing in Australia was predictable. Critics of the 'black armband' view of Australian history[54] poured scorn on the attempt to locate genocide in the Australian past. Most famously, Keith Windschuttle produced *The Fabrication of Aboriginal History* (the first volume of which was concerned with Tasmania) in order to deny, at length, that indigenous dispossession could be labelled genocide. The most recently published volume in Windschuttle's trilogy denies not only the allegation of genocide but even that there was a policy of child-removal and thus a 'stolen generation' at all. The debates that Windschuttle's work prompted crystallised into what have been dubbed Australia's 'History Wars'.[55]

Windschuttle's rejection of genocide is easily and indeed politically explicable, but some of the criticism of the application of genocide to Australian history has come from less predictable sources. For example, Inga Clendinnen, a historian and anthropologist who was among other things a Holocaust scholar, wrote:

> I am reasonably sophisticated in these modes of intellectual discussion, but when I see the word 'genocide' I still see Gypsies and Jews being herded into trains, into pits, into ravines, and behind them the shadowy figures of Armenian women and children being marched into the desert by armed men. I see deliberate mass murder.[56]

In doing so Clendinnen encapsulated many of the objections to the notion that genocide is part of Australian history, based on a sense not of what that history *was* but of what it was not. Indigenous dispossession may have been many things, Clendinnen seemed to be arguing, but it was not *that*. Or, to put it another way, Wybalenna,

Defining Terms

the 'Aboriginal establishment' on Flinders Island at which indigenous Tasmanians were confined and many of them died, may have been many things, but it was not Auschwitz.

Clendinnen famously went on to write evocatively about the first encounters between British settlers and indigenous Australians.[57] But in her rejection of the term genocide she articulated an almost instinctive reaction in Australian politics and culture. The argument went something like this: genocide was only committed by Nazis or other totalitarian ideological warriors, not by 'us'.[58] In this formulation 'genocide' conjures up images of the Holocaust. Henry Reynolds operated a similarly narrow understanding of genocide as the Holocaust in his investigations. In this there was also common cause with the likes of Windschuttle, who argued that there was no will to extermination on the part of 'the colonial authorities [who] wanted to civilise and modernise the Aborigines'. Again, the argument was that, as a consequence, there was no genocide.[59]

The implication of this critique is that genocide must look like the Nazi killing fields. Or at least it must look like a clichéd caricature of that 'Final Solution'. The Holocaust, which such an understanding of genocide relies upon, was the result of a unified process, a specific plan of extermination, enacted in specific sites like Auschwitz. I have already made clear that Wybalenna was not Auschwitz. What is more, in the 30 years of the most violent interactions between settlers and indigenous nations in Tasmania, and more obviously across the two centuries of destructive interaction in continental Australia, there was self-evidently no worked-through and unifying aim of putting to death the existing communities on the part of 'white settlers', their descendants or the British, colonial or Australian governments.[60] Thus, if one insists that in order to find genocide we must also find the avowed and unifying intention to exterminate all members of a single group, then we won't find it in either Australia generally or Tasmania in particular. If genocide must look like the Holocaust (or at least a caricature of the Holocaust), then it indeed did not play a role in either the Australian or the British past.

We certainly won't find genocide in relation to the entire indigenous community, or, to use the term that settlers would have used, the entire 'Aboriginal' community, of Australia either. That assumption, that 'Aborigines' were all part of a single ethnic group and culture, was itself born of a racist mindset – as I have said, in Tasmania alone there were nine different nations. Therefore, the idea that we can add up all of the murders of representatives of quite different nations across the vast continent of Australia and see a desire to exterminate, might itself be a perpetuation of the original colonial assumptions about the nature and essential similarity of indigenous societies.

That said, if we consider the individual nations in isolation then we might well be able to discern genocide more clearly – as there were obviously 'genocidal moments' in Australian history at which settlers and indeed the authorities sought to remove a particular group from a territory, and indeed did so using exterminatory violence.[61] The deployment of the Native Police Corps in Queensland in the 1860s, when they were used to 'disperse' clans from particular territories and did so using mass violence, offers many examples of this practice.[62] In Tasmania, the deliberate clearing of the North West clans from the territory of the Van Diemen's Land Company towards the end of the 1820s was also in these terms an example of genocide – in that it had the clear goal of the eradication of a particular ethnic and linguistic group in a defined region.[63] But, those who deny genocide in the Australian past would argue, even genocidal moments do not necessarily add up to genocide.

What the examples of Queensland in the 1860s and Tasmania in the 1820s also demonstrate is that if we consider genocide to be a state crime – and again the Holocaust draws us to that notion – then it might not appear to be applicable in the Australian case. Much of the violence in Australia was committed in apparent defiance of the state. Although they are few and far between, there are examples of efforts to punish the perpetrators of violence against indigenous peoples and communities on the part of the colonial and imperial state.[64] Colin Tatz has argued in relation to the same problem that genocide in Australia might be best regarded as 'private'. It was after all driven forward by individual settlers, rather than by either the colonial state or its metropolitan masters.[65]

Clearly there was no state project of extermination in either Tasmania or continental Australia, but this does not necessarily mean that we can find, as Henry Reynolds in effect does, that the state was not guilty of genocide or indeed that there was no genocide. After all, the lines between state and private action were not entirely clear. The violence on the Tasmanian frontier in the 1820s was in the service of a state-led cause – the project of settler colonisation and the creation of a new world. Dirk Moses and Mark Levene have argued separately that in those moments of violence we can see that the colonial project itself had a genocidal logic. It was not always evident, and indeed colonialism was spoken of in terms of protection and improvement. There was nothing approaching a 'Final Solution' that required, for its own sake, the extermination of indigenous Australians, but when communities resisted the colonial project exterminatory violence was unleashed[66] – most notably, of course, in Van Diemen's Land. Perhaps we ought simply to revise the idea of genocide as purely a state crime in the light of Australian history. After all, the frontier represented the most lethal theatre of violence in both Tasmania and later in Queensland and it was a space defined by the absence of the state.[67]

However, such observations still only pertain to extreme, indeed murderous, physical violence, something plainly not experienced by all indigenous Australians or even Tasmanians. This too might be evidence that the idea of genocide is not conceptually very useful in understanding the totality of the indigenous experience of the establishment of Australian colonies – because mass violence was just one form of dislocation that those peoples experienced.[68] Even in Van Diemen's Land perhaps fewer than 1,000 indigenous individuals met their deaths through violence on the frontier – although it is almost impossible to know how much violence has been forgotten as a result of the documentary deficit of an early-nineteenth-century colony in which the massacre of indigenous peoples was often kept secret.

Regardless of the deficiencies of the record, however, and indeed regardless of the precise role of lethal violence in the destruction of indigenous Tasmania, I am satisfied that it is both conceptually useful and morally correct to apply the label genocide to the British colonisation of Tasmania. This is not to say that this was a 'genocidal moment' within a more benign framework, but rather that colonisation itself amounted, in total, to genocide.

How, bearing in mind the objections cited above, can I assert this so confidently? For one thing, genocide does not refer only to lethal violence and nor does something have to look like the Holocaust to be genocide. Even if we are to use genocide only in a strictly legal sense then the authors of *Bringing Them Home* were quite right – the forcible transfer of children with the intention to undermine the viability of a community is defined as genocide in the 1948 convention. There is therefore no requirement for murder. But we must go beyond the formal legal framework – which after all was itself a compromised and imperfect articulation of the original concept of genocide.

As Dirk Moses has argued, Lemkin originally defined genocide as a 'total social practice'. Crucially, this encapsulated the cultural undermining of the communal basis of a population group as well as any violence done. Lemkin wrote:

> Genocide has two phases: one, destruction of the national pattern of the oppressed group; the other, the imposition of the national pattern of the oppressor. This imposition, in turn, may be made upon the oppressed population which is allowed to remain, or upon the territory alone after removal of the population and the colonisation of the area by the oppressor's own nationals.[69]

There is little doubt that colonial Van Diemen's Land meets these criteria, and bearing in mind Lemkin's cognisance of events in Tasmania it is not beyond the bounds of possibility that he had them in mind when formulating such an argument. After all, the settlement at Flinders

Island, which sought to enforce different ways of living, farming and indeed believing on indigenous Tasmanians, was nothing if not an attempt to 'impose the national pattern of the oppressor'.

That the British attempted to do this will become obvious as you read this book. The practice of child-removal that the *Bringing Them Home* report identified as genocidal was carried out in Van Diemen's Land precisely with the aim of eradicating the islanders' culture. The children who were removed were to be educated as white men. The removal of the indigenous nations from the land also enforced an explicit break from a shared past in Van Diemen's Land that amounted to cultural destruction, and led to the Flinders Island settlement in which islanders were subjected to a crude process aimed at cultural transformation, further evidence of the destructive aim as well as effect of policy. Moreover, many British people who were disgusted by violence in Tasmania believed that it would only be by abandoning their way of life – the way they ate, the way they lived, their spiritual beliefs – that indigenous Tasmanians would have any chance of survival.

Therefore it is precisely because the idea of genocide offers us a framework through which we might unify many of the different approaches to indigenous communities that it *is* conceptually useful for understanding the history of the British in Tasmania.[70] Some indigenous people in Tasmania died as at the hands of settlers who wished to exterminate them. Some died in the process of being removed from land that settlers wished to develop. Some died in the process of being removed from the land and 'civilised' into Europeans. Some died from warfare between the island's nations that was prompted by their declining resource bases, a result of the British presence. Some died of imported diseases. And, of course, some survived, but with little or no access to a culture that the British considered worthless and had attempted to destroy. This happened over the course of a colonisation played out during more than 50 years. Perhaps, then, genocide is not a description of an event at all, but the identification of a set of events, a process or an epoch. This is something that is only retrospectively visible.[71] And few could argue that the outcome of the British presence in Tasmania was anything but genocidal, with a population of several thousand reduced to a mere handful.

It is only the concept of genocide that captures the totality of a destruction that is not simply, to return to Inga Clendinnen's point, defined by deliberate mass murder. In what follows you will find perhaps fewer references to violence than you might expect in a book on genocide. Indeed, you will find that much of the book is dedicated to a discussion of the commitment of both the British government and its colonial representatives to the protection of the indigenous community. But, I will argue, such a commitment to protection and the 'progress' of the island's peoples was as much a commitment to eradication as the violence of the men on the Tasmanian frontier who openly practised and preached extermination.

But what about the role of disease? The British can hardly be held responsible for the ravaging of the indigenous Tasmanian population by diseases that the settlers did not themselves understand. It is not possible, for an epidemiologist let alone a historian, to delineate precisely the role that disease played in the destruction of indigenous Tasmanians and their communities. But we know, for example, that the precipitous decline of the population at Flinders Island was the result of disease rather than violence. As a result, it might appear that to label the Flinders Island settlement a site of genocide is illogical. Yet we also know that, perhaps knowingly, the British did introduce diseases into Australian populations. After all, the first contact with the people of what became Sydney led to a smallpox epidemic that devastated the community.[72] We also know that the settlers were certainly aware that the indigenous communities were apparently unable to cope with infections that Europeans could easily survive. As a consequence, the British both in Tasmania and at home interpreted indigenous population decline as the result of a *natural* process. But even those contemporary readings of the disaster in Tasmania ultimately understood that it was the arrival of the Europeans that was its root cause. Indeed, some iterations of the idea that the island's peoples were naturally slated for extinction relied on medicalised imagery – such as the idea that Tasmanians were destroyed by the 'breath of our presence'. Yet there was nothing natural about, for example, the deportation of indigenous Tasmanians into the confined spaces of the Wybalenna settlement and their forced cohabitation with an ever-changing cast of Europeans. As we will see, the authorities were aware that Flinders Island was literally killing its community, but that did not, until it was too late, force them to reconsider the utility of an institution that was anyway designed to destroy at the very least indigenous culture. Although it might be to overstate the case, it is worth remembering that Jews who died of typhus in Auschwitz were victims of genocide just like those who died in gas chambers.

The logic of the British presence in Tasmania, and indeed on continental Australia, looked forward to and indeed demanded a future free of the original owners of the soil. It is only the idea of genocide, incorporating both cultural and physical destruction, that can fully capture the totality of the project to undermine and destroy indigenous populations and their culture. In this analysis, I follow what Tony Barta identified as 'relations of genocide', in which the only outcome of the settler-colonial project could have been the destruction of existing societies. What is more, the British government knew explicitly that it had unleashed a destructive process that would eradicate those societies.[73] Its representatives disavowed, and indeed even regretted, the exterminatory impacts of their presence, yet they never faltered, never sought to roll back colonial development. Indeed, they even developed an understanding of the world that saw as inevitable the dying out of 'inferior' indigenous races.[74]

It is for these reasons that I believe that the term genocide is conceptually important and applicable in the Tasmanian case. Furthermore, I think it is even possible to identify a genocidal plan, and genocidal intent, thereby satisfying a more essentialist definition of genocide. Colonisation as a whole amounted to a 'plan' for a Tasmania, and indeed an Australia, free of indigenous peoples and their culture. This was a universal cultural assumption, it united protectionists and exterminationists, it was the common cause of the Colonial Office in Downing Street and the Tasmanian frontiersmen. Ultimately, there was among almost the entire British community a shared view that, to use Trollope's memorable phrase, the 'black men had to go'. The manner of their departure from history was contested, but there was a genocidal consensus that they had no part in the future. To put it another way, try imagining the colonisation of Van Diemen's Land proceeding in a manner that provided the island's original peoples with a future as inhabitants of Tasmania. Imagine if you like that those individuals committed to the protection of indigenous peoples had held sway, that disease had not destroyed the community held at Flinders Island. Is it possible to imagine a future in which indigenous communities flourished, practising their own culture and traditions? I would argue that it is not, because the avowed aim of colonisation was to destroy that culture and, at best, to save 'savages' from themselves.

It would, however, be intellectually dishonest to suggest that genocide is just deployed as an explanatory or conceptual device. There is a moral content to the accusation of genocide, just as there is to the rejection of the applicability of the word. Those who deny genocide in the Australian past do so in part because they do not wish to associate the Australian present with such an allegation. In international politics, the idea of genocide has a specific moral as well as legal force. Although the signatories to the genocide convention are not legally bound to intervene in reported cases of genocide, it is clear that various powers perceive that the moral case for their doing so will be greatly enhanced if a particular conflict can be labelled genocidal. Of course, this has had the regrettable impact of powers trying to avoid the use of the word in order to justify inaction – most notoriously in Rwanda in 1994.[75] In the politics of history and memory it is clear that the label of genocide conveys a particular moral message – hence the Turkish government's enduringly heavy-handed efforts to deny the Armenian genocide, and indeed other governments' enthusiastic embracing of the idea that the Turkish state committed genocide.[76] For victim groups, the label can also have a moral purpose – in that it appears to be the best way to articulate the depth of their suffering in any particular situation. Henry Reynolds reports for example the realisation of Wadjularbinna of the Gungalidda people of Northern Australia that she had been the victim of 'barbaric acts of genocide [...] a deliberate plan to deny me my true identity and try and destroy my place within a system of law and religion which connects me spiritually to the land, sea and creation'.[77] With reference to Tasmania, it is only genocide that can capture morally as well as conceptually the sheer scale of indigenous dislocation.

Yet it is in the moral case for the use of the term genocide that we are confronted again with the problem of comparison with the Holocaust. There is no doubt that the moral force of the term comes from association with the Nazi genocides. It was during World War II that Lemkin articulated his conceptualisation of genocide, and it is the Holocaust that modern globalised memory has elevated as the defining example of that crime. It is precisely because of associations with the Holocaust, the ultimate atrocity, that Turks, Americans and, as we have seen above, Australians deny that genocide occurred in their pasts, and it is for the same reason that Armenians, Native Americans and indigenous Australians assert that they have been victims of genocide.

Yet I have already asserted that genocide in Tasmania was not like the Holocaust, and in historical terms it was not. But paradoxically I do believe that the moral associations with the Holocaust that it creates are another reason that genocide provides a more pertinent framework for understanding the indigenous experience of colonisation than less morally charged concepts do. While there is no workable historical comparison between the dispossession and extermination of indigenous Tasmanians and the fate of Europe's Jews at the hand of the Nazis, there is a meaningful moral comparison.[78] While revulsion at the Holocaust is in part about the methods and the scale of the murder, there is something more fundamental that was and is repulsive about the Nazi project. What the Nazis sought to do was nothing less than to remake mankind in their own image – their desire was therefore literally to control and transform what it meant to be human. This, it seems to me, as well as the scale of destruction, is why the Holocaust now appears as the ultimate atrocity. It is certainly why I was drawn to Holocaust studies. But in the realisation that the Holocaust – through an attack on Jews and Judaism – was another in a long history of attacks on the nature of humanity, one is led inexorably to the conclusion that other historical episodes pose a similar moral challenge. And one of these is the settler colonisation of Australia and Tasmania, in which the British elevated themselves as the representatives of all humanity and quite deliberately consigned indigenous peoples to the past.

As a consequence, it is possible that observations about the moral similarities between the British settler-colonial project and the Nazi genocides might also cause us to revise the assertion that there is no sensible *historical* comparison between the Holocaust and the genocide of indigenous peoples. There is no sensible comparison to be made if one works backwards from the Holocaust, that remains true. If we attempt to fit genocide in Tasmania and Australia into the model of the Holocaust then we will inevitably fail. But self-evidently the crimes of settler colonialism pre-date the Holocaust. If we reverse the question, and ask whether, looking forward from the crimes of the settler-colonial era (throughout the European empires), we can usefully fit the Holocaust into a wider history of genocidal colonialism, then the answer is, of course, yes. We might well learn something about the Holocaust too, as a form of colonial violence come home to Europe, by considering the history of genocide in settler colonies – be that the British in Australia or, for example, the Germans in South West Africa.[79]

Of course, many historians might baulk at the suggestion that there is a moral context for the writing of history. Prioritising one set of values in this manner might be interpreted as a rejection of the noble dream of objectivity. And indeed it is. I have argued at length elsewhere that all historical writing is an ideological exercise.[80] This book is no different. It is grounded in a moral, ideological revulsion at genocide as an attack on difference and the magnificent variety of the human race and human cultures. An awareness that all historical narratives are ideological reconstructions does not necessarily lead us to a dangerous relativism, however. If it is replaced by a self-conscious, ideologically aware approach to the past that foregrounds the moral, ideological or political assumptions that anchor it, then history can be a means of coming to terms with the past and understanding the obligations that it places upon us. In this case, understanding that British settlers and indeed the British state were responsible for genocide in Van Diemen's Land might result in a more realistic appraisal of the legacy of empire than is on offer in contemporary discourse, and might make more meaningful public interactions with the idea of genocide in Britain today.[81]

Genocide plays a significant role in contemporary British culture. Largely through association with the Holocaust, it is generally represented as a kind of anti-symbol standing for all that Britain, and specifically its liberal sensibilities, is not. In contemporary cultural memory, genocide is often invoked as the ultimate atrocity. It is regretted, remembered and memorialised in a manner that suggests that such enormities occur in regimes and cultures very different to liberal Britain. Therefore, to suggest that genocide had occurred inside the British Empire, that British liberalism and ideas of progress were responsible for such an outrage, is self-evidently to challenge the complacency of modern memory culture.

There is one further justification for conceiving of what happened in British Van Diemen's Land as a genocide, one that will be explored throughout this book. Fundamentally, although they would use very different language, the British both in government and in wider culture understood the massive decline in population in terms that we would call genocidal today. Britain saw deliberate mass murder and extermination – or, as it was referred to at the time, 'extirpation' – in the 1820s and 1830s and continues to do so up to the present. The idea that indigenous Tasmanians had been exterminated was repeated over and over again, to the point that it became a cultural cliché. Intriguingly, therefore, and I hope to draw this out throughout this book, it was important in British narratives that there had been genocide in Van Diemen's Land. While it would be an exaggeration to say that British society and culture revelled in genocide, it is undoubtedly the case that the fact of genocide, and indeed the myth of the complete extinction of indigenous Tasmanians, told a powerful story about Britain and its history. The idea that the all-powerful Empire swept the helpless savages from history was repeated over and over, in scientific discourse especially, and displayed in museums, and as a consequence it is one of the primary aims of this book to understand how a clear conception of genocide has been woven into the British national story.

In their *Australia's Empire*, Deryck Schreuder and Stuart Ward argue history (and especially imperial history) is

> at its heart about memory – both that which lives in the popular imagination, and that which is put in place by careful and critical analysis of the past in all its protean and painful complexity. It becomes a civic memory which can be contested. It is also a memory which can be evoked for reasons of power, authority and cultural hegemony. It is not neutral territory, no matter how much we might yearn for a simplified past which legitimises the present.[82]

The present is the past and the past is the present. It is the aim of this book, using the example of the tragedy of indigenous Tasmanians, to demonstrate that genocide is very much a part of the British past and British history. And as such it is a call for that to be acknowledged in memory, in the British present, too.

TWO

Genocide in Van Diemen's Land

On 3 May 1804 a group of Oyster Bay people stumbled across the nascent British settlement at Risdon Cove. Although it is very difficult to say with any certainty what happened next, we know that the interaction between the two groups was violent and that some indigenous people were killed. These were the first casualties of a long conflict known in later years as the 'Black War', after which there were very few survivors. Twenty-six years after the British arrived perhaps only 700 indigenous people remained alive in Van Diemen's Land. In an effort to effect a permanent end to that conflict in October 1830, government men led the settler community in a military operation against them. Known as 'the Line' this was an attempt to confine the surviving population to a very small portion of the island. And for some of the participants it was more than just a territorial move: it was at last a concerted effort at extermination. This chapter traces the history of inter-communal relations between first contact and this attempted annihilation and crucially the role that the British 'home' played in this story.

While the massacre at Risdon Cove took place beyond the gaze of the home authorities of the British Empire in 1804, by the 1820s the idea that indigenous Tasmanians were locked in a spiral of vengeance for whatever occurred that May was well established in London. The military operations enacted by the colonial government in Hobart from 1826 onwards not only came with the approval of the British government but were reported in the British press and other publications.

Yet the role that the British government is awarded in the most recent accounts of genocide in Tasmania is that of an ultimately ineffectual restraining hand. To use the most modern language, the British government between 1826 and 1830 is portrayed as having been engaged in an unsuccessful project of genocide-prevention. Henry Reynolds argues that although British policy towards indigenous peoples was confused and contradictory the government in London was essentially the source of restraint – that in their entreaties against violence the British held back a settler population that from the mid 1820s wished to destroy the island's original population, who were attacking them in a war for control of the land.[1]

The central aim of this chapter is to critique the idea that the British government has some kind of alibi for the genocide that took place on territory that it controlled, and that was enacted by men whom it had sent to the other side of the world. This is not to say that the British government either established or endorsed a deliberate campaign of mass murder in Van Diemen's Land. However, it was committed to the development of the colony at all costs and continually sanctioned policies that had a destructive impact on indigenous communities. Ultimately the British government established a genocidal consensus that looked forward to a colony without indigenous Tasmanians.

FIRST CONTACT

When John West looked back at the history of Tasmania in the 1850s he could see an island transformed by an apparently all-powerful British invasion, by the 'triumph of colonisation'. The island itself had been revolutionised by the British presence: its original population had declined to just a handful of survivors, and it was thus easy for West to see the history of Van Diemen's Land in terms of the might of the British Empire.[2] Yet in 1804 the settlement must have looked rather different. The first efforts at settlement had failed, and the British began their Van Diemen's Land huddled in a few huts against the coast in the south-east corner of the island. Britain must have seemed a very long way away indeed. According to James Boyce the British government rather forgot about Van Diemen's Land in its first decade. It did not reply to the assiduous correspondence of the colony's first lieutenant governor, David Collins, between 1804 and his death in 1810, leaving the administration of the island to the larger parent colony of New South Wales.[3] The few sources we do have for these early years point to a somewhat desperate state of affairs, a colony whose 'distress is beyond conception', where food was scarce and hunger a defining feature.[4]

As strangers in a strange land the settlers would have felt an acute vulnerability, which set the tone for the incident at Risdon Cove in May 1804. Although it is easy to be lulled into thinking of the all-powerful British arriving in Van Diemen's Land and sweeping away all before them, the reality was rather different. It was the British who were confined to a small portion of the island in 1804, while indigenous communities roamed across large swathes of it, as they had done traditionally. As such it may well have been the British who were the more afraid when an indigenous group approached their settlement in May 1804.[5]

It is almost impossible to construct anything approaching a reliable narrative of what happened in Risdon Cove that May. The settlement had been established in September 1803. The land was particularly attractive as it encompassed traditional kangaroo-hunting grounds of the Big River and Oyster Bay peoples, which appeared to the British as naturally occurring parkland, but which had in fact been created by 'firestick farming'.[6] On 3 May 1804 a group of between 300 and 600 approached the settlement – probably engaged in hunting for kangaroo or perhaps congregating for a corroboree.[7] According to original eyewitness testimony the group intended to attack the settlement, although reports of their hostile intent may have been exaggerated in order to justify later settler violence. Certainly witnesses to a later enquiry stated that the Oyster Bay people were unarmed.[8] Whatever the intent of the indigenous Tasmanians who entered the Risdon Cove settlement, the settlers sought either to force them away or to engage them in combat. All we can say with certainty is that the indigenous group were fired upon by the British and that loss of life ensued.

The Last Man

What is much less certain is the number of indigenous people murdered. Robert Knopwood, the first chaplain of the settlements in Van Diemen's Land, recorded in his diary being called to Risdon Cove to perform the baptism of a boy whose parents had been killed in the attack.[9] Knopwood later told the Aborigines Committee, which oversaw the inquiry into the massacre, that five or six people were killed.[10] Another witness to the same committee suggested that a 'great many of the Natives [were] slaughtered and wounded'.[11] The committee itself concluded that as many as 50 were killed, although it acknowledged that that figure might have been an exaggeration. Edward White also testified that the remains of some of the dead were preserved by Jacob Mountgarret, the settlement surgeon, suggesting that the practice of collecting human remains was established at the beginning of the colony's history.

What is undeniable, however, is that the memory of that day became centrally important to the way that the authorities in Van Diemen's Land and the British Colonial Office understood and explained any violence between the indigenous and settler communities. Lieutenant Governor Collins warned that after the 'affray at Risdon Cove' he was fearful of the 'vindictive spirit of these people'.[12] His successor Thomas Davey recalled with shame the actions of 'British subjects' who had so 'ignominiously stained the honour of their country' at Risdon. Another lieutenant governor, George Arthur, did the same. When the British government published a report into the possibilities of further colonial development in Van Diemen's Land at the beginning of the 1820s, it was reported that relations between the two communities were governed by 'the spirit of hostility and revenge that [the indigenous community] still cherish for an act of unjustifiable violence formerly committed upon them'.[13]

In fact the British government was so attached to the narrative that saw the indigenous community as seeking revenge for the Risdon Cove massacre that the Colonial Office criticised the government in Hobart when it attempted to offer an alternative explanation. Looking back from a distance of more than 25 years, the Aborigines

Committee, which had been established by Lieutenant Governor George Arthur to administer and advise on policy towards the clans, reconstructed the massacre as the foundational event in settler-indigenous relations. But the committee argued that it was unable to say for certain whether violence since 1804 was a result of a desire for revenge on the part of the indigenous community, or of some more fundamental 'lurking spirit of cruelty and mischievous craft' on the part of 'the Natives'.[14] The then Secretary of State in London, George Murray, refused to allow such speculation to pass. On the contrary, Murray advised that the British government was convinced that hostility in Van Diemen's Land began with the violence of the 'white' community at Risdon Cove.[15] Such a view was a repudiation of the suggestion that indigenous Tasmanians somehow lacked a human response, and might be seen as acceptance of responsibility by the British. At the same time the government still subscribed to a version of events that constructed the islanders as irrational. They were believed to have been locked in a spiral of revenge. Crucially, the British government's narrative of the origins of violence in Van Diemen's Land also did not imply that violence was the inevitable outcome of British colonisation.

George Augustus Robinson recorded in his diary the importance of indigenous memories of Risdon and a desire for revenge as an explanation for the conflict that followed. 'It is very certain,' Robinson wrote in November 1829, 'that the natives to this very hour foster in their minds a remembrance of this wanton massacre of their fellow beings, and are anxious to atone for this aggression by the blood of their enemies.' In his ensuing account of the conflict, Robinson described the usurpation of traditional hunting grounds as one of the consequences of colonisation. The more obvious interpretation of the narrative that Robinson recounted was of course that violence was aimed at ending settler disruption of food supply. Yet such an understanding eluded him, as it did the British government. Instead Robinson did not allow anything to disrupt the sense that the 'devouring spirit of revenge' was the root cause of conflict.[16]

Of course, we can only speculate as to why, for Robinson and for London, the 'memory and vengeance' narrative was more appealing than the suggestion that the indigenous population were simply defending their territory. But what is clear is that the vengeance narrative suggested that it was not the occupation of the land per se that caused them to attack settlers, but rather that sufficient effort had not been made to demonstrate that the colonial development of the island was for the good of all. In other words it was not colonisation that was at fault, but the failure of its implementation.[17] It was not the fault of the British authors of colonisation but that of the settlers who carried it out.

The idea that the island's peoples had been prompted to an indiscriminate vengeance by the massacre, a passion which sustained them and their descendants over the next 30 years, tells us much about the assumptions that the British brought with them to Van Diemen's Land. Tasmanians were not, they supposed, capable of rational thought or action. Indeed the belief that indigenous peoples across the Empire were essentially childlike, incapable of meaningful communal or political action, underpinned the very basis of the British occupation of the land. It was widely assumed that an imagined failure of such peoples to exploit the resources of the land provided the moral and legal basis of colonisation.

Whether or not treatises like Emer de Vattel's *The Law of Nations* provided an adequate legal basis for the ownership of the land is a matter of ongoing dispute.[18] But the assumption that indigenous peoples were incapable, that they required the presence of the colonists to benefit from the possibilities of their land, was undoubtedly well established. It was an idea that also underpinned perhaps the most powerful assumption that the colonial authorities brought to their relations with peoples they encountered – that the island's communities required their protection. When in 1805 Lieutenant Governor David Collins announced that Tasmanians benefitted from the 'king's peace', that they were now subjects under British law, he was giving practical voice to that belief.[19] It was an assertion that would be repeated by his successors Davey, Sorell and Arthur. Again we might use these repeated statements as evidence of the benign intentions of the British. But the consistency of these public reminders of the duty of protection might be read in another way, as pointing to the threat the settlers represented for the existing population rather than the benefits they brought. After all, reminders that the indigenous community enjoyed the protection of the Crown were also warnings that settlers should desist from violence.

Such reminders of the legal obligation that settlers owed indigenous peoples do not mean those obligations were enforced. There were no prosecutions for either the maltreatment or the murder of indigenous Tasmanians in colonial Van Diemen's Land, but we know that violence was regular, especially before 1808.[20] Again the sources are scarce, but Robert Knopwood's diaries are replete with examples of confrontation – often it appears the result of islanders' attempts to expel settlers from their traditional hunting grounds. Most of the conflict appears to have occurred when settlers left the settled areas of the island, often in search of food. On 19 May 1807 Knopwood recorded the return of a man who had been absent from the settlement for 19 days:

> the natives had nearly killed him and his dogs. The governor's people were out with him when a battle ensued and they killed one of the natives [...] It is very dangerous to be out alone for fear of them.[21]

For those looking on from afar, the colonists at Van Diemen's Land appeared to be under siege from a hostile population. The government newspaper, the *Hobart Town Gazette*, for example, detailed attacks on settlers and their livestock after 1814.[22] Contemporary accounts tended to record more assiduously indigenous attacks on settlers than incidents in which the latter were the aggressors.

That Knopwood (who was a magistrate as well as a priest) points to the murder of indigenous Tasmanians as having been carried out by government men suggests that the will to prosecute for such crimes was limited. And again the violence occurred when settlers were pursuing the resources on which the original inhabitants' lives depended. This was, then, a conflict about rather more than a spirit of violence and revenge. Knopwood also pointed to the practice of taking children into white homes throughout the early history of the British colony. He had performed 26 baptisms by 1820.[23]

Reports of violence between the indigenous community and the settlers are undoubtedly sporadic in those first years of the colony, and we must presume that this represents a very small fragment of the total.[24] James Bonwick recounted in the 1870s that he had been able to find no records relating to the 'first six years of the settlement', for example. However, he pointed to a government declaration of 1810 that threatened punishment to anyone proved to be involved in the 'abominable cruelties which have been practised on [the indigenous population] by the white people' as evidence of a culture of violence. In New South Wales it was reported that violence was endemic in these years.[25] Again, we must assume that the silences in such documentation disguise much bloodshed.

In June 1813 Lieutenant Governor Davey issued a proclamation that attempted to halt violence on the frontier, a further suggestion that this was a widespread problem. Davey complained that 'the resentment of these poor uncultivated beings has been justly excited by a most barbarous and inhuman mode of proceeding against them'.[26] In 1830 witnesses to the Aborigines Committee recalled that violence between the two populations was consistently present, especially on the frontier, in the first two decades of the colony's existence. They reported:

> as the white population spread itself more widely over the island, and the settlers came more frequently in contact with the Natives, many outrages were committed which no interposition of the government, however well disposed, could, with the means at its command, have been able to prevent.

Notwithstanding the tendency of a government committee to believe that it had been impossible for the government to prevent bloodshed, it is telling that the authorities could accept that, for those on the frontier, 'it was as if the life of a savage had been unworthy of the slightest consideration'.[27] While the Aborigines Committee believed that such behaviour was 'disgraceful to the British character', it also noted with regret that it was much more a defining feature of British interactions with indigenous peoples than the conciliation and friendship that was supposed to govern inter-communal relations. As such the government in London might have suggested that relations between the communities were to be governed by the spirit of amity and kindness, but the harsh colonial reality was somewhat different.

However, it would be equally misleading to suggest that the evidence of the early colony points only to conflict between the populations. The same sources that suggest violence also remember cooperation and coexistence on a number of levels. Knopwood's diary suggests that food and resources were not only a source of conflict. He often describes giving food to a 'party of natives' that came to his land, suggesting that at times they would eat together.[28] Indigenous communities certainly adopted some aspects of settler culture – not least by drinking tea and keeping dogs, which had not been present on the island before the arrival of the British.[29] The most resonant example of such cross-cultural cooperation and coexistence were the mixed-heritage communities that began to emerge and become established in Van Diemen's Land: 'George Briggs [for example] lived with Woretermoteryenna [...] on Clarke Island, with their daughter, Dalrymple (Dolly) Mountgarret Briggs. Dolly was then sent to Launceston, where she was educated by the Mountgarret family and baptised by Robert Knopwood.' Dolly Briggs later married the stockman Thomas Johnson and was awarded a grant of land, pointing to the potential success of communal interaction.[30]

The Last Man

DEVELOPMENT

Although there was a regularity to settler–indigenous clashes in the first years of the colony, this does not mean that it was an all-consuming concern for the colonial authorities. Lieutenant Governor Sorell did not even mention the indigenous population in the instructions that he prepared for his successor in 1824.[31] And there was very little attention to the matter paid in accounts of the colony prepared for London before the 1820s. That said, there was a perception in London that Van Diemen's Land was witness to ongoing conflict between settlers and the original population from the beginning of the 1820s. The *Morning Post* reported in November 1821 that 'the natives of Van Diemen's Land [...] have been always hostilely inclined' to the British presence. The paper also confirmed the assumed importance of the Risdon Cove massacre when it explained this disposition as the result of a 'fatal quarrel at the first settling'.[32] More positive guides to emigrants also remembered the Risdon Cove massacre as the original offence that established the violence of settler–indigenous relationships – one history of the colony regretted that 'but for an untoward accident an amicable intercourse might, ere this, have been established between the settlers and the natives'.[33] As we can see, the idea that the colonisation did not inevitably result in conflict was well embedded.

That the *Morning Post* was writing about Van Diemen's Land at all speaks to a shift in attitude in Britain during the 1820s. In its first years Van Diemen's Land, and for that matter its parent colony New South Wales, had been regarded as primarily a penal settlement. But in the aftermath of the Napoleonic wars and the attendant problems of economic recovery, around 1820, perceptions changed and free migrants increasingly began to see the possibility of an Antipodean future. This was not the 'shovelling out' of Britain's paupers, however, but a middle-class emigration of people (largely men) with enough capital to qualify for free land grants. It would not be until later in the 1820s that emigration would be seen as a possible solution to Malthusian population problems, leading to the assisted-migration schemes of the 1830s and the development of systematic colonisation.

In 1819 the British government appointed John Thomas Bigge to inquire into the potential for development in the colony of New South Wales, including a particular focus on Van Diemen's Land. Bigge recommended that the colony was ripe for especially agricultural and pastoral development owing to the 'pre-eminent fertility of the soil'.[34] He envisaged the emigration of 'gentlemen of means' in order to promote colonial development and exploit the extant convict labour force.[35] Tellingly, Bigge gave little or no thought to indigenous peoples in his projection of the Tasmanian future, and it is difficult to disagree with John West's judgement in 1850 that the report was 'astonishing' in its 'indifference' to them.[36] Bigge predicted that 'there is no reason to presume that the black natives are numerous or that they will oppose any serious resistance to the extension of future settlements'.[37] He was proved spectacularly wrong, but his report was an indication of the degree to which government behaved as if the island's original population either did not matter or indeed was not even really there.

The Bigge report signalled a new attitude to the Australian colonies. As a consequence, the history of Van Diemen's Land in the 1820s is on one level that of an astonishingly rapid colonial development. This development was, in line with Bigge's suggestions, driven by the movement of middle-class men and their money from Britain, albeit crucially supported by government. Donald Macleod of Talisker on the Isle of Skye might be a typical example. Macleod left for Van Diemen's Land in 1820. He travelled to Australia with his seven children and two servants, lured by the promise of a land grant of 2,000 acres and, crucially, the offer of free convict labour to help develop the estate. According to Eric Richards this was 'patrician or family migration', which aimed to preserve or at least replicate the existing social order abroad. It was entirely dependent on the state because it relied on the existence of convict labour.[38] The British state did not encourage only the relocation of individuals to Van Diemen's Land, but the movement of capital too. The government licensed companies, like the Van Diemen's Land Company, as a means of aiding imperial development and looked to emigration to spread British wealth.[39] As the 1820s wore on the idea that Van Diemen's Land offered considerable possibilities for sheep-farming, and might therefore be a possible solution to British difficulties in the international woollen trade, also took hold. Accordingly, John Helder Wedge left Britain with 29 merino sheep in 1824 to work for the Van Diemen's Land Company. He was escaping debts from an unsuccessful venture in farming, and was appointed a surveyor in the colony. He would return in the 1830s along with ephemera he collected from his pursuit of indigenous Tasmanians in his capacity as a surveyor, pushing back the boundaries of the Vandemonian frontier.[40]

The British press reflected these changing attitudes, regularly printing letters from the colonies as a form of pro-emigration propaganda.[41] In this discourse Van Diemen's Land emerged as a kind of English Elysium, a place that was much the same as England, only better. 'All English fruits and vegetables are much finer than in England,' claimed the *Hampshire Telegraph* in December 1823, and could be grown with neither skill nor toil: 'you turn up the ground, you put in your seed, you sleep, and it grows.'[42]

Such paeans to 'our Australian paradise' were also represented in a wider emigration propaganda,[43] aimed specifically at enticing emigrants to Van Diemen's Land to enjoy the 'fineness of the climate there'.[44] Although such literature was aimed at men of capital somehow disenchanted with home, it was clearly seen as essential to demonstrate how very British – or English – it was on the other side of the world.[45] As Lieutenant Charles Jeffreys instructed readers in 1820, North America might have been attractive to those who wished to emigrate for 'political' or other 'ignoble' motives, but for 'settlers who carry with them British predilections, and who still enjoy British laws, with British manners and comforts [...] the settlements in Van Diemen's Land [are] more suited to their expectations.'[46]

Genocide in Van Diemen's Land

While Van Diemen's Land's essential Englishness was a central trope of this discourse, so was the idea that the island also represented a wilderness 'untouched by the hand of man'.[47] Such rhetoric displayed scant understanding of a population that had been present for some 40,000 years. Some emigrants' guides literally pretended that indigenous peoples did not exist, making no mention of them at all.[48] Others urged a form of colonial development that envisaged no competition for settler control of the land. Indeed it was the sheer emptiness of the island, according to these propagandists, that made it so attractive for development – the possibilities were scarcely imaginable.[49] It is little wonder that Van Diemen's Land appealed to 'ambitious, avaricious men'. For the reading men of Britain there appeared to be money to be made and land to be had.[50]

The sunlit colonial future that emigrants were promised did not include the indigenous population. Where they were represented, indigenous Tasmanians were constructed as peoples without culture, 'more barbarous and uncivilised' even than the population of continental Australia.[51] Grotesque racial characterisations of the 'inferior' Tasmanian abounded: they had 'jaws elongated like the Ourang Outang [...] they are dark, short in stature, with disproportionately thin limbs and shapeless bodies, entirely naked. Add to this frizzled hair and a most hideous expression or countenance.'[52] Such images might have raised alarm, or been off-putting to potential migrants, as might the universal view that the indigenous Tasmanians were (after Risdon) implacably hostile to their 'new neighbours'. Yet such concerns could be set aside, because the idea that the population was 'rapidly diminishing' abounded too.[53] These were peoples of the past, hurtling to oblivion. It was widely assumed that only the British would see Van Diemen's Land's future.

By the mid nineteenth century the idea that the indigenous peoples of all of Australia, and indeed throughout European empires, were expiring was commonplace. This was often interpreted as a natural process (or in Charles Darwin's case as the outcome of evolutionary advance[54]), and it became a rather convenient way to avoid confronting the impact of European colonisation on these societies.[55] It is intriguing to note the presence of this extermination discourse much earlier in emigration propaganda. In its 1820s incarnation it seems to have been rather more than just an evasion narrative.[56] Because it was part of a concerted effort to promote the development of the colonies, it was not a retrospective explanation for the decline of indigenous peoples but part of an ideological vision of the future. Therefore, this discourse of development in Britain hinted at the genocidal logic of the expansion of the colony.

When George Arthur was appointed lieutenant governor in Van Diemen's Land in May 1824, he shared this vision of an expanding and developing colony.[57] Although Arthur is remembered chiefly for the severity of his penal system (as well as his supervising of the genocide of indigenous Tasmanians), the significance of his commitment to the development of the colony, the expansion of its territory and the rapid growth of its population should not be underestimated.[58]

In line with this shifting conception of the importance of Van Diemen's Land, the new lieutenant governor was instructed that he must correspond directly with the Colonial Office 'upon all public questions which may arise within his government'.[59] Of course, the Colonial Office could not hope to dictate policy from the other side of the world, if only because it took so long to convey instructions between Hobart and London. As Arthur's predecessor Sorell had pointed out in 1817, he left London with a set of instructions on how to deal with the problem of bushrangers (escaped convicts) that were quite inappropriate by the time he got to Hobart some eight months later.[60]

In part it was hoped that London would not have to dictate policy anyway. When James Stephen, permanent undersecretary in the Colonial Office, told Arthur that he saw the colonists as 'good children' and the Colonial Office as 'considerate parents', he was writing to someone whom he considered a personal friend.[61] As he wrote in July 1824, there were 'few persons beyond my domestic circle, of whom I think more frequently or whom I would more gladly see than yourself'.[62] Stephen and Arthur were from the same world. Both men had emerged from the campaign against the slave trade, and both would have considered themselves evangelical reformers. Both were committed to the development of Van Diemen's Land and indeed of Australia more generally. As Stephen reflected towards the end of his career, Australia was to be 'built up from sea to sea as a white man's country'.[63]

Together, Stephen in London and Arthur in Hobart presided over the massive development of the colony. Nearly 2 million acres of land were granted between 1823 and 1831, a several-hundredfold increase on the amount of land granted prior to Arthur's arrival.[64] Indeed, in 1823 there were some 1,027 separate land grants made in Van Diemen's Land. That there were no grants at all in 1822 and just 116 in 1821 gives some indication of the great surge in development that the colony experienced.[65] The population ballooned from 12,643 in 1824 to 24,504 by 1830, and more than 40,000 by 1835.[66] The expansion in the number of people on the island was nothing compared to the explosion in the cattle and particularly sheep populations. By 1831 there were some 682,128 sheep on the island.[67] Such a number also meant that Van Diemen's Land became an important provider of wool for British markets. Indeed more wool (in monetary terms) was imported from Van Diemen's Land in 1831 than from the larger parent colony in New South Wales.[68]

Arthur's evangelical background and his role in the abolition of the slave trade in his previous posting in Honduras suggested that he would be a friend to the nations of Van Diemen's Land. Certainly he approached them with the desire to 'conciliate' and, in the language of colonisation, to share with them the benefits that he believed empire could bring. Arthur's first action towards the indigenous community, like his predecessor's, was to issue proclamations declaring them to be 'under the protection of British law' and warning settlers to desist from violence against them.[69] He encouraged settlers instead 'to exercise the utmost forbearance towards Aborigines, treating them on all occasions with the utmost kindness and compassion'.[70] But like his friend Stephen in the Colonial Office, whatever the strength of Arthur's commitment to improving relations between the two groups, it was secondary to his commitment to colonial expansion. Ultimately this vision of development did not include the indigenous population.

'THE BLACK WAR'

As a consequence of the evolving attitude to the question of colonial development in London, and perhaps the growing sense of the economic contribution that the colonies might make to metropolitan Britain, Arthur was issued with a new set of instructions to guide his dealings with indigenous communities. London still desired that they be treated with kindness, and ideally that they be 'civilised' – in other words transformed and forced to abandon their culture. But the Colonial Office also made clear that if the 'native inhabitants' were to attack the colony it was the '*duty*' of the governor to 'oppose force with force'. Even more significantly than that, indigenous people who threatened the colony were to be treated 'as if they proceeded from subjects of any accredited state'.[71]

Whereas previously London had little to say on the subject of settler–indigenous relations in the Australian colonies, beyond their requirement that 'the savages' be treated with kindness, this represented a profound shift. Aboriginal Tasmanians (and indeed all indigenous Australians) had been subject to the 'king's peace' and theoretically at least treated as equal under the law and as British subjects. But Secretary of State Henry Bathurst was now instructing the governors of New South Wales and Van Diemen's Land that it was possible for a state of war to exist between the settlers and indigenous communities. Such a declaration had contradictory implications. It meant that colonial governments (and indeed individuals) could justify much more easily the use of force. Previously the protection of the Crown had to be formally rescinded through a declaration of martial law in a particular territory. Yet it also meant that the British government was coming close to recognising indigenous communities' sovereignty in their territory – in the words of John Connor it was 'the closest the British government ever came to accepting the reality that the Aborigines were not misbehaving British subjects, but were sovereign peoples defending their lands in war'.[72]

While it implied indigenous territorial rights, overall the Bathurst declaration signalled the commitment of the British government to the defence of its colonial possessions. If indigenous peoples' equal status in the eyes of the law had previously been of little practical importance, from the mid 1820s there was also a mechanism by which it could be abandoned. When the colonial authorities did indeed turn to use military force against the indigenous clans, it was therefore instructions such as this that provided both further legal and moral foundation for such campaigns.[73]

After 1824 the colonial government in Hobart adopted force more and more as the means to manage relations with clans who were themselves attacking expanding settlements more frequently. The authorities embraced violence more formally in 1828 through the adoption of martial law. Whatever the specific motivations for any particular policy changes, the turn to violence was a direct result of the will to develop and expand the settlement. In other words, it was the result of pressure exerted from Britain, and indeed from the British government, and it was carried out within a legal framework constructed in the mother country. As the settlements, and particularly farmlands, expanded, indigenous ways of life were more and more disrupted. The idea of individual ownership of the land was alien to a population that had operated a communal system of land use. When, for example, the settler J.C. Sutherland ordered 'the natives' from *his* land in March 1824 it must have appeared to those expelled like the simple theft that it was.[74]

Indeed, it was more than that. To the indigenous community their relationship with the land was central to their existence, as both the source of food and a repository of culture and memory. To be removed from the land was thus nothing less than an existential threat. As a consequence, serious and sustained resistance against that threat appears to have begun in the latter part of 1823. One group, known in the colony as a 'tame mob' because they sometimes entered settled districts, was implicated in a number of violent attacks on stock-keepers on the east coast of Van Diemen's Land. In the face of increasing violence, the authorities in Hobart did attempt to fulfil at least one half of their obligation to apply the strictures of British law to settler–indigenous relations. Following the campaign to rid the colony of so-called bushrangers – escaped convicts who had terrorised the community in previous years – they sought to apply the full force of the law to individuals guilty of violence against the settlers. The apparent leader of the mob, Musquito, who was originally from New South Wales and who had previously been employed by the colonial authorities in pursuit of escaped convicts, became the first victim of this judicial process. After the authorities reneged on an agreement to return Musquito to continental Australia, he united with indigenous Tasmanians from the Oyster Bay people and led resistance against colonisation. He was ultimately arrested, tried and executed by a military court in February 1825.[75]

The trial and public execution of Musquito and an accomplice was aimed to act as a deterrent to the indigenous population, who were treated as criminals rather than opponents in war. Such a policy reflected a misunderstanding of the nature of indigenous violence, which Arthur believed was the work of individuals and not therefore indicative of any wider or more profound rejection of colonial development. It was as if he understood this violence in the same way he had the threat posed by the bushrangers or escaped convicts, as the *criminal* actions of individual malcontents rather than manifestations of any systemic or structural issues. However, there was a clear relationship between the expansion of the frontier and the levels of violence between settler and indigenous communities. As the frontier grew the number of violent incidents increased. Although documentation is necessarily fragmentary, and there was a natural inclination for settlers to record attacks on themselves and not those in which they were the instigators, we can see a clear relationship emerging.

There were just 11 violent incidents in 1824; the yearly total had risen to 72 by 1827, 144 by 1828, and 222 by 1830.[76] It therefore appears that the indigenous community responded to the profound threat represented by development in Tasmania with increasingly severe (and numerous) attacks on the settler population. In turn an increasingly paranoid settler population themselves reacted with ferocity, and a spiralling cycle of violence ensued. It is almost impossible to calculate the number of victims from these clashes, and we can only speculate as to the true figure that lies behind the documentary evidence. A police report from Launceston dated 27 May 1827 was typical. It records the death of William Knight, who was 'killed by the black native people'. It then refers to 'an attack made upon the murderers the next day by Corporal Skinner and his party'. It does not record the number of indigenous casualties.[77]

If such violence on the part of the island's original inhabitants was an attempt to roll back colonial development, the aggression of the settlers appears to have been inspired by the increasing desire to exterminate at the very least individual clans. Gilbert Robertson, who would lead one of the roving parties established by martial law in the colony from 1828, reported an incident to the Aborigines Committee that appears very much like an attempt to destroy an entire group. He stated that

> 20 Natives have been killed for one white man; great ravages were committed by a party of constables and some of the 40th regiment sent from Campbell Town; the party consisted of five or six; they got the Natives between two perpendicular rocks [...] the party killed them by firing all their ammunition upon them and then dragging the women and children [...] and dashing out their brains.[78]

There are many other examples, from newspapers in the colony, from the diaries of settlers and indeed from discussions within government, of the settler community calling for a campaign against the natives.

The Last Man

George Hobler, for example, in an attempt to demonstrate to his family in England the realities of colonial life, recorded in his diary an incident in which he and his men sought a group of indigenous Tasmanians at night in order to 'slaughter them' as they lay around their fire.[79] George Augustus Robinson reported several conversations with men he described as 'extirpationists' during his own 'friendly' and 'unarmed' pursuit of the indigenous population.[80]

When in November 1826 the authorities in Hobart declared that it was permissible for the settlers to use force against the indigenous population in order to drive them from the land, they portrayed a 'treacherous and sanguinary' community that repaid 'kindness' with 'murder'.[81] In this way the government was feeding a settler perception of indigenous Tasmanians as their permanent and irretrievable enemy. In this context government pleas that indigenous peoples still be treated with kindness or forbearance, and its insistence that settlers should not desire their eradication, were an irrelevance. The reality is that the decision to sanction the use of force was an acknowledgement, after the fact, of a war that was ongoing between the communities, one that had become, for some settlers at least, a war of extermination.

Genocidal intent was expressed by private citizens and rhetorically opposed by the government. Scholars such as Colin Tatz have as a consequence characterised genocide in Van Diemen's Land as taking place outside the reaches of government and the state, in keeping with the wild conditions of the frontier.[82] In such a formulation Governor Arthur's declaration of November 1826 was concerned less with confronting the 'outrages' of a violent indigenous community than with reining in a settler population who, on its fringes, were bent on the eradication of their antagonists. Yet in so doing Arthur made the indigenous community the 'open enemies', to use a phrase from the declaration, of the colonial state.[83] And the legal basis for this effective declaration of war was the instruction from the British state of 1825 that force should be used to protect the development of the colony. Whatever the desire for 'conciliation' and 'friendship', then, from November 1826 Britain was in effect at war with the original population of Van Diemen's Land. This was a war that by 1828 would involve 450 soldiers in the interior of the colony, as well as large numbers of mobilised men from the settler communities.[84]

This of course does not mean that Governor Arthur, or the British government he represented, acquiesced in the settlers' desire for extermination. But they did, together, provide the framework through which those exterminatory desires could be channelled. And, inevitably, the government's licensing of the use of force, its legal provision for a state of war, did not bring an end to violence but intensified it. Lyndall Ryan points to at least 70 attacks by indigenous groups on settlers and their property between September 1827 and March 1828 and argues that these followed Governor Arthur's urging greater use of force in the middle of 1827.[85] In November 1827 the lieutenant governor called for the 'hearty cooperation of all persons [...] for the common defence and protection of the community'.[86]

In the face of such violence, Arthur wrote regularly to London to seek counsel on how best to proceed. Both he and the British government were trapped in a situation in which they provided a means and a justification for settler violence that they apparently abhorred. And indeed in such correspondence Arthur hinted that the problem was as much *settler* violence as anything else. In January 1828 he outlined what he saw as the options in response to continuing calls to adopt 'harsh measures' – in other words to launch a full-scale drive for extermination. In this letter he suggested that the best plan was to attempt to confine the indigenous population to a portion of the island, 'which should be strictly reserved for them, and to supply them with food and clothing and afford them protection from injuries'.[87]

Such a vision of protection was in keeping with the British government's original instructions that every effort should be made to 'civilise' the indigenous community and bring to them the assumed benefits of the British mode of life, combined with its later recommendations that resistance be met with force. As such it is important to consider what the full implications of Arthur's idea of permanent protection really were. As Arthur himself acknowledged, it would lead to the transformation of the islanders' way of life. No longer would the communities be able to pursue their nomadic, migratory culture. Instead they would be reliant for sustenance on a colonial authority that wished to enclose them permanently. Such an apparently humanitarian vision, then, entailed its own particular form of cultural disruption and dislocation. In the twentieth or twenty-first century this kind of population movement would be called deportation or ethnic cleansing.

Just three months later, and in what Lyndall Ryan has interpreted as an absence of direction from London,[88] Arthur took decisive action to wrest control of increasingly chaotic clashes between indigenous Tasmanians and the settlers. On 15 April 1828 the colonial authorities announced their intention to seek the territorial solution to the ongoing violence that they had outlined previously.[89] Indigenous peoples were, as Arthur relayed to the Colonial Office two days later, going to be permanently excluded from the settled districts of the island, 'until their habits become civilised'. They were to be confined to territory in the west of Van Diemen's Land.[90] The settled districts were to be permanently protected by a 'line of military posts' and indigenous Tasmanians were to be prevented from entering them. In addition, any persons currently in the settled districts were to be 'expelled by force'. The government was prepared to face 'such consequences as may be necessarily attendant' on such a measure.[91] As the island's nations were at war and likely to react violently to such efforts, those 'consequences' were thus understood to be lethal.

London eventually approved both the prototype plan that Arthur outlined and the proclamation that was eventually issued. In other words, the government approved the violent separation of the communities. When Secretary of State William Huskisson wrote to Arthur in May 1828 his sanction of the proposed confinement seemed to be given with an air of hope rather than expectation. Indeed Huskisson, while offering no real solution, acknowledged that there was a contradiction between indigenous Tasmanians' desire to lead a nomadic life with full access to the land, and the British need for expanding their settlement.[92] Ultimately those mutually exclusive ambitions could only be resolved by the use of force. Huskisson's successor George Murray acknowledged as much when he instructed Arthur in August 1828 to adopt any measure that could 'check the incursions of the natives'.[93] Indeed, in Murray's subsequent approval of the declaration that announced indigenous peoples' permanent exclusion from the settled districts of the island, he wondered whether there was any real solution that did not rely on 'absolute force'. Was there any other way that 'ignorant beings' could be induced to acknowledge British authority, he wondered? Especially 'when possessed with the idea which they appear to entertain in regard to their own rights over the country, in comparison with the colonists'.[94]

In writing to Hobart in such terms, Murray seemed to reconfirm the priorities of the British government. In doing so, and in highlighting the government's preparedness to sanction 'absolute force', he demonstrated that the 'security of the lives and property of the settlers' was the most fundamental obligation on colonial governments, despite all the rhetoric of the need to 'protect' and conciliate. Such an instruction had lethal consequences. In acknowledging that the 'Aborigines of Van Diemen's Land' were convinced that they had prior claim to the territory, Murray also revealed that London was capable of understanding the reality of the conflict in which they were engaged. This was not a vengeful population possessed of some demonic spirit, but a community that was seeking to defend its land, to repel the British invaders. This was a war for the land and the British (in Hobart and in London) knew it.

In approving the authority of absolute force, Murray also anticipated Governor Arthur's next legislative move – a declaration of martial law in the colony. This pronouncement, made in November 1828 after the measures adopted in April failed to stem the tide of violence, represented in effect a full-scale declaration of war.[95] According to Henry Reynolds, martial law represented the colonial authorities' wholesale embracing of violence. The intention was to demonstrate to the indigenous population the full might of the British Empire, or, to use the Colonial Office's phrase, to make clear the authority of absolute force. This was to be done through the institution of several 'roving parties' or brigades, who were authorised to seek out indigenous groups at large within the settled districts of the island and effect their capture and eventual expulsion as per the territorial divisions announced in April. It is worth reiterating that although it was a policy designed in Hobart, it was carried out within a legal framework established by London.

There is little doubt that the militarisation of the community, and the sanctioning of force contained within the move to martial law, escalated violence – after all, it established bands of armed men 'scouring the bush' for indigenous clans.[96] It also incentivised the settler pursuit of indigenous peoples by providing bounty for each captured adult and child, and offering the possibility of a ticket of leave for any convict involved in any form of capture.[97] Yet it cannot be argued that this was an example of the colonial government's embracing of the desire to exterminate that abounded in the settler community. Governor Arthur wrote to the commanders of all roving parties in order to reiterate 'that the government puts forth its strength on this occasion by *no means whatever with a view to seeking the destruction of the Aborigines*'. Indeed, the very opposite was true: martial law was intended to bring about an end to the conflict, which Arthur feared would otherwise end only in the 'annihilation of the natives'.[98] As such, both the British and Tasmanian governments, somewhat contrarily, urged force and counselled restraint.

This contradiction is eloquently demonstrated by the reports of roving parties in the field that were sent regularly to the colonial government. Jorgen Jorgenson's reports openly acknowledged that 'indiscriminate slaughter' was not the aim of the parties, which were concerned 'to place the native tribes in a situation that they may be captured *without* the parties in pursuit being compelled to shed more human blood'.[99] Yet he also reported that there were plenty of volunteers for parties which had previously been involved in violence that went far beyond that envisaged by the government.[100] It is difficult

Genocide in Van Diemen's Land

to escape the impression that such men understood that it was their approach to the clans that had been licensed by the government in the move to martial law.

As with all previous measures, the intensification of government action simply led to more violence. Perhaps the most notorious example is the roving party of John Batman, one of the 'founding fathers' of the settlement that would become Melbourne. Batman formed a group that was active from August 1829 and was directly sanctioned by the government. The party included two indigenous men brought from Sydney in order to aid the pursuit of the clans of Van Diemen's Land. Batman's own account of his party's first encounter with indigenous Tasmanians is particularly brutal and suggests the inherent violence of the unique form of protection sanctioned under martial law. Batman wrote:

> the natives arose from the ground and were in the act of running away into a thick scrub, when I ordered the men to fire upon them, which was done, and a rush by the party immediately followed. We only captured that night one woman and a male child about 2 years old [...] next morning we found one man very badly wounded in the ankle and knee. Shortly after we found another, 10 buckshot had entered his body, he was alive, but very bad [...] [We] learnt from those we took that 10 men were wounded in the body which they gave us to understand were dead or would die [...] on Friday morning we left the place for my farm with the two men, woman and child, but found it quite impossible that the two former could walk, and after trying them by every means in my power, for some time, found I could not get them on. I was obliged therefore to shoot them.[101]

The Colonial Office would not have explicitly approved of the implications of the move to martial law that were played out in the horrendous scene described by Batman. It was Murray's wish that policy be carried out in the correct 'spirit' and it is not clear that Batman's murder of two wounded men conformed to that.[102] Yet the Colonial Office did approve the policy itself, and indeed as we have seen had anticipated it. George Murray wrote to Arthur in August 1829, stating that he saw no alternative to the sanction of martial law in view of the 'determined spirit of hostility manifested by the black or aboriginal Natives of Van Diemen's Land and the acts of barbarity which they have committed on defenceless settlers'. He also requested to be kept constantly up to date with developments.[103]

Of course, Murray's approval contained all the usual qualifications, that is, that such a policy must benefit the original population as well as the settlers, and as such could be interpreted as evidence of the good intentions of the British government. So numerous are the reminders from the Colonial Office that indigenous peoples should be protected that we must take seriously the idea that this was their intention. But was it a reasonable expectation? Given that the Colonial Office was aware of escalating violence, that it was aware that the island's communities had been moved to violence because they regarded themselves as having a greater right to the land than the settlers, and that it was prepared to sanction 'absolute force', I think the best that can be said is that Murray and his office were trapped within a mindset that they could not recognise made little sense even on its own terms. They were committed to a path that continually sanctioned a greater and greater degree of force, while arguing that force should be avoided. With every approval they opened up new possibilities for violence even while they continued to condemn violence itself. The British government preached protection, while contrarily approving of measure after measure that would escalate violence. It was, at the very least, a form of self-deception.[104]

It is also worth considering the implications of Colonial Office's claims that martial law would only be justified if it ultimately benefitted indigenous Tasmanians. This betrayed a further founding assumption of the colonial project that was essentially destructive – the belief that it was the colony itself that could protect, even save the original population. In other words, it was only through submitting to the power of the colony that they would find peace. According to this perverse mindset, the use of military force to defend the colony against attacks was also the best means of protecting indigenous Tasmanians.

Martial law did not restore order to the colony. As the threat to the survival of the island's original inhabitants became more organised and overt, attacks against the settlers became more frequent, more deadly and more coordinated. Four settlers were reported to have been killed in February 1830 alone, along with numerous instances of arson and robberies, which often involved the theft of arms and gunpowder.[105] In Arthur's reports home on the conflict in 1829 and 1830, indigenous violence was usually highlighted, painting a more and more detailed picture of desperate colonists under siege.[106] It is almost impossible to speculate as to the number of indigenous casualties during this period, although Henry Melville argued (in what was a calculated exaggeration) that the impact of martial law was to reduce the size of the original population by two-thirds.[107]

Whatever the reality of the conflict, Arthur's correspondence read as increasingly desperate. His April 1830 statement that the 'aboriginal Natives of this colony are and ever have been a most treacherous race'[108] represented a marked change in tone and it must have been clear even to the most optimistic observer in Britain that the colony was unlikely to save the lives, let alone the souls, of the indigenous population, such were the levels of violence between the two communities. Murray responded to the comprehensive report that the Hobart Aborigines Committee had compiled in March of that year with a further endorsement of Arthur's policy. That report had told of a 'sentiment of alarm' spreading throughout the colony as the attacks on settler property escalated to the extent that they even suspected in Hobart that the indigenous Tasmanians had 'lost the sense of the superiority of the white man'.[109] Murray's reaction perfectly captured the contradictions of government thinking towards the management of the colonies and the problem of resistance to colonisation. The fundamental priority remained the security of the colony and as such he recommended that 'the settlers [...] evince a more determined spirit

The Last Man

of resistance to their opponents'. But at the same time Murray warned, famously, that the 'extinction' of the indigenous population of Van Diemen's Land would leave 'an indelible stain' upon the reputation of the British government.[110] As such he urged violence and restraint at the same time.

AN INDELIBLE STAIN?

Such is the importance of that instruction, both in history and historiography, that it is vital that its phrasing is considered very carefully. It is worth quoting at length. Murray wrote:

> the great decrease which has of late years taken place in the amount of the Aboriginal population, render it not unreasonable to apprehend that the whole race of these people may, at no distant period, become extinct. But with whatever feelings such an event may be looked forward to by those of the settlers who have been sufferers by the collisions which have taken place, it is impossible not to contemplate such a result of our occupation of the island as one very difficult to be reconciled with feelings of humanity, or even with principles of justice and sound policy; and the adoption of any line of conduct, having for its avowed, or for its secret object, the extinction of the native race, could not fail to leave an indelible stain upon the character of the British government.[111]

The Colonial Office did not approve a policy of extermination. We have already seen that as much was clear. But it was of course aware, because George Arthur had been alerting it continually to the fact over the previous two years that there were elements of settler society that preached extermination. As such Murray was making very clear that London was set absolutely against that discourse. We can also detect an acknowledgement that the root cause of indigenous depopulation was the very presence of the colony. These observations have underpinned the interpretation, by scholars such as Henry Reynolds, that Murray's instruction represented a deliberate effort to set the British government against the actions of the settlers and thus against genocide.

However, I think it is important that we recognise the limits of Murray's regret. He was not arguing that the fact of the indigenous population's 'extinction' would bring opprobrium on the British, but rather that if it were discovered that this had been *the desired aim of British policy* they would be deserving of condemnation. Thus, far from providing an alibi for imperial responsibility, Murray's despatch suggests that the British government recognised the possibility of the extermination of the original population of the island, and that the cause of that was, to use Henry Reynolds's words, the 'colonising venture itself', but could offer only regret in response, precisely because it was committed to the colony above all else. It is as if Murray anticipated the strictures of the genocide convention, and sought to remind his officers that such an outcome was only acceptable if the British had not intended it.

Murray's warnings could do nothing to stem the tide of violence in Van Diemen's Land. And, articulating a very personal sense of despair, Arthur and policy makers in Hobart decided to move decisively against the indigenous community.[112] In a movement that became known as 'the Line', and that might well be the nearest thing to a state-organised action against an entire ethnic group anywhere in the history of the British Empire, the settlers of Van Diemen's Land were militarised, armed and formed into a wholesale campaign to pursue and effect the capture of the remaining indigenous population. A force of nearly 3,000 men was created to sweep across the island in pursuit of their enemy. The operation lasted for six weeks between 7 October and 24 November 1830.[113]

The idea of a general movement of this kind had been the subject of some discussion for months,[114] and Henry Melville painted a picture of a community at fever pitch in the period leading to October.[115] Public meetings were held in September, and it was presented as nothing less than a solemn duty for settlers to volunteer for service in 'the Line'. The campaign was portrayed as a matter of survival for the colony.[116] Although it was surrounded, in terms of the proclamations from the governor at least, with the usual rhetoric of conciliation and humanity, it is difficult to escape the view that for at least some of the colonists the time for their war of extermination had arrived. Even the government was using existential rhetoric and its calls for unity were powerfully utopian: 'all minor objects,' its call to arms demanded, 'must give way to this one great and engrossing pursuit.'[117] It is not clear that when the settlers talked of 'going after the natives' they intended that any would escape alive.[118] Such rhetoric is not surprising when one remembers that colonists genuinely believed that indigenous Tasmanians could murder all of them if the opportunity arose.[119]

In the event 'the Line' was a spectacular failure, in that few of the settlers' assailants were captured. Reports vary, but Robert Knopwood suggested that two people were captured and two were shot.[120] The now very small indigenous population easily evaded the organised community, thanks to their much superior knowledge of the land. It was scant return for an operation that had cost more than £30,000. But attacks on settlers and their property did decline in the immediate aftermath of the operation and by August 1831 Governor Arthur was proclaiming it a qualified success. 'The Natives,' he wrote to the Secretary of State for the Colonies, 'evidently awed by the force which was then put in motion, have [since] conducted themselves in a far more peaceable manner.'[121] One of the leaders of the action, the curious Jorgen Jorgenson, firmly believed that 'the Line' pacified the indigenous community through its display of force.[122]

BRITAIN: A RESTRAINING HAND?

Henry Reynolds argues that the prosecution of 'the Line' represented a fundamental policy breach with London. He suggests that in pursuing the islanders so indiscriminately, and in a manner that at the very least appeared to its participants to be a campaign of extermination,

Governor Arthur deliberately ignored instructions from the Secretary of State, George Murray, both in the 'indelible stain' despatch and in other correspondence.

In September 1830 Arthur had received a despatch from Murray that instructed that a criminal investigation be launched against a representative of the Van Diemen's Land Company, Alexander Goldie. Goldie had been involved in the murder of an indigenous woman on the company's land that even by Tasmanian standards was particularly brutal. The woman had died from an axe to the neck, while lying injured as the result of an affray between an indigenous group and some company men. The Solicitor General in Van Diemen's Land, Alfred Stephen, had been deeply disturbed by the potential implications of the killing. He believed that it was in a sense legal, under the auspices of the declaration of martial law and in turn under Bathurst's instruction. But Stephen was also concerned that, if martial law really did mean that such actions were now legal, the rule of law had, in effect, been entirely abandoned.[123] On hearing of the case the Colonial Office had been equally disturbed and had urged investigation. Indeed, Murray suggested to Arthur that this might be the moment to make good the commitment to legal protection and that he was 'certain' that 'nothing […] will tend more effectually to check the evil than to bring before a Court […] any person who may have been instrumental to the death of a Native'. He further instructed Arthur that he should make sure that that was 'distinctly understood' by everyone in the colony.

For Reynolds, Murray's despatch represented a challenge to the entire legal basis of martial law and as such the campaign against the indigenous population. He argued that it was a revocation of the 1825 instruction that force should be used in defence of the colony and was a return to the idea that the guiding principle of policy towards indigenous peoples should be a commitment to protection.[124] But Arthur did not launch a prosecution and instead organised the community to mobilise further force. By not proceeding with an investigation, and instead intensifying the campaign in a manner that at the least threatened further loss of life, Reynolds suggests that the colonists acted decisively against the wishes of the metropolitan government. In so doing, Reynolds provides the alibi on which many interpretations of British actions in Van Diemen's Land have rested.

It is, however, difficult to share the conviction that this affair demonstrates that the British set themselves entirely against racial violence in Tasmania. And even if Murray was dismayed by the Goldie affair, it was a brief moment in which the British government was forced to face the logic of its own policy. Murray was soon replaced as Secretary of State and his successor retrospectively approved both of 'the Line' and of Arthur's decision not to prosecute Goldie.[125] And there is certainly little evidence of an enduring breach between Arthur and the Colonial Office.[126] More than this, however, such an interpretation ignores the degree to which the events that were played out in Van Diemen's Land were the result of the *British* prioritisation of the development of the colony, regardless of its impact on the island's existing communities.

THE VAN DIEMEN'S LAND COMPANY

Perhaps this can be best explained further by investigating the particular example of the Van Diemen's Land Company, and the links between the genocidal displacement of an indigenous community and the wider political and cultural imperatives established in London. The Van Diemen's Land Company was created in London during 1824 and 1825 by the government and a group of investors, led by wool-industry expert James Bischoff, who were looking to exploit the potential of the colony for sheep-farming.[127] The investors were attracted by the possibility of a large land grant from the Colonial Office, the promise of subsidised convict labour and the reduction of import tariffs on wool.[128] They were drawn to the potential of Van Diemen's Land through a guide written by Edward Curr, which had suggested the availability of land for sheep-farming in the colony.[129] Curr had migrated to Van Diemen's Land in 1820. After briefly returning to England, where he wrote the book, he was appointed the chief agent of the company. He led its first expedition in the north-west of the colony, where its land would be granted, after the company was formally chartered in November 1825.

Although privately financed, the company was a very clear example of the commitment of government in Britain to colonial expansion. It was created (like the Australian Agricultural Company before it) by government charter and was specifically given responsibility for the development of the colony – in terms of both infrastructure and capital investment. As well as a grant of 250,000 acres of land, on which the company would only pay quit-rent after ten years if it had failed to save the treasury money, the company was charged with acting in effect as a bank within the colony in order to facilitate further investment.[130] The amount of land available, the costs of employing convicts and the nature of the development needed were all matters of careful negotiation in the formation of the company. The fate of the North West clans who inhabited the lands that the company was to take over was not. They did not merit a single mention in negotiations and they do not feature in the early annual reports of the company either.[131]

In part of course this was because the government believed that these were 'wastelands', that they were 'uninhabited' and not in use.[132] Yet this does not mean that the government or indeed the investors believed that the land was literally empty. They were only too aware of the presence of the indigenous population. Indeed, the original orders of the company's chief agent, Edward Curr, in 1826 were remarkable because of the clarity of his recognition of what the grant of land actually entailed: 'it should always be kept in view that in taking a large tract of the country for the necessary purposes of cultivation the original possessors will be deprived in great degree of their hunting grounds.' He warned other company men to be careful in their dealings with these peoples, suggesting chillingly that 'the surest way to prevent bloodshed is to be always prepared to repel and punish aggression.'[133] Curr's logic was precisely that which had been emanating from Downing Street.

And the company's agents were indeed always prepared to repel aggression. James Boyce suggests that the company was responsible for massive reductions in the population in the north-west of the island from some 600 to 700 people in 1827 to just 100 by 1832.[134] Several massacres were reported to the company's directors in London, invariably carried out by the convicts assigned to the company. The first, in February 1828, was at Cape Grim, where anything between three and 30 people were killed by convicts including Charles Chamberlain – who had been sentenced to a lengthy period of transportation.[135] Chamberlain boasted that 30 men, women and children had been murdered that day.[136] As we try to disentangle the responsibility for violence and its relationship with British colonial policy, we should not forget the role that men like this played, themselves displaced and brutalised by the British state. Their violence was directed at the only people in their world less powerful than themselves.[137]

Rhetorically at least the company and its agents were committed to the protection of the peoples whose land they sought to invade. In that sense the Van Diemen's Land Company could be another example in the history of the restraining hand of London in relations between the settler and indigenous communities on the island, and it has been interpreted as such.[138] The company's directors always counselled that efforts should be made to 'conciliate', for example in their voluminous correspondence with their agents on the ground in the colony. But the directors' faith in conciliation was founded on one central assumption: that the original population would accept the reality that the development of their land was self-evidently a good thing. If they refused to accept this, and resisted, then like the British government the company's only way of resolving the logical contradiction of its position was through the use of force.

Therefore, attempts to resist usurpation came to be interpreted by the Van Diemen's Land Company, as they did by the British government, not as the legitimate defence of territory but as the disruption of development. In that sense, the company believed in its right to meet such attacks with violence. If nothing else, it was the only way to protect its investment. It also believed that violence itself might help the indigenous population realise that they could not meaningfully resist the invasion of their land. The directors wrote to Edward Curr in April 1829 that they were

> aware that a knowledge of the strength and power of the company must be first proved to exist and fully impressed upon the natives and on that account the court [of directors] send you by the Friendship [a ship] some Fire Arms, particularly pistols which they conceive will be of more use than muskets because they can be carried about the person; you will therefore be fully prepared for war.

The men of the company were supposed to use these weapons of war in order to 'prevent hostile contact with the Natives and to promote Friendship and conciliation', but if the indigenous population refused to keep their side of the bargain then the result was inevitable.[139]

Hence, when a group of company men went after the islanders they encountered at Emu Bay in August 1829, which ended with the death of one of the latter by axe, they were doing the bidding of the governments in Hobart and London. Alexander Goldie himself recounted that he and his armed men had gone after the indigenous group and that he had, on hearing gunshots, cried out 'as loud as he could do not hurt them'. But it was too late. The injured woman was then killed in order to end her suffering.[140] It is also notable that both Goldie's account of this killing and Batman's of the earlier encounter transform killing into an act of mercy.

We cannot therefore accept the rhetoric of conciliation and protection at face value. The directors of the Van Diemen's Land Company, like the government whose interests they served, believed in only one future for the island. The destruction of communities in the north-west of Van Diemen's Land was therefore the result of the British commitment to development, whatever the apparently benign intentions of its protagonists. It also might be noted that the directors of the Van Diemen's Land Company in the first years of its operations only made a return on their investment because of the appreciation of the value of the land that they had been given by the British government, which had been stolen from indigenous Tasmanians.[141] The direct relationship between dispossession and development is clear. As Cassandra Pybus wrote so eloquently about the British in Van Diemen's Land more generally: 'they had come to Van Diemen's Land to prosper and multiply, to make farms or to run prisons. The Aboriginal inhabitants were superfluous to their ambitions and a hindrance to their achievement.'[142]

It is true, as Henry Reynolds argues, that both the company directors and the government were appalled by specific instances of violence. And the so-called Goldie affair is a clear indication of this. The directors, following the reaction of the Colonial Office, expressed open disgust for the brutality of the murder in 1830, stating that it was 'as much opposed to the laws of God and nature as it was to the orders and interests of the company'.[143] Like the government, their dismay was so vocal because they were being confronted with the logic of their own policy. And also like the government, in the end the directors were content to let the matter go following the recording of their protest. The British could, as we know, not be seen to be pursuing a policy of annihilation.

Like Governor George Arthur, Edward Curr received no sanction from his employers over the affair or any other specific atrocity. The new Secretary of State for the Colonies, Lord Goderich, advised Arthur that ultimately he had been correct to ignore the 'instructions of Sir George Murray'. He had also been correct to proceed with the militarisation of the community in 'the Line' and as such to lead a campaign against the indigenous population that had 'inspired the natives with no little dread of your power'.[144]

BRITISH MEN

Of course, it was not just the imperatives for development set in London that linked British state and society with the destruction of indigenous communities in Van Diemen's Land. The protagonists in this story in Tasmania were to all intents and purposes *British* men. Though Van Diemen's Land should not just be seen as having been somehow transplanted from the other side of the world, there is little doubt that many of those who chose to emigrate did so in pursuit of an Antipodean England.[145] And an important part of their pursuit of that fantasy became the campaign against the original population. Michael Steel emigrated to Van Diemen's Land in 1823. Son of a 'yeoman farmer', he left England in the aftermath of an agricultural depression that threatened his livelihood. Yet although he sought opportunity in Van Diemen's Land, he hardly left England behind, and indeed returned in 1840 in order to find a wife. Oscillating between home and the New World, Steel also wrote home with tales of the 'extremely ugly' indigenous population.[146] He wrote regularly of violence between the two communities and of pursuing 'those vagabonds' with the intent to kill, reporting that 'neither the Dogs nor their masters could stand the bullets of white men'.[147]

Let's consider John Helder Wedge again as a further example. Wedge emigrated in 1824, having been appointed as a government surveyor and with a land grant of some 1,500 acres. He was responsible for a survey of land belonging to the Van Diemen's Land Company and actually secured the extension of its original grant. He was in that sense responsible for literally extending the frontiers of development in the colony. Wedge returned to England in the 1830s to nurse his ailing father and brought with him curiosities from his Vandemonian adventure. These included spears and other weaponry, which were then deposited in a museum in Saffron Walden in Essex. Later Wedge would return to Van Diemen's Land and serve in the legislature, after the award of self-government in 1856.

It is difficult to discern Wedge's particular involvement in violence against the indigenous community. His diary is replete with details of hostile exchanges on company lands, and he himself was armed against them – in self-defence, of course.[148] It was only natural then that he participated in 'the Line'. Like so many other witnesses, Wedge only really testified to defending himself against attack. Also, on his return to England Wedge protested against the ill-treatment of indigenous peoples at Port Phillip on the Australian mainland and was sure, because of his experiences in Tasmania, of the possibilities of 'conciliation'. Wedge was also convinced in 1830 that indigenous Tasmanians could not be allowed to 'remain at large' in the colony. He took a number of children into his home during his time in Van Diemen's Land,[149] and made some efforts to learn their language.[150] Yet he also abandoned one of those children as 'incorrigibly bad'.[151] Whatever the reality, Wedge is a clear example, like Michael Steel, of the entanglement of those involved in violence in Tasmania with home.

Regardless of when the Colonial Office approved the policy of 'the Line', the reality is that from 1828 onwards Downing Street had sanctioned a policy that amounted to a territorial solution to the conflict between the two populations in Van Diemen's Land. One way or another, both the colonial government in Hobart and the metropolitan government looked forward to a future in Van Diemen's Land in which the island's original inhabitants were confined within a specific territory. Such restrictions would only, it was envisioned, be lifted as and when they became civilised. Of course what becoming civilised really meant was accepting the reality of the colony and the colonial future of the island. As this future could not accommodate indigenous modes of existence and especially land use, this was a genocidal consensus.

In the aftermath of 'the Line' and its failure, Arthur proposed a change in policy and decided to pursue more decisively the idea that the separation of the island's communities could be achieved by conciliation or peaceful means. After all, the military solution that he adopted had not worked. The third chapter of this book will discuss this attempt at conciliation, and its role in a policy of deportation that deserves the label 'ethnic cleansing'. As a final comment on the relationship between the British government and genocide in the

1820s, however, we might note Lord Goderich's reaction on learning of the failure of 'the Line'. As we have already seen he was satisfied that it had left the indigenous population in awe of imperial power. But he feared that it would not last, and that their 'spirit of animosity and love of plunder' would return.[152] One wonders what he thought would happen then. He had surely noted Arthur's own warning of November 1830 when he informed Downing Street that the spirit of 'self-preservation' among the settlers would 'compel [them] to destroy the indigenous population'. Yet Goderich simply informed Arthur that he would leave the next move to him. He cannot have expected that the result would be anything other than the destruction of indigenous life in Tasmania.

THREE

Ethnic Cleansing

Violence was only one route to the final removal of the indigenous population from Van Diemen's Land. The confinement of the island's clans, which had been the object of policy since April 1828, through martial law and then 'the Line', was in the end achieved by what was known as the 'Friendly Mission' of George Augustus Robinson. After his appointment to oversee a mission to the people of Bruny Island in 1829, Robinson – together with a small group of islanders – led a roving embassy to negotiate with indigenous groups until August 1834. It was these negotiations that brought an end to the most serious violence, with an agreement brokered in December 1831. To many in Britain, and indeed Tasmania, Robinson's mission demonstrated what could be achieved with the 'amity and kindness' that was supposed to have defined British relations with the islanders from the outset. The 1831 agreement was only the beginning of Robinson's story, however, and he spent the next three years on an expedition throughout Tasmania to 'bring in' the remaining indigenous groups. By 1834 the vast majority of the surviving population had been expelled to Flinders Island, housed in a settlement known to its inhabitants as Wybalenna. In what looks very much like a state-endorsed campaign of ethnic cleansing, by the end of Robinson's mission there were almost no indigenous Tasmanians remaining in Van Diemen's Land.

This chapter will explore the 'Friendly Mission', its deportation of indigenous Tasmanians and its relationship with Britain. Again, it has been argued recently that these policies were pursued *despite* the

The Last Man

British government. James Boyce's *Van Diemen's Land* suggests that the deportation of the remaining indigenous population after the beginning of 1832 represented a breach with Downing Street. Boyce writes: 'at no time during the next five years was the actual policy of forced removal ever presented to, let alone sanctioned by, the Colonial Office. This crime was to be primarily a local affair.'[1] I disagree. Indeed, not only did the British government, to use the words of the Secretary of State for the Colonies in 1832, 'approve the removal of these people', but their deportation was simply the implementation of a policy agreed between Hobart and London during the 1820s. Furthermore, deportation represented a fulfilment of the *British* discourse of colonisation and civilisation, and articulated the original assumptions of British politicians about the nature of the relationship between the original inhabitants and the colony. By 1835 the policy of removing the remnant also articulated the increasingly widespread assumption that the indigenous Tasmanian community was doomed to disappear.

THE 'FRIENDLY MISSION'

According to some interpretations, George Arthur in effect pursued two different policies towards indigenous Tasmanians in the 1820s.[2] Alongside the strategy of licensed communal violence, he had long been attempting a more measured negotiation with indigenous groups too. In March 1829 (and therefore in the context of martial law) George Augustus Robinson had been appointed to run a small establishment for the inhabitants of Bruny Island, which lay off the south coast of Van Diemen's Land. He would form close relationships with that community, and from there *together* Robinson and his indigenous associates set off on a journey on which they would negotiate with other communities in order ultimately to bring an end to the fighting that had blighted the island.[3]

George Augustus Robinson was born in London in 1791, the son of a builder. He himself was employed in the building trade in Kent, London and perhaps also Edinburgh in the first decades of the nineteenth century. Apparently facing a crisis in 1823, and unable to support his growing family, Robinson emigrated to Australia in search of employment – part of the wave of free migration that itself intensified the conflict for resources in Van Diemen's Land. It appears he only settled on Van Diemen's Land as a destination (rather than New South Wales) while en route from Britain, arriving in Hobart in January 1824. He immediately began work as a builder. Over the following five years Robinson continued to trade, with varying degrees of success. He was also active in the burgeoning Wesleyan community in the town, a reflection of his utterly committed Christian faith.[4]

According to Robinson himself, he was concerned 'with the deplorable state and condition of the Aboriginal inhabitants' from the first moment he arrived in Hobart. Arthur appealed for someone to administer the Bruny Island settlement in March 1829, and Robinson seized the opportunity to act on his curiosity about whether the indigenous Tasmanians 'could be instructed and whether anything could be done for their moral, religious and material improvement'.[5] Undoubtedly Robinson was attracted by the land grant that came with the position and indeed the social status that he thought such a role might have bestowed. At the same time all of the available evidence suggests that he was also morally and religiously committed to the idea of 'ameliorating' the plight of and living in harmony with people with whom he wished to share the gifts of 'civilisation'.[6] Robinson wished to put into practice British instructions regarding the treatment of indigenous communities. This could be best achieved, he believed, by creating a kind of model village, transforming the population into an ersatz European peasantry whom Robinson would teach to farm the land and crucially to worship the Christian God.[7] At the same time, Robinson discerned at the beginning of his appointment that the outcome of the current war was likely to be the destruction of the indigenous population. Thus he saw his task as nothing less than saving indigenous Tasmanians from extinction, as well as showing them the path to eternity.[8]

As much as those involved in the physical pursuit of the indigenous population were driven by imperatives set for them in metropolitan

London, so were Robinson and, through his support of Robinson's activities, George Arthur. We have already noted that Arthur came from an evangelical, humanitarian community and was closely associated with the abolition movement. Robinson, although from an entirely different social group, had also imbibed much of the rhetoric of that evangelical teaching on race. Consider Robinson's reflections of November 1830, which drew heavily on the rhetoric of abolitionist discourse that suggested that all men were brothers:

> Poor unbefriended and hapless people! I imagined myself an Aborigine. I looked upon them as brethren, not, as they have been maligned, savages. No, they are my brethren by creation. God has made one blood of all nations of people and I am not ashamed to call them brothers and would to God I could call them brethren by redemption.[9]

Robinson's task was also therefore a profoundly religious one: he understood his interactions with his followers as 'decisively the work of God'.[10] He saw indigenous peoples as (potentially at least) his brothers in Christ.

Yet there was a deep paradox at work here too. As we have seen, Robinson's vision of rescue was a spiritual mission: he believed that he could save the souls of the population by enacting their religious and cultural transformation. As such, while he was motivated by a deep care for the island's peoples, and his journals do attempt to record some aspects of their culture, he was also dedicated, absolutely, to the transformation and therefore eradication of that culture. This desire is eloquently symbolised by Robinson's fierce determination that indigenous peoples must abandon their itinerant life and become sedentary. He wanted to transform their vision and understanding of the land and its ownership. At the settlement on Bruny Island allotments would be fenced, for example, and as such the land would no longer be held in common. Thus Robinson may not have wished to preside over the physical destruction of indigenous peoples but nor would their cultural survival have represented a success to him either. In this ambition for the transformation, indeed erasure, of indigenous culture, Robinson articulated the logic of the British colonisation of Van Diemen's Land. It is therefore no exaggeration to say that such was the extent of the genocidal consensus that even those individuals most sympathetic to the island's existing communities did not envisage a future for them in Van Diemen's Land.

Governor Arthur first discussed the idea of a permanent 'Aboriginal settlement' with the Colonial Office in January 1828 in the context of his plan to divide the island. Permission was sought from London for the expenditure to provide food and clothing for the indigenous population. Arthur acknowledged that they would be prevented from living off the land in their traditional manner by his plan and it was therefore assumed they would require government support. Ironically, at this time Arthur dismissed the idea that the settlement ought to be located on one of Van Diemen's Land's outlying islands. He felt that to separate communities from their land would represent too great an injustice.[11] This concern was abandoned just two years later. The settlement at Bruny Island – traditionally the home of the Nuenonne people of the South East nation – was, however, part of this vision to confine indigenous peoples within their traditional territories.

Robinson encountered 20 individuals on Bruny, including Woorraddy and Truganini, who would become central figures in his later mission to the rest of Tasmania.[12] Although he undoubtedly showed an interest in the people he met – and attempted to engage with them – he was from the outset utterly committed to their transformation. One of the first things he did was to separate the children of the community from their parents. He planned to build a separate dormitory for them and advised George Arthur that the children could be more easily westernised. He wrote: 'these children appear to be destined by Providence as a foundation upon which the superstructure of Your Excellency's benevolence is hereafter to be erected [...] rousing them from that torpid inactivity in which they have so long slumbered.'[13]

The Last Man

From the beginning, however, the settlement became associated with death and disease for the indigenous population as mortality rates were unusually high. Robinson's journal recorded several deaths in the winter and spring of 1829.[14] He also observed that the community wished to leave the settlement, unwilling to stay somewhere that had the stigma of disease.[15] It was no surprise therefore that the Nuenonne were prepared to leave the settlement with Robinson to attempt negotiation with other indigenous groups from February 1830.

Negotiations began a year into the period of martial law, and therefore in Robinson's mind his mission represented an alternative to the policy of extermination currently being pursued by much of the rest of the settler population. Indeed, his journey through the Tasmanian bush was in a sense a mission to the settlers as well as to indigenous peoples. He constantly referred to meeting with settlers, and clearly had vigorous debates with what he described as 'extirpationists' as to the future of policy towards the indigenous communities.[16] In that sense, although the policies of conciliation and pursuit appeared different from one another, they did interact. Indeed, Robinson himself could be spurred into action by the decrees emanating from Hobart. In July 1830, for example, he was quick to collect some of the indigenous Tasmanians who had submitted to him after it was announced that a bounty would be offered to anyone who captured the enemies of colonisation alive.[17]

Robinson's mission did not, and indeed could not, prevent attacks on the settler population. As we have seen in the previous chapter, violence reached a new intensity in 1830. It was, therefore, the perceived failure of conciliation, in the mind of the lieutenant governor at least, that led to the intensification of action against the indigenous population in the spring of 1830. Arthur lost faith in the idea that the island's peoples could be reconciled to the colony at that time. He wrote to London to inform the Colonial Office of this, which gives us some indication of the priority that the Colonial Office placed on such efforts too. George Arthur clearly felt that he needed to demonstrate that London's preferred approach had failed. Indeed,

Ethnic Cleansing

Secretary of State George Murray's famous warning that the extinction of indigenous Tasmanians might leave a stain on the reputation of the British Empire contained an eloquent statement of the British commitment to 'conciliation' as a means to 'reclaim the Natives from their original savage life, and render them sensible of the advantages which would ultimately result to themselves, and to their descendants, from the introduction amongst them of the religion and civilisation' of the British.[18] The directors of the Van Diemen's Land Company also continually extolled the virtues of conciliation to Edward Curr,[19] entertaining great hopes when Robinson brought his mission to their land in the middle of 1830 that the indigenous population might be reconciled to the presence of the company.[20] Thus there can be little doubt that across the spectrum of people concerned with Van Diemen's Land in London, the British favoured conciliation as the route to bringing peace to the island.

But what did conciliation really mean? As Murray's despatch made clear, it involved a fundamental commitment to the transformation and indeed anglicisation of indigenous life in Tasmania. We should not be surprised at this. Let us not forget that as the chief agent of conciliation, Robinson envisaged the creation of a settled indigenous community under his supervision. Lyndall Ryan argues that by September 1830 Robinson was already thinking of a sanctuary for indigenous peoples away from Van Diemen's Land.[21] And certainly, at the end of 1830, as 'the Line' progressed, Robinson had begun moving communities away from the Tasmanian mainland and from the clutches of the settlers.[22] In part this was inspired by a desire to save them from their bloodthirsty enemies, but it was also inspired by a desire to enforce cultural change.

If the military operations of 1830 were in part a response to the limited success of conciliation, in the aftermath of the failure of 'the Line' Arthur would turn once again to Robinson. Arthur noted that Robinson's efforts in the bush had been rather more successful than that of the militarised community. And the scale of that success is notable. 'The Line' appeared to have captured next to no one. Yet in November 1830, in the middle of the six-week military operation,

Robinson could report to Arthur that he had with him on Swan Island a further 13 members of the 'most hostile tribes'.[23] He later recorded in his journal his joy at his success: 'They are parts of different nations [...] they all seemed filled with joy. The sensation I felt was great. I had the satisfaction to know that I was their deliverer, and that I had preserved their lives.'[24] At this point Robinson intended that the final location for the 'Aboriginal establishment' would be Gun Carriage Island. His self-image as their saviour might speak to Robinson's incredible conceit, but it also demonstrates that he genuinely believed that 'the Line' represented an existential threat. Thus Robinson believed that he was both literally and metaphorically delivering indigenous Tasmanians from barbarism.

One of the central conundrums when considering Robinson is the question of *how* he managed to persuade people to accompany him. His own self-regard and the construction of the story of his mission in which he was the central character led immediately to characterisations of him as an almost mystical figure.[25] His self-image as redeemer certainly had some metaphysical connotations. But as Henry Reynolds points out, the success of the 'Friendly Mission' was rather more prosaic. It took place in a time of war, a war that was almost universally understood to be one of extermination from which there would be few if any survivors among the indigenous population. As such, while Robinson and his indigenous representatives did not employ force, they did rely on the threat of violence elsewhere to help them persuade others that their best chance of a future lay with them.

Henry Reynolds believes that we should assert more clearly the role of the indigenous ambassadors themselves in the process by which Robinson convinced others to join them. Negotiations with hostile tribes were always begun by Robinson's representatives. They clearly had discerned that indigenous Tasmanians faced an existential threat in the settlers, and that Robinson might offer them a means of ameliorating that threat.[26] And, at least according to his diary, Robinson was also crucial in emphasising the danger that the settlers really posed. For instance, in November 1830, he told one group (quite truthfully) that if government soldiers found them 'they would be cleared off the island'.[27]

Indeed, Robinson's report of his persuading 13 people to follow him to Swan Island in November 1830 emphasises for us the degree to which he relied almost entirely on convincing indigenous Tasmanians that their lives were in danger. He constantly reminded his charges that they were all being pursued, and this was the means by which he drove his party to Swan Island: 'Having made them some tea, I hurried them to set off, telling them the sooner we got away the better as the soldiers was [sic] coming.'[28] Indeed, the idea that accompanying Robinson was an entirely free choice appears fanciful in the light of his journal. As they made their way to Swan Island Robinson reflected on the difficulty of preventing 'the natives absconding', and when they finally reached the boat that would take them to the island he 'ordered the crew to keep strict watch all night that the people did not get away'.[29]

The constant interactions of violence and conciliation suggest that we might revise the view that they were two different policies being pursued on Van Diemen's Land. Instead they might be better characterised as two different approaches to the same problem with a shared goal: the separation and removal of the indigenous population. Although Robinson's approach was less likely to end in physical destruction, neither policy envisaged anything approaching a future for that population in Van Diemen's Land. As Robinson wrote to Arthur from Swan Island, in the midst of the failed military efforts of 'the Line', 'the whole aboriginal population could be brought together by the same method that has hitherto been adopted.'[30] More than that, when conciliation was adopted as the state-endorsed policy after the failure of military attempts to quell and confine the indigenous population, it became inextricably linked with a vision of an ethnically cleansed Van Diemen's Land. Thus, when Arthur relayed the Aborigines Committee's deliberations to London in February 1831, he outlined a vision of conciliation and deportation that represented the fusion of the two apparently separate approaches that had hitherto been pursued into a new genocidal vision of the island's future.

The Last Man

DECEPTION AND DEPORTATION

Arthur explained to London that the island's original inhabitants were not going to be destroyed, but placed 'in safety with their countrymen at the intended Aboriginal establishment on Gun Carriage Island'. At the same time as this operation, permanent military outposts were going to be created in order to protect the most exposed settler populations.[31] Therefore conciliation, deportation and military force were now all parts of a single policy of ethnic cleansing. Robinson's task was, London was informed, nothing less than the removal of the *'entire* black population' of the island.[32] Lest London be in any doubt about what the potential consequences of such a policy might be, Arthur made it very clear for them:

> even if they [the deported indigenous population] should pine away, it is better that they should meet with their death in that way, whilst every kindness is manifested towards them, than that they should fall a sacrifice to the inevitable consequences of their continued acts of outrage upon the white inhabitants.[33]

In the Colonial Office, the Secretary of State for the Colonies, Lord Goderich, enthusiastically endorsed these proposals, as he had the proposals for military action. If he had any concerns, they are not evident, and he agreed quickly to the plans for deportation in October 1831. Goderich remained sceptical that they would succeed, and did not believe that the entire community could be removed in this manner, but acknowledged that 'there were hopes [that Robinson would succeed] in persuading a considerable number of them to migrate to one of the islands in the Bass straits'.[34] The following May, Goderich would remind Arthur once more (in the context of reports of further violence) that the Colonial Office had 'approved' of the plan for 'the removal of these people to a neighbouring dependency of Van Diemen's Land'.[35]

Goderich stressed in his correspondence, however, that what he

Ethnic Cleansing

supported was *voluntary* movement by the indigenous community. He referred to the 'black population who have already consented to their removal', for example. Therefore, might it be argued that British endorsement of a deportation policy was rather limited and specifically that it did not endorse the use of force? Again, I think it is important that we ask what voluntarism really meant in this context. The answer to that question seems to reveal that there were few practical limits to London's support for deportation. Later in 1831 (or in 1832 when it received the correspondence) it must have seemed to the Colonial Office that once again Van Diemen's Land was heading for disaster. A fresh outbreak of violence in the colony culminated in August 1831 with the murder of Captain Bartholomew Thomas while he was attempting to conciliate a 'tribe of natives which had approached his farming establishment'.[36] Thomas's body had been mutilated, and Arthur confided that such violence led him to believe that the settler population would once again try to move decisively against the indigenous population. Knowing of such violence, it seems fanciful that the British government could have entertained any belief that men and women who refused to accompany Robinson might have been able to live free from molestation on the Vandemonian mainland.

It was in the context of heightened tension after the murder of Captain Thomas that Arthur and the Aborigines Committee in Hobart resolved once again that they would pursue vigorously a policy of removing the indigenous population from Van Diemen's Land and that this would be achieved through Robinson's mission.[37] Thomas's murder left Arthur in the bleakest despair as to the perceived treachery of the islanders.[38] Knowing this, we should not necessarily view the policy of conciliation and deportation as a step back from the licensing of violence in martial law and then 'the Line'. Those policies were designed to expel the indigenous population *within* Van Diemen's Land, and as such the turn to conciliation was the first time that Arthur's policy moved decisively against the idea of a future of any kind for them anywhere on the island. While the outcome of the military policies might ultimately have been extermination, it was not their intention.

But from the latter half of 1831 onwards, *the aim* of policy was, decisively, to remove all indigenous people from the island. As such, the turn to the apparently more benign aim of conciliation actually represented a radicalisation of policy. And it was agreed in London.

Robinson was the agent of this policy, and he and his ambassadors successfully negotiated an agreement with the most significant clans remaining at large on the island in the final months of 1831. The terms of that agreement itself are something of a mystery, and as such it can only be imperfectly recreated. Robinson conducted a complex web of negotiations from August onwards that involved some indigenous leaders in a meeting with Governor Arthur in October 1831.[39] Intriguingly, Arthur's own report of that meeting does not mention the views of those leaders like Mannalargenna who were present – only Robinson's view that a permanent 'home for […] the Natives who form Mr Robinson's party and whom he considers perfectly conciliated' needed to be established.[40] This was to be a settlement on the Tasmanian mainland, but it never materialised.

After October, Robinson was led by his guides in search of the Big River people. Again, the context for such negotiations was the continuing existential threat that the settler community posed to the existing population. This was something that Robinson at least was satisfied continually to remind the indigenous community of, and one suspects that the government made clear that it also was unable to control that communal desire for violence. Robinson's journal is full of examples of his emphasising the violence and threat posed by the wider white community at the time. As he reminded his followers in October 1831 during an argument about the inability of the mission to find further indigenous clans: 'was [sic] the white people to see us the whole country would be in alarm and parties would be sent out and we should be in danger of being shot.'[41] Not that Robinson needed to issue such warnings to keep alive the memory of 'the Line'. It was also etched into the landscape itself and he and his party often came across structures built 'at the time of the line' – a physical manifestation of the enmity that the settlers harboured.[42]

Ethnic Cleansing

On 31 December 1831 Robinson met with the leaders of the Big River people, and secured an agreement that they would accompany him. From this point on, in effect the war was over. His official report on the agreement stated that there was

> not the slightest doubt in my mind but that a decidedly final termination to the numerous and wanton aggressions of these benighted people has been achieved and that no further apprehension need be entertained of any further inroad upon the tranquillity of the colony from the same source – the whole of the sanguinary tribes being now removed.

Robinson continued:

> The chiefs assigned as a reason for their outrages upon the white inhabitants that they and their forefathers had been cruelly abused, that their country had been taken from them, their wives and daughters had been violated and taken away, and that they had experienced a multitude of wrongs [...] They were willing however to accept the offers of the government and they placed themselves under my protection accordingly.[43]

Why were they now willing to accept the offers of the government for protection? We will never know for certain, but it seems likely that Robinson and his indigenous representatives succeeded in persuading them that there was no other realistic hope. Robinson's journal referred, just a few weeks before, to a conversation with a group of 'natives' (unnamed) during which they confessed that they realised that they would be unable to drive the 'white man' from their island. Their communities had been witness to a demographic disaster, and, despite their ability to disrupt the colony, the war was now clearly unwinnable.[44] As Henry Reynolds argues, the agreement with Robinson simply represented the best way to ensure 'the survival of the Tasmanians as a people'.[45] Thus, agreement was the result of Robinson, and more particularly the indigenous people who accompanied him, persuading others of this fundamental reality.

Henry Reynolds and James Boyce contend that these negotiations involved a deliberate deception on the part of the colonial authorities. They suggest that in the meetings in October and December Arthur and Robinson had pledged to allow the community to live, free of molestation, on the Tasmanian mainland, and it was on these grounds that they consented to be permanently resettled. Reynolds also argues that the agreement would have involved some pledge to allow the community the freedom to practise their own culture. According to this interpretation, the agreement represented a treaty between the colonial authorities and the island's original inhabitants, in which the latter agreed to surrender their land to the British. Certainly the indigenous community themselves developed a communal memory of the agreement that reflected that understanding. When the survivors petitioned Queen Victoria more than 15 years later, they referred to themselves as the 'Free aboriginal inhabitants of Van Diemen's Land [who] were not taken prisoners but freely gave up our country to Colonel Arthur [...] after defending ourselves'.[46] And indeed Robinson himself had made clear in 1831 that the 26 people from the Big River and Oyster Bay tribes who had surrendered in December 'ought not to be looked upon as captives. They have placed themselves under my protection and are serious for peace'.[47]

Certainly, such an agreement did indeed represent a deception on the part of the authorities and Robinson as the communities were to be permanently removed from Van Diemen's Land. As we have seen, throughout his contact with various groups Robinson was manipulative. He also made clear in his dealings with the Aborigines Committee that he did not believe that it was necessary to regard any agreement with the islanders' leaders as binding. Despite Robinson's claims that he believed the indigenous population to be capable of reason, the manner in which he characterised them in discussions with the colonial government does not really bear this out. Arthur could then report to London in April 1831 that, according to Robinson, 'no

Ethnic Cleansing

dependence could be placed in their [the leaders of the indigenous community] observance of any treaty, even if they could be induced to enter into it', and as such any measures should be adopted to attempt to persuade them to 'resort to the Aboriginal establishment' then to be situated on Gun Carriage Island.[48]

As a consequence, there is no evidence that the British government at least ever *believed* that it had entered into any agreement with the indigenous community or that it should be bound by any such agreement, other than that indigenous peoples would be protected in their new island home. Indeed there is some doubt as to whether the Colonial Office in London would have consented to any other arrangement that acknowledged the original inhabitants as having any rights to land in Van Diemen's Land itself. After all, even George Murray, the Secretary of State who came closest to questioning Arthur's policy, remained of the view that the indigenous population's claim to have any rights to the land was fanciful.

When the British government learnt that an agreement had been reached, by whatever means, it rejoiced that peace had been restored. But it also reaffirmed its commitment to the existing policy of removing the survivors from the mainland. In that sense it might even be suggested that the terms of any agreement are actually somewhat irrelevant, as there seemed to be no authority on the British side – Robinson, the governor or indeed the government in London – that believed that any such arrangement need divert them from the task of deportation and ethnic cleansing. Indeed, Lord Goderich seemed to react to news of 'the happy termination of the hostilities which have so long existed between the Native tribes of the Colony and the settlers' by transferring all future responsibility for policy to Hobart. 'I should ill discharge my duty,' Goderich opined,

> were I not also to express to you the sense which His Majesty entertains of the humane and truly Christian temper by which the whole of your proceedings towards these ignorant and misguided people have been distinguished. I am satisfied that

the same desire which you have earnestly manifested of treating them with kindness will suggest to you any precaution which may be necessary to prevent them from being molested in their proposed retreat and I feel therefore that I cannot do better than to leave to you all subsequent arrangements for their protection.[49]

After he had effected the capture of the Big River people with the agreement at the end of 1831, Robinson supervised their removal to Flinders Island. In time it was assumed that Robinson would become the supervising agent of that community, but first he was instructed to continue his mission to round up the surviving indigenous communities on the mainland. George Arthur required that Robinson effect a 'permanent' solution to the problem of inter-communal violence.[50] Accordingly Robinson left Hobart in February 1832 in order to supervise the forced removal of indigenous Tasmanians remaining in the west of Van Diemen's Land. In the meantime, the 26 Big River and Oyster Bay people who had surrendered to Robinson on 31 January travelled to Flinders Island, where they joined a community of 66 survivors from the 'Black War'.[51]

POPULATION CLEARANCES

Robinson's movement, and therefore his task, was continually relayed to London.[52] I can find no evidence that his mission was somehow deliberately kept secret. In April 1832, for example, Arthur informed Goderich that Robinson would be proceeding to the property of the Van Diemen's Land Company 'in the hope of falling in with the Natives which had been troublesome there'.[53] It was perfectly clear to those in London who read the correspondence from Hobart that Robinson's task was to round up *all* of the survivors of the indigenous community. In March 1833, for instance, the Colonial Office was told, as part of a lengthy justification for his enhanced salary and pension arrangements, that Robinson had proceeded 'immediately into the interior' the year before in order 'to prosecute his friendly mission to the Aborigines with a view to his bringing in *the whole* of the natives still at large in the island'.[54] For Robinson himself it was of absolutely crucial importance that his task was to find 'all the natives' because he discerned that that was the way in which he could gain most financially and in terms of notoriety: 'By taking the whole I gain not only the reward but celebrity,' he wrote in September 1832.[55]

Robinson's continuing success was again the result of implied force and deft negotiation. A combination of his stress on the dangers posed by the white settlers and the commitment of his indigenous guides to the idea that he could protect their community from the hostile population persuaded others that Robinson represented the best hope. Throughout his journals Robinson suggested that he was at the mercy of his guides, and as such it is really they, not he, who decided when contact could be made with other communities. But at the same time Robinson himself continued to emphasise the threat that other settlers posed to the island's peoples and this again called into question the idea that those who accompanied him did so voluntarily. For example, in July 1832 Robinson reminded a group of North West Tasmanians that they did not have to go with him, but simultaneously warned them that the consequence of not doing so would be to face violent hostility without protection.[56]

At times Robinson also resorted to the explicit use of force. In September 1832 he threatened Woorraddy with a gun.[57] He carried firearms constantly from October of that year.[58] In May 1833 Robinson also effected the removal of the few remaining indigenous Tasmanians in the vicinity of Macquarie Harbour using the threat of firearms.[59] He reflected on this in his diary, acknowledging the extremity of his actions but justifying them on the basis that he had the 'satisfaction to know that their removal is for their own good'.[60] This was a theme that Robinson would return to again and again in an internal dialogue aimed at defending his actions. In August 1833 he compared the people he was depriving of their liberty to the insane in an asylum: 'if the medical office considered diet and medicine requisite, surely the same means could have been resorted to oblige them to receive it as is done with insane persons in the lunatic hospitals.'[61]

Robinson completed the final leg of his mission between December 1833 and August 1834 with an attempt to capture the remaining inhabitants on the west coast of the island. The sheer effort of roaming the bush for so long is testament to the central aim of Robinson's project – that of completing the removal of *all* indigenous Tasmanians. During this final journey Robinson repeatedly reflected on the possibility of his not meeting the terms of his commission, a failure that would be caused by his leaving any of the islanders at large.[62]

With the expedition to the west coast, Robinson completed his mission. Further inhabitants would be discovered over the next decade and transferred to Flinders Island. And, of course, an indigenous community, including children born of relationships between the island's women and the so-called sealers, men who hunted seals in the islands around Tasmania, would remain throughout the history of the colony. Further to this, it is impossible to know how many indigenous children were brought up by white settlers on the island. Certainly the apparent prevalence of white families taking in, or indeed stealing, children in the early years of the colony suggests that it is likely that more indigenous children were taken than we have records or awareness of. But as far as the government of Van Diemen's Land was concerned, Robinson's expedition that ended in August 1834 represented the final moments of indigenous life in Tasmania. The colony was after this point represented as, in the famous words of Charles Darwin, 'enjoy[ing] the great advantage of being free from a native population'.[63]

Robinson himself did not head for Flinders Island until June 1835. It was there that he would ultimately attempt to fulfil his original vision of a model village in which the (by then) 112 residents of Wybalenna would be transformed. During his long 'Friendly Mission' nearly 300 people had surrendered to Robinson, a community that had been continually hampered by disease and deprivation and indeed death. But despite the high mortality rate, Robinson's mission represented

Ethnic Cleansing

the purest articulation of the vision of protection that had originally been constructed in London and played out in Van Diemen's Land. Indeed, death alone was not enough to shake Robinson's faith in his mission. Although he reported in October 1833 that his community had been visited by a 'dire malady' of 'epidemic' proportions, he was still able to recommend his 'Friendly Mission' as a prototype for the treatment of indigenous peoples throughout the British world. He wrote to Arthur: 'I trust the time is not far distant when the same humane policy will be adopted towards the aboriginal inhabitants of every colony throughout the British Empire.' This was therefore not a local crime, but the implementation of an imperial ideology. Robinson believed that, through the ethnic cleansing of Van Diemen's Land, the colonial authorities had saved the indigenous peoples of the island. His was the fulfilment of the original British vision of a benign colonisation of benefit to all. It is worth quoting Robinson here at length:

> in reflecting upon these operations a pleasing circumstance presents itself to our view, namely that it cannot hereafter be said that those people were harshly treated, that they were torn from their kindred and friends – that they were forced from their country. No their removal has been for their benefit and almost every instance with their own free will and consent they have been removed from danger and placed in safety at a suitable asylum provided for their reception and where they are brought under moral and religious instruction.[64]

While it would be difficult to disagree with James Boyce's judgement that the systematic ethnic cleansing of Van Diemen's Land represents 'the black hole of Tasmanian history', it is impossible to concur with his view that this was a history written and enacted in Tasmania alone. Together the colonial government and the Colonial Office in London developed an understanding in the context of the violence of 1830 and 1831 that there was no future for indigenous Tasmanians on the island. The first attempts at achieving this, in 'the Line', were military, and then the task was accomplished in the wake of that show of force by a project of conciliation understood in London and Hobart to involve the deportation of the survivors from Van Diemen's Land. London was sceptical that it would succeed, but not unaware that such a project was being attempted.

One of the reasons that Boyce cites for the British ignorance of the project to ethnically cleanse Tasmania was that there was no rational policy reason for the project – the implication being that the British, whose stewardship of the Empire was so often governed by perceptions of economic rationality, would have objected if they had known, on these grounds alone. But such a view takes a rather narrow view of the utility of the deportation of the remaining 'Aborigines'. The removal of indigenous peoples was not necessary in terms of conflict – the war was over. But the overwhelming commitment to the development of the colony, in both London and Hobart, suggests another purpose. Indeed, in 1835 Charles James Napier wrote a critique of colonisation that lambasted the settler colonies precisely because they did not make enough of the labour of their existing populations, but tellingly he argued that the means for remedying this might be permanently to separate indigenous and settler communities until the former had been civilised.[65] British newspapers also reported that the deportation of indigenous Tasmanians was aimed at transforming them into useful citizens.

Furthermore, the removal of the indigenous community did have an obviously economically rational benefit – it drove up the price of land in Van Diemen's Land. George Arthur confided in 1837 that 'once the Aborigines had been pacified', property 'almost suddenly rose in value from 50–100 percent'.[66] Revenue from the sale of Crown lands in 1836 was some 13 times what it had been in 1831 before the conflict had ended.[67] In the colony the 'removal of these blacks' was welcomed as being central to the further development of the land, especially in freeing space for grazing sheep.[68] There were over 200,000 more sheep in Van Diemen's Land in 1836 than there had been in 1831.[69] The British government may have regretted the decline in population and the 'necessity' of the confinement on Flinders Island, but there is no doubt that it welcomed the apparent consequences. Indeed, on retirement Lord Glenelg, Goderich's successor in Downing Street, did not remember Arthur's chief contribution in terms of settler–indigenous relations but rather recognised his contribution to 'advancing the social prosperity' of the colony.[70] Although the Colonial Office was portrayed by its critics at the time as a barrier to development in settler colonies, it is clear that it was itself still concerned to ensure that the colonies prospered – even if only to prevent them being a drain on the treasury.

Robinson's accounts of both the process of removing the indigenous population and his time as their commandant at Flinders Island indicate that he too was aware of the contribution of his activities to the economic well-being of the colony. One of his biographers has alleged that he was entirely motivated by his own financial gain.[71] This seems an exaggeration, as Robinson did believe that he was acting in the best interests of indigenous Tasmanians. But what cannot be denied is that he did not feel that his recompense for the 'Friendly Mission' adequately reflected the economic benefits that he had brought.[72]

From the arrival of George Arthur in 1824 the priority of both the colonial and metropolitan governments was the development of the colony. The indigenous population was seen first as an existential threat, and then as barrier to that development. This is not to say that the original motivations for the movements against them were purely economic – that would be too crudely deterministic an explanation. At first, as we have seen, the colonial government understood that it was defending itself against the island's existing inhabitants. But the war from 1824 onwards can be understood as, in effect, a competition for resources. Thus, if we are looking for a reason for London and Hobart's collusion in a project to remove all indigenous peoples from the island of Tasmania when there was apparently no benefit to be gained in terms of the protection of the colony, then we should not ignore the common commitment to colonial development as a factor. Indeed, deportation was simply the continuation of the policies, such as martial law, that were aimed at the economic defence of the colony.

Robinson's story was also one that was told and retold in Britain itself, and as such his mission, the ethnic clearance of Van Diemen's Land, was not just linked to Britain, and indeed Britons, through the Colonial Office. During the 1830s, just as the narrative of violence had been relayed to British audiences in the previous decade, the removal of indigenous peoples and crucially a sense of their decay and decline was represented in Britain too – on the stage and in gallery exhibitions as well as in the published word. The next chapter of this book continues our exploration of the political entanglements between Britain, the British government and the decline of the indigenous Tasmanian population, concentrating on the period *after* 1835. We shall, however, return to Robinson, the conflict he helped bring to an end and the population movement that he supervised, in later chapters by considering the way in which the island's peoples were being represented to British audiences during the process of their destruction. It will become clear that at the very centre of British understandings of the colonial experience in Van Diemen's Land was a perception that the Empire had largely destroyed the indigenous community. In other words, a perception of what we call genocide was central to the British understanding of the colony they had created. But, for now, suffice it to say that in the Colonial Office there was contentment that George Augustus Robinson's 'Friendly Mission' had been successfully completed. Van Diemen's Land was now free of the burden of an indigenous population and could face an unencumbered route to its colonial development and future.

FOUR

Cultural Genocide

Despite government endorsement of the deportation of surviving indigenous Tasmanians to Flinders Island, fears of their imminent demise haunted British politics in the mid 1830s. Having achieved the abolition of slavery, evangelical reformers in Britain became increasingly concerned by the consequences of settler colonialism as an equivalent moral problem. It appeared to former abolitionists that wherever the British encountered indigenous peoples they invariably destroyed them. As a consequence, and prompted in part by panic at the massive decline in the population in Van Diemen's Land, between 1835 and 1837 a select committee was set up in the House of Commons to investigate the impact of British settlements on 'Aboriginal' communities across the Empire. It was chaired by the former abolition campaigner Sir Thomas Fowell Buxton, and represents a moment when indigenous Tasmanians became a live issue in British political life.

When the committee reported its findings to Parliament, it recommended that colonisation become more Christian, that it aim to save rather than destroy the communities it encountered. In articulating such ambitions it had Van Diemen's Land in mind as an example of the crisis that colonialism caused in indigenous societies. Intriguingly, however, according to the select committee Van Diemen's Land also represented the possibility of a better future for British relations with existing communities in the Empire. Indeed, the committee and the British government turned to the Flinders Island settlement as a model for their vision of Christian colonialism. Not only were the 'ethnic clearances' in Van Diemen's Land more than just a local affair, then, the Flinders Island settlement that they produced became a *pan-imperial* space. It was the laboratory in which an imperially sanctioned experiment was conducted: to protect, save and transform 'native' peoples from wild children of nature into 'useful' imperial subjects. The culmination of George Augustus Robinson's 'Friendly Mission' became, albeit briefly, the celebrated 'humanitarian' solution to the problems of inter-ethnic relationships in the British Empire. Flinders Island was portrayed as humanitarianism in action. However, looking back from the twenty-first century, it was cultural genocide in action too.

This chapter will begin with an investigation of the select committee, its discourse concerning Van Diemen's Land and an analysis of how that discourse came to be represented in the politics of 'protection'. Yet the hopes invested in the Flinders Island community were short-lived. Whether it had originally been motivated by a desire to protect or destroy, by the middle of the 1840s even its most enthusiastic supporters had been forced to admit that the settlement had failed. As a consequence, faith in the ability of British civilisation to redeem indigenous peoples soon gave way to despair at the inevitability of their decline, because the numbers on Flinders Island seemed inexorably to fall. The idea proposed during the 'Black War' that this decline was somehow inescapable appeared to be confirmed. As the population dwindled further, and despite efforts by the 'free people' of Van Diemen's Land to assert their rights and vitality, this suggestion – that indigenous peoples were destined to fade away in the light of the British Empire – took firmer and firmer hold, within both government and wider political culture. If the notion that indigenous Tasmanians might be saved and transformed produced a new faith in the British imperial mission in the late 1830s, a new faith that the British might not repeat the mistakes of Van Diemen's Land, then the idea that they appeared doomed by Providence to extinction embedded imperial conceit even further a decade later. Desperate, primitive, 'Aborigines' were contrasted with the thrusting men of modernity from the 1840s onwards. From then on, British engagement with

Cultural Genocide

indigenous Tasmania and the genocidal consequences of colonialism was confined to charting the apparently unavoidable extinction of the 'Tasmanian race' down to the death of Truganini in 1876, after which the original islanders were believed to be only a memory.

I will chart these shifting understandings of Flinders Island, and changing attitudes and policy towards 'Aborigines', within the metropolitan British government. What are the implications of the narrative that unfolds here for our understanding of the relationship of the British government and indeed a wider British political culture to genocide in Tasmania? When thinking about this issue we *could* use the humanitarian campaigns of the 1830s, just as we could use the rhetoric of government that apparently protested against extermination, to construct a narrative that identifies the British state, and especially its metropolitan centre, as the avowed opponent of destruction. It is after all the case that in humanitarian circles the plight of indigenous Tasmanians, and the massive reduction in population since the founding of Van Diemen's Land, led to a perception of a crisis of colonialism, and calls for the refounding of the colonial project on humanitarian terms.[1] Thomas Hodgkin, who had fought for abolition, argued that the crisis facing 'Aborigines' was a more 'enormous evil' than slavery precisely because it threatened the extermination of entire peoples.[2] Thus we *could* argue that when we see genocide in Tasmania we are not looking at a genocidal moment in the British past at all, but British efforts to prevent or at least ameliorate the effects of what we would call genocide.

However, by placing the humanitarian campaign for the 'civilisation' of indigenous peoples in the context of longer-term British policy towards Tasmania and other Australian colonies, we can begin to see that that too was a discourse of destruction. Thus this chapter must begin with an analysis of humanitarian discourse and its prescription for remedying the injustices of colonialism. I argue that the vision for the 'protection' of communities articulated by humanitarians amounted to a prescription for cultural genocide imposed on Australia from London.

The Last Man

I will then show that this (from one vantage point) hopeful vision was soon transformed. It seems that the stubborn refusal of indigenous peoples themselves to accept the roles that they had been awarded led many British observers, inside and outside government, to the apocalyptic and pessimistic assumption that the decline to nonexistence of such peoples was inevitable. Both of these ways of understanding indigenous peoples and the future of empire amounted to visions of genocide. Indeed, I will argue that in the pictures of 'native' societies that were painted in Victorian politics we can see that the idea of progress at the heart of many liberal British identities was itself essentially genocidal.

THE SELECT COMMITTEE ON ABORIGINES (BRITISH SETTLEMENTS)

Thomas Fowell Buxton had been the leader of the parliamentary anti-slavery movement. He had been drawn to the issue of 'Aboriginal' communities within the Empire in the 1820s, and consistently raised it with the Colonial Office in the aftermath of the successful abolition campaign.[3] The presence of evangelicals in Downing Street, such as Thomas Spring-Rice, Lord Glenelg and James Stephen, ensured that he had a sympathetic hearing. Indeed, Stephen wrote to Buxton in 1837 to make clear that he regarded their working together on righting the 'cruel wrongs which our country has inflicted on such a large portion of the human race' as the most vital work of his career.[4] As well as the suffering of indigenous Tasmanians, Secretary of State Glenelg was in particular concerned by the treatment of the Xhosa people in the Cape Colony, who had been engaged in war with the colonial authorities following the annexation of Queen Adelaide Province in 1835. Buxton's concerns pre-dated this – he had publicly called for the establishment of a select committee in the House of Commons in July 1834 – and it was set up with the support of government in the following year. Buxton suggested that a committee be established in order to discuss how the 'rapid decrease

Cultural Genocide

that was taking place among the native inhabitants of the colonies' might be arrested.

The 16 members of the committee included Sir George Grey, Undersecretary of State in the Colonial Office, something that confirms the close association between campaigners and those operating colonial policy in government. They would hear testimony from some 47 witnesses over the next two years, nearly all of whom would point to the injurious treatment of indigenous populations at the hands of the Empire.[5] The virtual elimination of all of the original islanders in Van Diemen's Land acted as a constant reminder of the possible consequences of failure for the select committee.

The driving force behind the committee was its recognition of indigenous communities' right to enjoy the benefits of civilisation, rather than any right to the land. Using the language of the abolition movement, the select committee, and the report that it produced, argued that peoples across the Empire were brothers in the human family. Witnesses were reminded that it sat for 'practical purposes',[6] in order to discuss 'what measures ought to be adopted with regard to the native inhabitants of countries where British settlements are made [...] to lead them to the peaceful and voluntary reception of the Christian religion'.[7] There was therefore little understanding of the worth of indigenous culture. Therefore, the select committee was not concerned to bring an end to colonial encounters but to ensure that those encounters were more equitable and of demonstrable 'benefit' to indigenous communities.

One of the missionaries who gave evidence on Van Diemen's Land provides us with a typical example. James Backhouse, a Quaker who arrived in Hobart in 1832, came closer than anyone to recognising that the cultural differences between settlers and the existing community were not a simple matter of superiority or hierarchy. He recorded in his diary of his time in Van Diemen's Land that its 'natives [...] exceeded Europeans in skill in those things to which their attention had been directed from childhood'. As such neither European nor Tasmanian might be dismissed as defective he argued, just culturally distinct.[8] Backhouse, echoing the language of the abolition movement, welcomed indigenous Tasmanians as members of 'the human family'. Yet there were very clear limits to his appreciation of indigenous culture too, and it did not extend to a belief that that culture should be allowed to endure. Backhouse visited the Flinders Island settlement, for example, and reported enthusiastically on the project of 'civilisation' that was under way there, even before Robinson had completed his 'Friendly Mission'.[9] Backhouse's understanding of protecting indigenous communities and respect for cultural difference could apparently also accommodate the project to ensure their cultural eradication. The same could also be said of the select committee itself.

The events in Van Diemen's Land played a curious role at the select committee. In some senses its members were haunted by the idea of the 'Black War' and the notion that the island's peoples had in effect been exterminated.[10] Indeed, the idea that the purpose of humanitarian campaigning on the Empire was to prevent other communities from sharing the fate of 'the natives of [...] Van Diemen's Land' was commonplace throughout the 1830s and into the 1840s.[11] In the preparations for the hearings, James Backhouse directly advised Buxton that 'before long they [indigenous Tasmanians] will become extinct'.[12] But, at the same time, because of the Flinders Island settlement, Van Diemen's Land represented a possible solution for the committee. In the same letter, Backhouse had confirmed that the population was 'making some progress in civilisation' and that they 'appear very happy. There is reason to believe much more happy than they have been for a long time in their own land.'[13] George Arthur himself enthusiastically welcomed Buxton's investigations, and offered his own experience in the search for a comprehensive means to 'protect' indigenous communities.[14]

The select committee heard and then published evidence on Van Diemen's Land that very much conformed to the picture of conflict that was already available in the public sphere. The idea that indigenous Tasmanians faced extinction was routinely proposed, as was the narrative that identified the Risdon Cove massacre as the original offence that roused the community to vengeance. William Broughton, who had served as chair of Arthur's Aborigines Committee in Hobart, testified that the 'ferocious' inhabitants of Van Diemen's Land had been provoked into vengeful violence by the settlers.[15] Generally speaking the evidence provided by missionaries from across the settler colonies painted a picture of settler–indigenous relations that could be recognised in Van Diemen's Land too. Most notably, violence was routinely identified as the result of the delinquency of the settlers rather than a fact of colonisation itself. Thomas Hodgkin discussed with Buxton and his colleagues the phenomenon of Europeans being unleashed on 'savage nations' without 'much restraint from the hand of European authority'.[16] The select committee thus reflected the powerful, class-based discourse that suggested that the settlers, as the surplus population of Britain, represented its human dregs.[17] Violence against 'Aboriginals' was not therefore understood as a consequence of the British Empire itself; rather, the Empire had created a means by which Britain's own savages might be shipped abroad.

As many scholars have pointed out, it is important that we don't misunderstand the committee and conclude that it was somehow anti-imperialist. In particular, it is simply not the case that the experience of the indigenous population in Van Diemen's Land had so chastened the British that there was a significant portion of opinion arguing, on humanitarian terms, that the extent of empire needed to be rolled back. There is no doubt that the report Buxton and his committee finally produced in 1837 represented a searing critique of the impact of colonialism, alleging that 'every law of humanity and justice has been forgotten and disregarded' in the expansion of Britain's settler colonies.[18] But it was a *settler-led* colonialism that Buxton and his humanitarian colleagues were attacking, not the centrally sanctioned colonial policies of the metropolitan government.[19] Indeed, the overt concentration in the select committee on the 'sin of the settlers' appears in part to have been a device to protect the idea of colonialism itself.[20] As one of Buxton's humanitarian successors, Henry Fox Bourne, wrote, criticisms of colonisation were 'in no spirit of opposition to colonies or colonisation, in no attempt to prevent the growth and outspread of the English race, but with a desire to make that movement better'.[21]

Thomas Hodgkin was one of a number of witnesses, including George Arthur, who argued that the response to the crisis in indigenous populations should be the appointment, by London rather than the settler regimes, of 'Aboriginal protectors'. Their task would have been both to prevent settler attacks and to supervise the 'civilisation' of indigenous populations, and thus to make colonialism 'better'. The idea of 'protectors' was based, in Arthur's case at least, on the experience of Robinson in Van Diemen's Land. The select committee adopted such proposals and recommended that in future relations between settlers and indigenous communities be regulated by the appointment of 'protectors of the natives'. In its final report the committee outlined the 'duties' of such a post, which would include 'supplying [...] employment', and, most importantly, the education of children. Thus the select committee, although it was scarred by the experience of indigenous Tasmanians, also heard proposals for what was essentially a Vandemonian solution to the sufferings of others.

Yet this was not the only irony of the proposals for the protectors. They also represented a dual extension of the colonial project. First, as direct appointments from London the protectors would strengthen the role of the Colonial Office in the affairs of an individual colony. The Colonial Office had in effect handed control of 'Aboriginal policy' in Van Diemen's Land to George Arthur in 1832. The select committee suggested that that be reversed and that control be transferred back to London. Secondly, while strengthening the formal bonds of empire, this vision of protection relied on the rhetoric of 'civilisation', itself a powerful colonial ideology that implied the providential destiny of British, Christian civilisation.[22]

With this in mind, it is difficult to agree with Henry Reynolds's assessment that the significance of the select committee lies in its articulation of indigenous communities' right to their land.[23] Certainly, some witnesses to the committee did refer to the British theft of territory, and Buxton's final report excoriated Britain for its failure to recognise that 'the native inhabitants [...] have an incontrovertible right to the land'.[24] However, the main thrust of the committee's witnesses, and indeed its conclusions, was an attempt to sanctify the mission to and with it the transformation of indigenous communities rather than a preoccupation with land rights. The problem with the taking of the land was, in the eyes of the committee, not the theft per se but the fact that it had been seized with no sense that the original owners should 'benefit'.[25] What is more, Buxton did not recommend that treaties be signed with indigenous authorities – for that would have been to set too high a store by their authority structures and political arrangements. Instead, the committee recommended, again on the Flinders Island model, the separation of 'Aboriginal' communities into reservations paid for by the sale of other lands. It is true that, theoretically, the islanders' rights to the land were recognised in such an arrangement, but at the same time they would have been limited to reservations, something that would have lessened their contact with (growing) colonial societies and made them the target of missionaries who would seek to enact their 'moral and intellectual improvement'.[26] The reservations also *required* further territorial expansion in order to finance them.

In the Australian context, the select committee met at a time when the Empire was expanding. The new colonies of South Australia and what would become Victoria were both founded in the mid 1830s. It is true that the negotiations for the formation of those colonies did involve some recognition of the right of indigenous peoples to the land. However, this did not imply that those peoples could act as any form of brake on colonial development. Ultimately the Colonial Office envisaged a system in which the sale of Crown lands would help finance the creation of reservations where the population would be protected by the Empire, in the fashion recommended by the select committee. Of course, these reservations would also leave the rest of the land empty for development. Thus the select committee, in very practical terms, contributed to the formation of a system of colonial development, albeit one that included the amelioration of the plight of indigenous populations. It seems to me that such amelioration fell far short of recognising the territorial rights of existing communities.

The commitments to 'protection' and 'improvement' implicit in such proposals should not be misunderstood. They envisaged a radical reorientation and indeed transformation of traditional ways of life. Children would be separated from their families – indeed, some even went so far as to suggest that they should be sent to England. European ways of farming were to be foisted on populations whose profound cultural and economic relationships with the land were thought to count for nothing. The committee hid (even from themselves) the potential and essential destructiveness of this project behind language which talked of the 'intellectual improvement of mankind'.[27] But, even for Buxton's humanitarians, the aim of colonisation remained the 'gradual extinction of savage barbarism'.[28] In essence the select committee thus contributed to what John Docker has labelled an 'honourable colonisation', extending the iron fist of colonial development and the usurpation of the land within the velvet glove of rhetoric that suggested that the colony itself was the saviour of those it displaced.[29]

In the aftermath of the select committee, Buxton, Hodgkin and other campaigners formed the Aborigines' Protection Society. This was to become a humanitarian organisation that would promote a version of 'honourable colonisation' throughout the rest of the century. Rhetorically at least the version of colonialism that the society promoted was of a different order. It promised the dawning of a hopeful, 'new and better era' in which peoples would be protected from the ravages of a settler population. Again, it might be comforting to suggest that the meetings of these humanitarians in Exeter Hall on the Strand demonstrate that there was a significant body of opinion in London that was dedicated to the welfare of indigenous peoples, and wished to prevent their further dispossession and dislocation. And in rhetorical terms this is true.

But the good men of the Aborigines' Protection Society did not oppose, at any level, the colonial project itself. Like the select committee that helped them to form the organisation, they believed, honestly

Cultural Genocide

and wholeheartedly, that colonialism itself could 'rescue and elevate the coloured races'. Protectors would ensure that the savage settler population could not physically injure indigenous peoples, while the missionaries would protect communities from themselves.[30] Such a vision was enacted on Flinders Island with disastrous consequences.

FLINDERS ISLAND AND THE 'PROTECTION' OF INDIGENOUS AUSTRALIANS

The Colonial Office sympathised with the vision of Christian colonialism proposed by the select committee and the Aborigines' Protection Society. After all, it articulated the same assumptions that had governed policies towards indigenous peoples over the previous decade, and under which the Colonial Office had sanctioned the ethnic clearances in Van Diemen's Land. Downing Street's endorsement of the deportation of survivors in Van Diemen's Land had after all been based on a belief in the duty of protection. Since his arrival as Secretary of State Lord Glenelg had attempted to act in the humanitarian mode. He went to great lengths to ensure that relations between settlers and peoples across the Empire were governed by the rule of law rather than force. Towards the end of Richard Bourke's tenure as governor of New South Wales, for example, Glenelg instructed him that it was not possible for a state of war to exist between the agents of empire and indigenous peoples, who were British subjects too.[31] In doing so, Glenelg apparently confirmed a shift away from the policy of Lord Bathurst that had underpinned the first military campaigns in Van Diemen's Land. Central to Glenelg's policy was the idea that settlers could and should face judicial investigation for violence against indigenous people. As a consequence, the Colonial Office supported, and indeed lobbied for, the prosecution of those involved in the Myall Creek massacre in New South Wales in 1838.[32]

Despite Glenelg's interventions, 'Aboriginal policy' across the Australian colonies remained essentially contradictory, as it had in Van Diemen's Land. While the Colonial Office repeatedly instructed its agents that violence should not be tolerated and that the perpetrators should face trial, they also *repeatedly* highlighted the circumstances in which violence actually *was* acceptable. As Glenelg wrote to the newly appointed governor of New South Wales George Gipps in December 1838:

> that while the Government afford all due protection to the person and property of the peaceable and industrious settlers, it may be clearly known by all parties that it will not shrink from enforcing the law against all those who, *not for the purpose of self-defence*, but wantonly, commit acts of violence or aggression against the aboriginal inhabitants.[33]

In other words, violence in protection of the colony, and the colonial idea, remained entirely acceptable.

After the select committee reported, however, the Colonial Office accepted that it required a more proactive policy of 'protection'.[34] The committee had succeeded in convincing Glenelg, and other officials, that 'Aboriginals' across Australia would be wiped out without the intervention of Downing Street. The Colonial Office turned to Van Diemen's Land for the solution to this problem, because it was there that a policy of protection had been employed and, as it understood it, had in effect saved the remnant population. There is of course an obvious and unresolved contradiction about this: Van Diemen's Land was also the site of maximum indigenous dislocation.

The idea that the Flinders Island settlement represented a potential model for the whole of the British Empire was not, however, developed only as a response to the select committee. The Colonial Office had long believed that Flinders Island was a practical articulation of the principles of humanitarian imperialism, although news that Robinson himself thought the settlement a failure did cause a temporary crisis of confidence in 1835.

When Robinson returned to Flinders Island in 1835, he did not expect to be staying long. The negotiations for the formation of the

Cultural Genocide

colony of South Australia had included discussions about 'Aboriginal protection' and it had been proposed that as the Empire's foremost expert on these matters Robinson be transferred to the new settlement to implement policy there.[35] In those negotiations it was suggested that Robinson wished to take the surviving indigenous Tasmanians from Flinders Island with him to the new colony. Robinson argued that this was necessary in order to ensure the survival of a community that was declining rapidly.

Such an argument caused consternation in Downing Street. The Colonial Office simply could not understand why it would be necessary to transfer the now 130 indigenous Tasmanians from Flinders Island. After all, it believed in Wybalenna as the solution to the potential extinction of Tasmania's original inhabitants, as the means of saving them. If in fact it was now part of the problem, Lord Glenelg not unreasonably demanded to know why this was the case and required a 'full and detailed report of the state and condition of the Natives at Flinders Island'.[36] Glenelg's dismay confirmed an enduring faith in London in the deportation-as-protection project that had been so enthusiastically articulated by Lord Goderich in 1832.

The reality of Flinders Island was complex, and defies easy characterisation. Like officials in London, in Van Diemen's Land men like Robinson and Arthur genuinely believed that the settlement could be the means of transforming and in effect westernising indigenous Tasmanians. According to the colonial mindset the settlement physically saved indigenous Tasmanians from settler violence, as well as from their own savagery. Children were separated from their parents in order to be educated as Englishmen, and eventually the settlement had European-style housing, individual allotments for cultivation, a weekly market and indeed a newspaper.[37] Such innovations were accompanied by regular church services, and were the basis of the moral and religious instruction the surviving indigenous Tasmanians would experience after their deportation from the mainland. As we saw in Chapter Three, Robinson also understood that Flinders Island was not a local project but might have been of pan-imperial significance.

But, alongside this rhetoric, and alarmingly in an institution designed to save (and confine) the indigenous population, death was a constant presence and 'scythed through the Aboriginal community'. Between 1832 and October 1847, 132 indigenous Tasmanians died in Wybalenna, most often from pneumonia. By contrast, in its first five years over 70 convicts worked at the settlement but only one died of disease.[38] At the end of 1835 Robinson suggested in his diary the burden he felt at the presence of death and disease:

> it is an appalling sight to view the mounds of earth now before us where the people are buried [...] each one reminds us that the body of a native lies there. This is their repository of the dead [...] These numerous graves contain only the bodies of Aborigines.

Robinson continued his lamentation for the dead by explaining it as the result of Providence: 'God's will be done. To these poor people the affliction is heavy indeed.'[39] He recognised the tragedy of Flinders Island, that its existence was based on the desolation of the indigenous community at British hands. Around the same time he raged in his private journal against the theft of land: 'we are the usurpers.'[40]

While there was a contradiction in some of Robinson's views of the settlement he led in 1835, there was a consistency in his depiction of its community. For all Robinson's evangelical rhetoric that cast the indigenous Tasmanians as his brothers, he did not regard people like Walter Arthur (an indigenous boy who had been educated in Hobart and then sent to Flinders Island in 1835 and renamed in honour of George Arthur) and even Truganini as *like him*. Robinson constructed them as having no agency, no hand in controlling their own history. They were at the mercy of God and the anointed British Empire. At his most optimistic Robinson believed they would be transformed, 'civilised', into Europeans. At his most pessimistic he believed they were doomed to extinction. According to scholars like Henry Reynolds and Lyndall Ryan, Robinson was in fact trapped in a mindset that meant he could not understand or appreciate what was really occurring on Flinders Island. The picture they paint as an alternative is of a Creole community, the result of a cultural hybridity, where the indigenous Tasmanians indeed had agency, where they were able 'to pick and choose among the many things that colonial society had to offer'.[41] One of those things was of course language: many of the inhabitants spoke English, combining it with their own languages.[42] And indigenous Tasmanians were not simply the unwilling participants at Robinson's many religious services either, but, especially through the evangelical Walter Arthur, developed a Creole Christianity of their own.[43] They also used the accommodation that Robinson provided on their own terms, at times incorporating their brick huts into communal life, at times abandoning them for a life outside the settlement.

Yet whatever the reality of the Flinders Island community, throughout the Empire it was the fantasies that mattered most: the fantasy of Wybalenna as an instructional institution that would supervise indigenous Tasmanians' route to the freedom of civilisation, or the fantasy of a wretched charnel house in which they slipped inexorably into history. The most important version of the former, a myth of the settlement as a laboratory of civilisation, was constructed by George Augustus Robinson himself in a report dated June 1837, which had been prepared in response to Glenelg's anguished request of 1835. Robinson's narrative is important because it is the longest and most comprehensive description of life on Flinders Island, but also because it was the document that reaffirmed the Colonial Office's view that Flinders Island offered a potential model for protection across the Empire.

Apparently without irony Robinson reported that the 'only thing to be deplored' about the settlement on Flinders Island was the 'mortality' of its inhabitants. Such was the scale of the problem, he repeated his statement to what was by then, although unbeknownst to him, Her Majesty's Government that without intervention indigenous Tasmanians would 'in a very short period of time' become 'extinct'. Yet this was the only qualification in the otherwise utopian picture that Robinson painted. In an effort to reassure the Colonial Office that the policy of removal and deportation that it had itself endorsed was not the root of extermination, he asserted that the Tasmanians' extinction was the will of Providence and would thus have occurred anyway. Indeed, Robinson argued that as extinction was providential, this reaffirmed the humanity of the deportation policy because it ensured that the dying Tasmanians would have some chance of access to a 'knowledge of God' that would ensure their smooth passage to eternity.[44]

Robinson claimed great success in the project of 'civilisation' at Flinders Island and also offered a comprehensive definition of what that ambition practically amounted to. He wrote that removal had bestowed 'manifold [...] advantages' on the 'aborigines'. As well as receiving religious instruction, the indigenous community had been 'taught' the skills of husbandry and now 'dig and plant their own potatoes' as well as growing large quantities of strawberries. As well as being sedentarised in European houses they had also accepted the idea of private property.[45] They participated in a regular market at which their manufactures could be sold using a currency created for the purpose.[46]

Robinson also extolled the virtues of the 'Aboriginal' police force that he had created on the island. This consisted of 'four special constables' nominated by the entire community whose duties included preventing the passage of those who attempted to abscond from the settlement.[47] The existence of the police is the only issue over which Robinson's description of his practical attempt to implement a humanitarian imperialism differs from the version of 'protection' outlined in London by the select committee. In their final report they had rejected the idea of 'Aboriginal' police forces, because 'the instinct and passions of uncivilised men' ensured that they 'become victims of their own zeal' when awarded such power.[48]

In her biography of George Augustus Robinson, Vivienne Rae-Ellis dismissed his report as a work of pure fiction, calculated only to achieve his (and the settlement's) transfer to the Australian mainland.[49] While it is difficult to discern Robinson's real motivations, there seems little doubt that his depiction of the settlement was 'part aspiration and part imagination'.[50] His private journals seem to suggest that he genuinely did believe he was transforming the indigenous community,[51] while as we have seen the survival of their culture was the more notable feature of life at the settlement. Despite in that sense dwelling in the imaginary, we also know from his journals that Robinson was in fact unable to ignore the suffering that the settlement brought. As such Robinson seemed to inhabit both fantasy and reality, and perhaps his understanding of the settlement will thus remain elusive.

Whether Robinson's picture of the settlement was an elaborate fiction or not, it was accepted enthusiastically in London. Glenelg's scepticism and concern about the settlement was forgotten, and he accepted that Robinson had 'suggested plans for the civilisation and improvement of the Natives' that could be implemented throughout Australia. Thus Robinson's report ensured that Flinders Island became the practical manifestation of the recommendations of the select committee.[52] The report was sent round the colonies as a potential basis for the policy of protectors. In January 1838, for example, Glenelg instructed Governor Gipps about the outcome of the deliberations of the select committee and about Robinson's 'success' at Flinders Island. Gipps was told that Her Majesty's Government's response to Buxton's recommendations would be to appoint Robinson as chief protector in New South Wales and that he should establish an 'aboriginal settlement comparatively so far advanced in civilisation' as Flinders Island.[53]

The fantasy of Flinders Island was therefore rather more important than any reality, because it was the former that had a practical policy impact. Government enthusiasm for Robinson's imaginary account also tells us something of the fundamental priorities of the Colonial Office, and its vision of both the purpose of colonial expansion and its impacts. Remember that Robinson freely acknowledged that Wybalenna had a problem with the mortality of its inhabitants. But this fact was not enough to invalidate its purpose in either his eyes

The Last Man

or that of the British government. Despite an acknowledged population decline of 50 per cent, the settlement was not declared a failure. Perceptions of its success were therefore determined not by the survival of the indigenous community, but by the degree of their transformation, or, to put it another way, the decline of their own culture and the degree of their adoption of 'civilisation'. For humanitarians such as Glenelg, it was this that decided whether or not colonial expansion could be justified. As Frederick Chesson wrote towards the end of the century, 'we may hope to satisfy our conscience as a nation [if we] spread the blessings of civilisation among races which have hitherto been hopelessly degraded by barbarism.'[54]

After receiving the report, the Colonial Office aggressively pursued a policy of 'protection' across the Australian colonies that attempted to replicate Robinson's fantasy island. Four protectors were to be appointed, overseen by Robinson as chief protector. Robinson had originally been proposed by George Arthur, but his recruitment was confirmed through London.[55] His fellow protectors were also appointed in Downing Street, and their duties were established there too. Indeed it was Glenelg who outlined the responsibilities and function of the protectors to colonial governments in January 1838. Thus the system of 'protection' represented a formal expansion of centralised imperial control – an implementation of the select committee's vision that the settler population could not be trusted with such delicate and crucial work. The duties of the protectors were to include those areas that had apparently proved successful on Flinders Island. Like Robinson, Downing Street argued that 'protection' required that indigenous populations turn to the cultivation of the soil and the construction of buildings. Moral and religious teaching was central, as was the idea that indigenous children should be separated from their parents and educated 'extensively' in order to claim them for civilisation.[56]

London's interventions in the 'protection' of indigenous populations did not end with Lord Glenelg's tenure in the Colonial Office. His successors similarly bombarded colonial governors with instructions,

Cultural Genocide

to, at least in Gipps's case in New South Wales, their evident exasperation.[57] Governors were repeatedly reminded of their 'sacred duty of making systematic' efforts to reveal to the 'former occupiers of [the land] the blessings of Christianity, or the knowledge of the arts and advantages of civilised life',[58] and of their responsibility to attempt to educate children away from their families and communities.[59] In October 1840 the Secretary of State, Lord John Russell, wrote from Downing Street to Sydney, outlining very clearly that the price of colonisation and civilisation was the destruction of the communal lives and cultures of peoples across Australia:

> it would appear [...] impossible that any nation subject to [indigenous laws and customs] could ever emerge from a savage state, [and] even that no race [...] could in no other respects remain long in a state of civilisation if they were admitted to the operation of such barbarous customs.[60]

Both the select committee report and Robinson's depiction of Flinders Island were embodiments of the discourse of humanitarian imperialism in the latter half of the 1830s. Both could be used to point to the fact of the benign intentions of one version of British imperialism at this time. That both received such a favourable reception in Downing Street was a result of the dominance of humanitarian thinking within the Colonial Office at this time too. Yet there is a dual irony here. First that humanitarian thinking created an interventionist Colonial Office, which sought through the office of protectors in the Australian colonies to control 'Aboriginal' policy directly. That desire in turn articulated an embedded colonial discourse that characterised the settlers as, essentially, savages themselves. Second, the discourse of protection was markedly destructive. As Patrick Brantlinger has suggested, it was a form of 'white supremacism' insistent on 'transforming savage customs and cultures into Christianity and white civilisation'. Its aim was nothing less then the eradication of indigenous culture throughout the colonies in Australia. In other words, its aim was genocide.[61]

The Last Man

The system of protectors that the British government established in response to the select committee of 1835–7 became the foundation of policy towards peoples in Australia throughout the next century. While enthusiasm for the policy waned in Britain during the 1840s, it returned in various guises, especially after the Australian colonies were granted self-government and the British withdrew from attempting to control policy in this area. The separation of children from their communities became a central plank of the enduringly genocidal policies towards those communities. When the Aborigines Protection Board was established in New South Wales in 1883 and in Western Australia in 1886, both were welcomed by the Aborigines' Protection Society in London, the group that had grown out of the select committee.[62]

In 1875 the report of the Royal Commission on the Condition of the Aborigines of Queensland recommended action to abate the decline of the indigenous population there. It is a familiar set of recommendations: that protectors be appointed, that 'Aboriginal reserves' be created, that the building of houses and the cultivation of land be encouraged and that a special effort be made to Christianise the young.[63] The Native Police Force, which Robinson specifically identified as an important element of his vision of protection, was not dealt with by the board of inquiry. As Alison Palmer has shown, however, the Native Police in Queensland became an agent in extermination.[64] Indeed, this was recognised at the time by the campaigning Aborigines' Protection Society, who lobbied the governor of Queensland on the issue. But even then we cannot identify the society as simply the British opponents of extermination. They welcomed all of the other measures in the report, including those that we would now consider to be genocidal.

In the event, Robinson's report and the appointment of 'protectors' represented the high-water mark of humanitarian hopes that colonisation could be shown to be demonstrably beneficial to indigenous communities. Humanitarian influence in Britain had already begun to fade in the late 1830s. Symbolically, Buxton lost his parliamentary seat in 1837,⁶⁵ and Glenelg had left the Colonial Office by September 1839. Although his successor, Lord John Russell, continued to be sympathetic to the principles of humanitarianism, he gradually began to accept that he could not direct the transformation of indigenous societies from London.⁶⁶

In general terms, there appears to have been a growing pessimism about the possibilities of Christian colonialism throughout the 1840s. Catherine Hall reports that missionaries in the West Indies were beginning to face the limitations of their influence, and lamented the failure of freed slaves to transform themselves according to the 'missionary dream'.⁶⁷ And even within the group that remained most steadfastly committed to humanitarianism, the Aborigines' Protection Society, there was a growing alarm about whether British colonialism could in fact change course. The society's 1844 annual report lamented that 'the tendencies of modern colonisation remain unchanged [and] the misery and ruin of the previous inhabitants must be the inevitable result'.⁶⁸

Of course, even when 'protection' had apparently offered a hopeful future, there had been a general sense that this might have come too late for indigenous Tasmanians. Both George Augustus Robinson and Arthur's successor as lieutenant governor of Van Diemen's Land, John Franklin, had suggested that 'this particular black family is doomed to become extinct'.⁶⁹ And James Stephen advised Glenelg in November 1838 that it was 'almost certain that in a very short time the last remnant of this race of men will have wholly disappeared'.⁷⁰ As the 1840s progressed the idea that Tasmanians were indeed doomed became fixed in political and popular culture in Britain. As questions began to be asked about the successes of the 'protection' policies enacted in response to the select committee, the idea that other 'Aboriginal' populations were destined to follow indigenous Tasmanians out of history became dominant. As the following discussion will demonstrate, this discourse of inevitable decline also operated a genocidal logic that suggested that the only futures for indigenous communities were transformation or death.

The Last Man

'I SHOULD NOT WITHOUT THE MOST EXTREME RELUCTANCE ADMIT THAT NOTHING CAN BE DONE'

As we have seen, the idea that indigenous Tasmanians were doomed to extinction had been a fixed part of Anglo-Australian discourse on settler–indigenous relations since the mid 1820s. Towards the end of the 1830s that discourse became dominant and was increasingly applied to all of the indigenous peoples in the Australian colonies. Just as the optimistic view of the possibilities that such peoples might be transformed by a Christian colonialism had been based on the Flinders Island settlement, so the gradual dominance of pessimism was, *in part*, informed by an understanding of the failure of that experiment. Declarations that indigenous Tasmanians were fated to die out were made most insistently by those, such as Henry Melville in his critical history of Van Diemen's Land (aimed at removing Governor Arthur), who wished to emphasise the iniquities of colonisation. In the late 1830s newspaper reports began to dwell on the 'horrors enacted at Flinders Island', highlighting the 'wasting away of a race once hardy, active and numerous' as a means of lobbying for a different approach.[71] Memoirists and travellers would do the same. John Lort Stokes, who had risen to be the commander of Darwin's *Beagle*, wrote two influential natural-history volumes titled *Discoveries in Australia* in the mid 1840s, in which he highlighted the plight of indigenous Tasmanians in order to suggest that never again should such unregulated contact between indigenous peoples and colonists be allowed. Stokes argued that all that could be done for the Tasmanians was to 'soothe their declining years'.[72]

Such critics of colonisation did not have to be aiming at the treatment of indigenous populations in particular to draw on the imagery of an extinguished race in their rhetoric. In the mid 1840s, when debate around colonisation focused on matters of cost, a ritual feature of the discussion was an emphasis on the predicted 'speedy' extinction of indigenous Tasmanians as a means to highlight in general terms the injurious effects of the Empire.[73] The idea of extinction, of

Cultural Genocide

extermination, was also a ritual of anti-transportation rhetoric – it was commonly cited as evidence of the urgent need to bring an end to convict shipments in order to prevent such atrocities in the future. John Dixon's memoir of Van Diemen's Land is just one example. In *Condition and Capabilities of Van Diemen's Land*, published in 1839, he 'predicted' the 'final extinction' of the indigenous communities confined on Flinders Island. He could not be clearer about who was responsible for the violence that preceded deportation: the 'callous-hearted monsters' who had been transported to Van Diemen's Land by the mother country.[74]

The apparent inevitability of extinction provided a prism through which the failure of the protection policies introduced at the behest of the select committee could be understood. The failure of that protection regime is perhaps best symbolised by the experience of those whom Robinson took with him when he left Flinders Island in February 1839. Robinson was prevented from transferring the entire community to Port Phillip on the Australian mainland because it was deemed too great a risk in the new colony of Victoria.[75] He did, however, take 15 residents of Wybalenna, including Walter Arthur, Woorraddy and Truganini.[76] Yet Robinson was unsure and to an extent unsupported in his new role.[77] He was unable to provide properly for his Tasmanian followers, five of whom he ultimately transferred to the 'care' of one his assistants, William Thomas.[78] Under the leadership of Pevay – who had aided Robinson in his mission to the clans on the land controlled by the Van Diemen's Land Company – this group became involved in violence and conflict with the settlers in the later months of 1841 and were implicated in two murders. They were arrested and two of them, Pevay and Maulboyheenner, were tried and executed on 20 January 1842. Of course, despite Robinson's protestations, the two men were prevented from giving evidence at their own trial. Their conflict with settlers was part of a general resistance to colonisation but they were portrayed as savages bent on violence – in keeping with the understanding of conflict in Van Diemen's Land in the 1820s. The indigenous Tasmanians' decision to abscond from the care of

Robinson's assistant protector displayed an understandable contempt for the protectorate itself, and they were typical of a population that in general terms Robinson was unable to sedentarise in the way that he had on Flinders Island.

The tragedy of Pevay was not shared by all the indigenous Tasmanians in Melbourne. Walter Arthur was successful in the new colony and was employed as a stockman. Yet in London it was not Arthur who appeared symbolic, although for many historians he now represents the possibilities of indigenous adaptation to the settler colony. Instead it was the tales of endemic violence that resonated.[79] Robinson himself sought to explain the problems he was experiencing in familiar terms – as a result not of dispossession and resistance to it, but of the character of the settlers, the 'depraved white men' pursuing the peoples whose land they had also usurped.[80] In London, however, the obvious fact that despite the hopes of Flinders Island Robinson had not remotely succeeded either in 'civilising' the peoples he encountered in Port Phillip or even in preventing violent confrontations between the two communities led to much darker premonitions.

Faced with the failure of the protectorates, James Stephen had suggested that the only solution was 'to make the Aborigines formidable to the Europeans'. 'If they could be armed, disciplined and taught to act in concert, there might be a chance for their salvation,' he wrote, before adding darkly, 'as it is, there is none.'[81] Stephen's pessimism was reflected elsewhere in the Colonial Office. When Lord Stanley succeeded Lord John Russell as Secretary of State he concluded that the protectorate system was failing. In despair, in December 1842 he wrote to Governor Gipps and effectively transferred responsibility for finding a solution to the crisis back to colonial governments. He ended that letter with an impassioned declaration, which merits lengthy quotation:

> I should not without the most extreme reluctance admit that nothing can be done; that with respect to them alone the doctrines of Christianity must be inoperative and that the

advantages of civilisation incommunicable. I cannot acquiesce in the theory that they are incapable of improvement and their extinction before the white settler is a necessity which it is impossible to control [...] I assure you that I shall be willing and anxious to cooperate with you in any arrangement for their civilisation which may hold out a fair prospect of success.[82]

Although Stanley was apparently reaffirming his commitment to the hopeful humanitarian assumptions that informed the commitment to 'civilising' missions in Australia, he was also signalling that he was ineluctably being drawn to a more pessimistic conclusion. What is more, by transferring responsibility he essentially confessed that he had no real sense of how a solution might be achieved.

Even the most hopeful of humanitarians appeared unable to escape the idea that indigenous peoples were dying. This is important for our understanding of how the concept operated and its relationship with the idea of 'civilisation' and protection. Once the apparent certainty of extermination in Van Diemen's Land had confirmed the possibility of racial extinction it became the prism through which all indigenous populations were viewed. As such it also became entirely self-fulfilling. Attempts by indigenous inhabitants – such as those by the indigenous Tasmanians whom Robinson took with him to Port Phillip – to resist 'civilisation' or to escape its clutches acted only to undermine the very idea that the benefits of that civilisation were available to their communities and supported the opposing notion that they belonged only in the past, that they could not be reconciled to colonial development. The very idea that peoples could be civilised, elevated or raised up had assumed that this was the only possible route to the future. When officials in the Colonial Office or members of the Aborigines' Protection Society protested that the idea that indigenous peoples were unable to receive the doctrines of Christ or the benefits of civilisation was itself a contravention of the Christian, humanitarian view that all men were brothers,[83] they also provided the grounds for disproving their own assumptions. The only way such peoples could demonstrate that they were not doomed was to 'civilise'.

Reactions to the community of Flinders Island in the 1840s offer the clearest evidence that the idea of permanent decline became a rhetorical prison in Victorian Britain, in terms of both how indigenous communities were imagined and policy towards them. After Robinson had departed from Flinders Island, the colonial government quickly concluded that there too efforts at 'civilisation' had been a failure. Under the care of Robinson's son, the settlement continued to be considered as a means for the transformation of the surviving indigenous people but the assumption that the community was ultimately doomed was pervasive. Under the pressure of that assumption the operation was gradually scaled down, so that by the time Henry Jeanneret arrived as commandant in the middle of 1842 the settlement was largely considered only as a means for providing care for a declining community.[84]

HENRY JEANNERET AND THE END OF THE FLINDERS ISLAND EXPERIMENT

In October 1842, husband and wife Walter and Mary Ann Arthur, Truganini and the rest of those who had survived their transfer to Port Phillip with Robinson returned to Flinders Island. According to Lyndall Ryan, those returning from continental Australia were much more assertive of their rights – refusing for example to engage in labour unless they were adequately recompensed.[85] Certainly Jeanneret, a Scottish-trained dentist who had previously been employed in the penal station at Port Arthur,[86] quickly became exasperated with them. Jeanneret was particularly critical of Walter Arthur, who had become de facto leader of the community. Jeanneret accused him of inciting disaffection.[87] Ultimately, Arthur did indeed assert the rights of his community, by protesting against Jeanneret's treatment of them, which he alleged included arbitrary imprisonment of those who were unwilling to obey his instructions. Arthur wrote to the

Colonial Secretary in Hobart, declaring: 'I am now in bodily fear of my life, and that of my wife, if we are put in gaol and suffer in health [...] I am lost, I cannot live.'[88]

The response of the colonial government to Arthur's allegations was to remove Jeanneret from his position. At which point Jeanneret himself turned to the imperial government in London, claiming that he had been defamed and demanding to be reinstated.[89] What had been a minor dispute on the outer reaches of the Empire was then transformed into a struggle fought in the metropolitan centre. And, once again, Flinders Island became an imperial space that represented discussion and debate about the very nature of colonisation. Jeanneret had professed himself to be committed to the project of transforming indigenous lives. But unlike his predecessor Robinson, his efforts at 'civilisation' appear to have been motivated by a complete revulsion at indigenous culture. He described a corroboree, for example, as producing 'scenes scarcely equalled in spheres of the grossest depravity'.[90]

In the first instance, Jeanneret's protests in London were successful. The colonial government was ordered to reinstate him in August 1845. However, the Colonial Office did not regard the dispute over the management of Flinders Island to be a conflict concerning the indigenous population at this stage. It was simply concerned about the operation of due process, and whether or not the colonial government had exceeded its powers in permanently removing Jeanneret, as an agent of the Crown, from his post.[91] Jeanneret was due to return to Flinders Island in February 1846.

Walter Arthur and the 47 remaining residents were dismayed. And their response was to petition not just the British government but Queen Victoria herself, in what Henry Reynolds has described as 'one of the most important, as well as one of the most neglected, documents' in post-invasion 'Aboriginal' history.[92] Arthur and the other elders of the community styled themselves as the 'Free aboriginal inhabitants of Van Diemen's Land' who 'freely gave up our country to Colonel Arthur then the governor after defending ourselves', and, in the light of their quiet cooperation in the establishment at Flinders Island, demanded Jeanneret not be allowed to return on the grounds of his mistreatment of their community.

The very fact of the petition demonstrates the enduring sense that London remained the ultimate arbiter in Van Diemen's Land, and the ultimate power in the lives of the indigenous community. It also suggested that the community accepted that authority as a balance to the potentially injurious rule of their colonial masters. The idea of the savage settler was not just held in London, it seems. Men like Robinson and George Arthur had clearly succeeded in embedding the sense that the imperial government at least had a protective intention.

In London the petition was interpreted not just as a request to prevent Jeanneret from returning, but as the articulation of a desire to abandon Flinders Island altogether.[93] This response seems to betray the enduring influence of humanitarian thinking in the Colonial Office and the residue of a commitment to recognising, in some sense, the indigenous community's right to the land. Indeed, Henry Reynolds suggests that London fundamentally accepted that indigenous Tasmanians had a right to their home.[94] At a time when the cost of the Flinders Island settlement was also a matter of public discussion, James Stephen wrote:

> why we should persevere in a policy at once so costly to the author, and so fatal to the objects of it, I cannot imagine particularly as the establishment has been created not so much with a view to any benefit to the [Aborigines] as from a regard to the interests of the colonists.[95]

Lord Grey, the Secretary of State for the Colonies, agreed. He echoed Stephen's sentiments and told Governor William Denison in Hobart that 'the marked decrease in numbers shows that the present position is anything but favourable to their [the indigenous community's] physical condition'. Grey further instructed that you will therefore [...] take the measures proposed [...] for withdrawing the natives to Van Diemen's Land, either collectively or gradually as may appear to be most advisable, and for breaking up the whole of the establishment; making such a provision for the care and maintenance of the natives, when so removed, as may be considered adapted to their wants. You will acquaint the memorialists that I have laid their memorial before the Queen, who was pleased to receive it very graciously.[96]

Grey's instruction was extraordinarily significant. For the Wybalenna community it meant their transfer back to the Tasmanian mainland, to an abandoned penal station at Oyster Cove. Forty-six people made the journey there in 1847. According to Reynolds, Grey's intervention also articulated the long-held humanitarian view that indigenous peoples retained some rights to their ancestral lands. Indeed, Reynolds suggests that Grey recognised the return of land as a means to try to forestall the predicted 'extermination'.[97]

The community themselves may well have been momentarily overjoyed at their return to their homeland,[98] but the British government was not undergoing a conversion to the idea that such peoples held land rights, or that they therefore might also have had some right to cultural survival. Instead, I think it much more realistic to understand the abandonment of Flinders Island by the British government as part of a slow but inexorable move within the Colonial Office towards the idea that the indigenous inhabitants of Van Diemen's Land in particular, and Australia in general, could not be saved from their inevitable doom. Grey was simply completing the journey that Lord John Russell had started in December 1842 – the settled view of the Colonial Office was that there was indeed nothing that could be done. The Flinders Island community was simply being allowed to go home to die.

Furthermore, this development in the British government's thinking was not disrupted by the actions of the indigenous community. After all, it might have been expected that the government would interpret the petition – in which the indigenous Tasmanians demonstrated a

The Last Man

faith in a Christian God and a respect for the authority of the Crown – as the fulfilment of its ambitions for the 'free people of Van Diemen's Land'. As a community they were expressing themselves politically, and as such might have seemed precisely to be progressing towards the 'civilisation' that the British had always dreamt of. But Stephen and the Secretary of State suggested in response that they believed Flinders Island had always been for the benefit of the colonists. In doing so, self-consciously or otherwise, they reversed their cherished beliefs of a decade previously. This was no hopeful projection of indigenous survival but an articulation of despair.

Although Grey restated his faith in 'small reserves' in which 'the Aborigines' might develop a bond 'with civilised society' in 1848, there was no conviction to his pursuit of that policy.[99] Returning the peoples of Van Diemen's Land to Oyster Cove had fulfilled the policies of the early 1840s that returned responsibilities to the colonial government from the centre. The protectorate policy was officially abandoned in 1849 when Grey conceded that he had come to the conclusion that the civilisation projects could not work. As A.G.L. Shaw wrote, Grey simply declared that 'unfortunately "nothing more can be done" for the Aborigines – "sacred duty" or not. "Express my regret at the failure of measures for this improvement," he noted, and that was that.'[100] The British government simply forgot its concern for the indigenous peoples of Australia from that point on.

The indigenous community was abandoned at Oyster Cove. The penal station there had originally been deserted because it was insanitary, but it was deemed fit for 'Aboriginal' habitation.[101] The community declined rapidly. By 1854 there were just 18 people surviving, and, based on his report on the future of the settlement, Governor Denison clearly viewed his only responsibility as the supervision of its inexorable decline.[102] Despite Denison's wish that the community should not suffer, the settlement at Oyster Cove was poorly funded and inadequately rationed. By 1859 all attempts at religious instruction had been abandoned. At this stage there were just 14 indigenous Tasmanians remaining there.

Cultural Genocide

In Britain, the gloom that Lord Grey articulated from the Colonial Office had not taken root only in politics, but in wider culture too. If Flinders Island had once offered hope, now the devastation of the community pointed only to despair. The idea that Tasmanians were doomed to extinction became embedded in a diverse range of cultural forms, and informed an assumption that all indigenous peoples would share a similar fate. Indeed, it became a cultural given, a shared belief, which fulfilled a number of different functions, all of which pointed to the ordained superiority of the British as well as the permanent inferiority of the traditional cultures that the British were fated to replace. Consider the example of the Empire exhibition at the Crystal Palace in 1851. The 'Great Exhibition' displayed the technology and achievements of the British from across the colonised world; it was the definitive example of mid-century confidence about British superiority. The Aborigines' Protection Society had welcomed the fact that there were to be some exhibits from indigenous communities, arguing that this was to suggest their role in the future of the Empire.[103] Yet the exhibits from Van Diemen's Land suggested only the past.[104] In total there were 349 items from the island on display, including fine carpentry made from Huon pine and jams made from fruits imported by the colonists to demonstrate the spread of English culture. Yet there were just four exhibits of indigenous artefacts – and all of those, including shell necklaces, baskets and a water pitcher, were attributed not to those who had made them but to the colonists who had collected them. These were represented in Britain's mid-century display of triumph, therefore, as the relics of a lost people.[105] Indigenous Tasmanians were represented in the Crystal Palace as a culture that had been swept away.

'THE LAST MAN'

When Bessy Clark died in 1867 there were only three survivors in the Oyster Cove community. By then the idea that the 'extinction' of the indigenous Tasmanians was fast approaching had already been fixed in

The Last Man

the public imagination in Britain,[106] which began to engage in a kind of nostalgic countdown of the remaining survivors, a countdown to the end of a race. The idea that William Lanne had become 'the last man', the sole male survivor, excited particular curiosity.[107] A public appearance by Lanne at Government House in Hobart, for example, was widely reported in the British press, and occasioned much reflection on the passing of these 'unhappy people'.[108] Although such reports were often reproductions of accounts in Tasmanian newspapers, they did contain efforts at explaining the disintegration of indigenous Tasmanian society. The narratives on offer were familiar: indeed, by now there was a certain ritual to them – peaceable peoples had been roused to a spirit of wild revenge by their treatment at the hands of ruthless settlers, the displaced and depraved convict population. Transfer to Flinders Island was equally reported as, in hindsight, a measure that ensured further declension because it attempted to contain the wild and roving spirit of peoples now understood to be beyond the reach of a settled, civilised life. Thus, although the means of the Tasmanians' destruction was to be regretted, it was of course still regarded as inevitable. The contours of this discourse will be explored further in the following chapter.

When Lanne's death was reported there were only two survivors of the Oyster Cove community. Mary Ann died in August 1871, leaving Truganini – according to the British – the sole survivor of not just her community but her entire race. As, apparently, the very 'last Tasmanian' of all, Truganini became a kind of colonial celebrity, 'the best-known Tasmanian Aborigine in the world'.[109] Of course, the reality was that Truganini was not the last. Intriguingly, this was openly acknowledged in British discussions of Tasmania. Such discourse itself demonstrates the depth of the 'pernicious myth' in that it is shown clearly to have been dependent on a racialised view of the world.[110] The mixed-race communities of Tasmania and its outlying islands were not considered to be fully indigenous, as if the 'blood' of an Englishman might be the antidote to the poison of Aboriginality. And of course it was assumed that mixed-race Tasmanians could not endure anyway. The

Cultural Genocide

'fecundity' of mixed-race women was universally doubted, and there was a more lurid and indeed contrary suggestion that the children of mixed-race associations were usually slaughtered, an idea that drew on the long roots of the allegation that indigenous societies routinely practised both infanticide and cannibalism.[111]

Despite the acknowledgement of the reality of mixed-race communities, Truganini became the symbol of her passing people in the 1870s. An interview with the 'merry as a cricket' 'last of her race' was published in the *Gentleman's Magazine* in London in October 1876.[112] The article, which was widely syndicated, appearing in a variety of other newspapers,[113] asserted as incontrovertible fact that it was the lot of 'savage races' to 'disappear at the approach of civilisation like the dew before the morning sun'. Its author painted a mournful picture of Truganini that conformed to the image of the Tasmanians as a community somehow out of time, marooned in the future. She was not capable of understanding the reality of the modern world, according to the *Gentleman's Magazine*. Her interviewer had come from Britain and argued that Truganini could not conceive of the distances that he (as representative of the men of modernity) had travelled. In fact, Robinson reported that Truganini had a very clear understanding of imperial distances in the 1830s.[114] But in the *Gentleman's Magazine* the 'last Tasmanian' appeared as an acquisitive, venal simpleton. By the time the interview was published, Truganini had died. She had become ill, and was pronounced dead in May 1876.[115] Her death was reported in *The Times* in July: 'A royal lady: Trucaminni [...] the last Tasmanian aboriginal has died of paralysis aged 73.'[116] And with that, as far as Britain was concerned, indigenous Tasmanians had fulfilled their destiny and were extinct.

Since George Augustus Robinson led his final captives to Flinders Island, indigenous Tasmanians and attempts to transform them had essentially played two apparently contradictory roles in British politics.

Broadly speaking, in the later 1830s and into the 1840s, although the idea that the Tasmanians themselves may be entirely exterminated was regularly proposed, the settlement at Flinders Island was seen as the hopeful possibility of the British Empire. It appeared to embody a humanitarian approach to the construction of empire and was seen as the means by which the gifts of civilisation might be shared. It was the prototype on which a policy of 'protection' was based, before being established across the Australian colonies in the 1840s. In effect, it was to say that what had happened to the existing population of Van Diemen's Land could be an aberration, and not become the norm.

However, even though it was seen as a replacement for a relationship of violence and indeed extermination between settler and indigenous communities and notwithstanding its actual impact, 'protection' was essentially a prescription for cultural genocide. The idea that peoples could be liberated from their own barbarism involved the intentional destruction of their culture. It was hoped that they would have been entirely westernised at the end of the process. That process of westernisation became in many ways more important than the preservation of life itself; in the words of Robinson the only problem with Flinders Island was the mortality rate among its inhabitants. In the eyes of the Colonial Office such a qualification was not enough to bring an end to a plan to replicate the Flinders Island model across the Australian colonies.

The vision of 'protection' cast indigenous Tasmanians as the basis for hope, but from (broadly speaking) the late 1840s onwards they became the basis of despair. 'Protection' had not arrested the decline of indigenous peoples in Australia, nor had it led to any notable successes in the project of 'civilisation' – and nowhere was this more true than in Tasmania, where the small remnant community apparently hurtled towards oblivion. As a consequence, the experience of colonial Tasmania came to be used as evidence that such peoples were inevitably doomed – predestined by either Providence or nature to decline to nonexistence. Such an apocalyptic vision was genocidal. Although explanations for the decline of populations varied, what they had in common was an attempt to incorporate what we would call genocide into much broader understandings of the world.

Because of the impact of the British colony of Van Diemen's Land on the existing community of Tasmania, genocide became a constituent part of a variety of British identities and cultures. While these discourses were many and various – from evangelical Christianity to race science – they did share one fundamental assumption: that the British nation and its Empire were at the apex of human progress. It is therefore no exaggeration to state that this very idea, the very notion of progress, that cultural shorthand for the spirit of the age, amounted to a genocidal vision of the world. It is to a more detailed analysis of the cultural role of the destruction of indigenous Tasmanians that this book now turns.

FIVE

'We have exterminated the race in Van Diemen's Land': Genocide in British Culture

It is curious that the destructive impact of the British Empire in Australia is often presented as rather irrelevant to the British past and present. 'White Australians still struggle to come to terms with *their* colonial past,' we were told (without irony) by a British newspaper in 2009.[1] The object of the final two chapters of this book is to challenge this assumed separation of a destructive, indeed genocidal, Empire from its British home. This will be achieved through an investigation of the representation of the destruction of indigenous Tasmanians in British culture in the nineteenth century. The following chapter will concentrate on efforts to come to terms with the legacies of colonial violence in Britain up to the present day. The book will end with an analysis of much more recent debates about whether or not the remains of the dead collected in Tasmania should be returned to the present-day Aboriginal community.

The final chapters of *The Last Man* are therefore interventions in ongoing debates about the importance or otherwise of empire in British culture, both in the nineteenth century and today. As such they are rather different in nature and conception to the first half of this study. They argue that genocide made a significant contribution to British culture, and indeed British identities. The campaign of extermination in Van Diemen's Land was written and rewritten in Britain, read and reread by British audiences. The appearances of indigenous

Tasmanians, usually claimed to have disappeared, in British culture were many and various – from art exhibitions to museums displaying human remains. In these representations, the genocide of indigenous Tasmanians contributed to a sense of Britain as a preordained, advanced imperial nation. As such genocide in Tasmania in various ways became a part of British identity.

Such arguments contribute to the debate about whether the Empire really was a significant feature in the lives and culture of Britain and Britons in the nineteenth century and beyond. In his *Absent-Minded Imperialists* Bernard Porter argues that in fact, and contrary to the assumptions of previous scholars, the Empire was not important in the reality of people's lives.[2] 'Ordinary' Britons, Porter argues, knew little of their Empire.[3] When it comes to the violence and brutality that sustained it, Porter again proclaims that although of course *colonists* were aware that the Empire was forged in violence, in Britain itself this was little considered.[4]

Porter of course considers the Empire as a whole, and finds that no coherent sense of Britain's imperial purpose existed. I take the opposite method and focus on a single case study in the shape of Van Diemen's Land and then Tasmania. By concentrating on a limited territory and set of events, I argue that, contrary to Porter's argument, Britons *were* surrounded by imperial stories, which told a consistent narrative about the nature of the Empire, and more importantly the nature of being British. That those narratives were also concerned with the destructive impact of imperial expansion rather belies any claims that Britons must have been ignorant of its brutal realities. Thus it will be shown here that Britons were faced consistently with the extermination of indigenous Tasmanians from the 1820s onwards, and that this was a narrative that emphasised British progress over 'native' backwardness. In other words, an understanding of genocide in Tasmania informed a British sense of racial superiority.

Porter is right when he argues that scholars cannot adequately identify how such ideas about empire, or in this instance Tasmania, were understood. In-depth analysis of the discourses in which genocide

Genocide in British Culture

in Tasmania was constructed will not reveal exactly what those events meant to the readers of the books I refer to, or the viewers of the paintings I describe. However, there is a consistency to the shape, texture and implications of these representations that allows us to speculate as to its function in British culture. We might note for example that any argument that severs the links between domestic experience and imperial brutality has distinct similarities to the suggestion (proposed by imperial apologists from the 1820s onwards) that the Empire was fundamentally built on good intentions, subverted by the settlers that carried it into being. When we come across the repeated suggestion that it was the 'savage settlers' who were responsible for violence done to the poor benighted 'Aborigines', we can see that such arguments supported the idea that the Empire was a benign force. An understanding of settler brutality supported a sense of Britain's imperial purpose.

What follows is a discussion of a series of different narratives of racial violence and cultural genocide in Tasmania, from across the nineteenth century. Particularly prominent representations – the paintings of John Glover in the 1830s and James Bonwick's book *The Last of the Tasmanians* from the 1870s – are discussed in more detail, while other narratives (such as those constructed in the scientific debate on human origins) are discussed within the context of the general discourses from which they emerged.

REPORTING GENOCIDE

I will begin by going back to the beginning of this book and considering how the 'Black War' was reported in Britain. First, it is worth noting that the ongoing conflict in Van Diemen's Land was recounted publicly as well as in private letters. A picture of desperate colonists under siege was developed throughout the 1820s, with settlers portrayed as victims of attack from the 'pitiless savages'.[5] Often, particularly fearful descriptions of settler–indigenous relations were provided in an effort to counter the emigration propaganda that constructed Van Diemen's Land as an English Elysium. 'The truth is,' wrote a correspondent in

The Examiner in October 1824, 'the natives of Van Diemen's Land are generally hostile towards the settlers [...] they show foreigners no mercy when they catch them alone and unarmed.'[6] Not that such reporting disrupted a continuous picture of Van Diemen's Land as a potential idyll, the 'most fruitful and healthy spot on the face of the earth'.[7] However, across the decade, as the violence in Van Diemen's Land intensified, its reporting came to dominate the way in which the colony was represented in Britain.[8]

Settler violence was part of this story, but was invariably represented purely as an effort to quell the 'restless', 'annoying' or 'troublesome' 'black natives'.[9] The offer of friendship, readers were informed, had been met only with violent and, by implication, irrational and unjustified violence – an idea that assumed the worth of colonisation. Yet in the face of such provocation the settler population remained apparently resolute, building an inheritance for their 'children and grandchildren'.[10] But, as the rhetoric surrounding the indigenous population reached a crescendo towards the end of the 1820s, the settlers themselves were portrayed as increasingly (but necessarily) violent. In April 1829 several newspapers reported that the 'natives' had, 'like the snakes', resumed a campaign of violence 'as the warm weather returned'.[11] And as such it was going to be necessary for the settlers to take 'vigorous and efficient measures' in response.[12] By this stage it was predicted that a 'war of extermination' would be the inevitable result of this enduring hostility. 'The Line' was similarly reported as a popular uprising against the island's original inhabitants: 'it would appear that the whole of the population of Hobart Town were up in arms to oppose the Aborigines,' readers were told in May 1831.[13] By 1832 newspapers were predicting openly that the settlers' response to further violence would be to 'hunt them down like wild beasts'.[14]

It is of course impossible for us to understand the impact of this colonial discourse. We might speculate that anyone leaving Britain after 1824 would have known, if they had thought about Van Diemen's Land at all, that one of the things that awaited them was a population that wished to disrupt settlement and development. We might even go further, and point out that some of the writing about Van Diemen's Land in the 1820s suggested that any future colonists would have to do battle for their land. Certainly it is clear from the discourse around settler–indigenous violence that the idea that settlement involved the takeover of 'wastelands' was a kind of collective fantasy. It was a post hoc justification that overlaid a very clear and widely shared conception that settler colonialism involved a struggle for control of the land. Indeed, the fact that the press in Britain were predicting a 'war of extermination' by the time of 'the Line' at the end of 1830 and into 1831 means we can say very clearly that they envisaged what we might call genocide.

It is interesting to note that this vision of genocide was perhaps itself a kind of colonial fantasy too. The government often acknowledged that what was occurring in Van Diemen's Land was a war – indeed, Governor Arthur even told London of his admiration for the military tactics and prowess of an indigenous population he had previously considered docile.[15] Yet the picture developed in the British press was not that of a war, a battle between evenly matched, or even *unevenly* matched, opponents. Instead, as we have seen, the picture was of an apparently friendly colonial population being continually tormented by the irritant of the 'Aborigines' or 'savages'. Ultimately, when they could bear it no longer, the settler population pursued indigenous Tasmanians with vigour, just as a hunter pursues its prey. The superiority of the white man was thus even built into the story of extermination itself: the 'black natives [...] would be swept away.'[16]

REPORTING ROBINSON

It was not only violence that was reported in the metropole. Robinson's endeavours ensured that he became something of a 'colonial celebrity'.[17] Certainly, the final removal of indigenous Tasmanians from the island was reported in the British press, just as the 'Black War' had been previously. Robinson's appearance in Hobart with the survivors of the Big River and Oyster Bay peoples provided a symbolic opportunity for discussion of the relative merits of 'extermination' and 'conciliation' as means of solving the problem of resistance in Tasmania. Press reports reminded readers in the summer of 1832 that 'a most inhuman attempt was made, some time ago, to exterminate them all', but that this had 'providentially failed'; instead the indigenous population would 'now be put in the way of being civilised and become useful members of the social state instead of being hunted down like wild beasts'.[18] Therefore it is tempting to suggest that such a discussion of events in Van Diemen's Land supports the thesis that Britain commonly represented a restraining hand in policy, and that the alternatives to genocide were preached in the public sphere.

However, on closer analysis of the reports from the *Hobart Town Courier* that were reprinted in Britain one is struck by the fact that the alternative to indigenous peoples' being 'hunted like wild beasts' was still represented very clearly in terms that we would consider genocidal. Such reports painted a picture of a dishevelled caravan being led through the streets of Hobart to the docks and an awaiting ship, which would effect their removal to 'Flinders Island'. And this deportation was represented as essential for the further development of the colony, freeing up 'large tracts of pasture' for farming. It was therefore plain, not just to the British government, that Van Diemen's Land would progress to the future free of the burden of a population who were represented as a break on development.

After the beginning of 1832 Robinson's 'Friendly Mission' appeared regularly in the pages of the British press. His 'colonial celebrity' was forged in the representation of his journey through the Tasmanian interior as a kind of classic imperial adventure.[19] And such reporting left little doubt as to the totality of Robinson's ambitions: his aim was the complete removal of indigenous Tasmanians from the mainland. It was therefore not just the ministers and officials in the Colonial Office who were aware of the desire to deport the entire population. Newspapers suggested that Robinson was pursuing 'every black native' in June 1834 for example, reporting that he was confident that 'the last' would soon be accompanying him. Of course, while such examples are representations in Britain, they were usually simply verbatim

Genocide in British Culture

repetitions of reports in newspapers from the colony. As such they also represented what the colonists themselves wished to tell a wider British world about their communities. And as far as reporting the ongoing 'Friendly Mission' was concerned, it was always made clear that the final aim was the total separation of the indigenous community. According to British newspapers, Van Diemen's Land was indebted to Robinson for having 'ridded us of enemies of the very worst description'.[20] Robinson's mission was thus understood both in Van Diemen's Land and in Britain as a continuation of the military endeavours against the indigenous population.[21]

INDIGENOUS TASMANIANS ON THE STAGE

Robinson's work, and the indigenous Tasmanian community as a whole, appeared in a number of cultural forms in 1830s England, all of which ultimately anticipated the end of indigenous life in Van Diemen's Land. William Thomas Moncrieff's play *Van Diemen's Land*, for example, brought the story of the islanders' resistance to the London stage in 1831.[22] Playing on British understandings of indigenous Australians, the central character in Moncrieff's drama was Bennelong, who in real life had been brought to London from New South Wales in 1793 and had for two years been 'adopted as a pet of the officer set'.[23] In the drama, after his return to New South Wales, Bennelong travels to Van Diemen's Land where he becomes a resistance leader. Yet Moncrieff's play is not just a straightforward presentation of settler–indigenous conflict. In common with many literary representations of Australia in the early nineteenth century, Moncrieff implies that, in some aspects, settler society is as 'savage' as the culture it has usurped. It is the settlers, and especially the wild convict population, who are responsible for violence against indigenous Tasmanians. As such, by proposing that Britain had, through transportation, exported its vices, Moncrieff's drama offers a critique of colonialism. Yet at the same time it is a defence of colonialism too. In the play, Bennelong is able to join forces with the respectable settler population to turn on the bushrangers who are terrorising both communities. Thus it offers a vision of a cooperative future for colonialism, albeit one that might have come too late for the population of Van Diemen's Land, whom Bennelong acknowledges in the play are being 'extirpated'.[24]

By using the example of Bennelong, Moncrieff tapped into an extant understanding of indigenous Australians in British culture – after all, Bennelong never visited Van Diemen's Land, but he had been displayed as a colonial curiosity or living example of 'primitive man' in England. Bennelong was just the first indigenous Australian to be represented in this fashion: later in the nineteenth century the public exhibition of 'native' peoples in ethnological exhibitions, which might properly be called human zoos, was frequent. They were presented according to a number of narratives, which demonstrated the importance of racial characterisations in the British view of empire. They were frequently infantilised, represented as the children of nature rather than as having any complex culture. Famously, John Heaviside Clark's description of 'native field sports' in New South Wales summarised the culture there as reducible to hunting, dancing and war.[25]

As the evangelical view of empire took further hold in the 1830s, representations of indigenous Australians tended to emphasise a potential for transformation as well as the essential simplicity of their culture. For example, the frequent depiction of children in Western dress was apparently an attempt to demonstrate the possibility of 'civilising' wild 'natives'. Indeed, this rhetoric of transformation had been central to the depiction of indigenous peoples by colonists in Van Diemen's Land itself. In 1829 the colonial government had used pictorial representations to try to communicate the pronouncements of Governor Arthur to the island's communities. These so-called 'proclamation boards' (see illustration No. 1) included images of indigenous individuals in British dress, which were designed to show the potential for peaceful interaction between the two communities.[26]

Of course, the idea that indigenous peoples could be 'civilised' was central to the British imperial mission and this was articulated by Moncrieff's play. However, as in that drama, such hopeful narratives

Genocide in British Culture

were often tinged with despair that indigenous Tasmanians were doomed. The most prominent representations of Robinson and his contact with the island's communities did not dwell on transformation, but implanted the notion that such peoples were retreating before the might of the British. Perhaps most important in this regard were the landscape paintings of John Glover, exhibited in London in 1835, which offered a vision of Tasmania as an island with only an indigenous *past* but an exclusively colonial future.

PAINTING THE COLONIAL FUTURE

Pictorial representations of indigenous Australians in the first half of the nineteenth century were relatively rare. Clark's *Field Sports* volume in 1813 was among the first, and was followed by the publication of some paintings by convict painter Joseph Lycett, whose *Views in Australia or New South Wales and Van Diemen's Land* in 1824 was one of the first examples of emigration propaganda that included detailed artistic renderings of both the Australian landscape and its inhabitants. Both subjects aimed to excite the imagination in representing the 'new creation' discovered in the Antipodes, and more importantly to stress the scale of the Empire's task in taming this wild land. Lycett's representations of Van Diemen's Land particularly emphasised the untamed landscape, probably in order to encourage a sense of the potential for development.[27] He did not include indigenous figures in his Tasmanian landscapes – perhaps as a further effort to emphasise the 'emptiness' of the land there.[28]

Therefore when John Glover exhibited a series of paintings in Bond Street in the summer of 1835, which included several depictions of traditional life in Van Diemen's Land, he broke new ground. But Glover's work was significant not just because of its novelty, but also because of his celebrity. Glover was an artist, a landscape painter, of international repute. Often referred to as the 'English Claude', he was an important figure in the European art scene in the first decades of the nineteenth century. His paintings of the Tasmanian landscape were thus bound to attract attention. Furthermore, Glover met George Augustus Robinson several times and his paintings of the island's inhabitants have been described as a tribute to Robinson's work.[29]

Glover first encountered Robinson soon after the former arrived in Van Diemen's Land in 1831,[30] and they had discovered a shared repulsion at settler mistreatment of indigenous peoples. They came across each other periodically throughout Robinson's 'Friendly Mission', and Glover painted Robinson's followers.[31] Their relationship culminated in Glover painting the work usually known as *Aborigines Dancing at Brighton* (see illustration No. 7) as a tribute to Robinson's 'services in having removed the hostile blacks'.[32] Robinson intended that the picture would be the frontispiece for his projected book on his Tasmanian experiences,[33] while Glover wished to 'shew the natives at corrobery under the wild woods of the country, to give an idea of the manner they enjoyed themselves before being disturbed by the white people'.[34] When Glover exhibited in London, then, he offered an interpretation of life in Van Diemen's Land to a British audience that explicitly acknowledged the removal of indigenous peoples from the colony. Glover's work is therefore one of the clearest indications that the ethnic clearances in the 1830s were very far from just a local crime, but were instead the subject of Empire-wide discussion and debate.[35] Of course, there were other artistic renderings of both Tasmania and indigenous Tasmanians that today are perhaps more evocative of colonial encounters in Van Diemen's Land. For example, Benjamin Duterrau's depiction of Robinson's agreement with the Big River people, *The Conciliation* (1840), is much more widely disseminated now than Glover's work (see illustration No. 8). But I have come across no records of Duterrau's or other works being exhibited in London, and as such have concentrated on Glover as an artist whose pictures of Van Diemen's Land could be viewed, and were discussed, in Britain during the 1830s.

Glover was at the forefront of a thriving art scene in London in the 1820s. He was among the first artists to exhibit alone, establishing a trend of single-artist exhibitions that contributed to a growing sense that painting could be a form of public entertainment.[36] But at the end

Genocide in British Culture

of that decade, when he was still a substantial presence in the British art world, Glover decided to follow his sons to Van Diemen's Land. Lured by the promise of an extensive land grant, and a return to the rural idyll of his childhood, Glover was one of those middle-class men of property and wealth whom government had been encouraging to emigrate to the island. He was rewarded with ownership of a 6,000-acre farm, and the paintings that he sent home first in 1832,[37] and then again in 1835, suggest that he was reinvigorated by the new landscape that he encountered. More than that, his artwork can be understood as a continuation of the emigration propaganda of Lycett. Indeed, his triumphant *My Harvest Home*, painted in 1835 (see illustration No. 2), shows a glorious harvest bathed in Antipodean sunlight, a celebration of the European presence in Van Diemen's Land and of the victory over the dark, forbidding and wild landscapes that had been depicted previously.[38]

Glover was of course aware that this triumph in Van Diemen's Land came at the expense of the island's original community. He arrived in February 1831 in the aftermath of the failure of 'the Line', and therefore in the midst of war between the survivors and the settlers. Although by August of that year Glover had himself noted that there were 'very few' indigenous Tasmanians remaining,[39] he did encounter them – both through an association with John Batman and at the site of his own land grant at Mills Plains, which was in a newly settled district and thus on the frontier.[40] And if the dominant feature of Glover's paintings was an exploration of the new landscapes that Van Diemen's Land presented him with, which have been defined as 'pastoral arcadias', then a second prominent subject for him, especially in the paintings he exported to London, was the displaced community.

Glover's exhibition of 'Pictures Descriptive of the Scenery and Customs of the Inhabitants of Van Diemen's Land' opened in his gallery in Bond Street in July 1835. It featured 68 paintings: 36 were Tasmanian landscapes, of which seven depicted the island's inhabitants.[41] The exhibition catalogue suggests that its purpose was largely to inform about the landscape. Brief descriptions attached to some of the works expanded on the peculiarities of Vandemonian flora and fauna. Glover was particularly fascinated with the eucalyptus trees, which were the subject of many of his pictures, and that 'however numerous [...] rarely prevent your tracing through them the whole distant country'.[42] Glover sought explicitly to differentiate his Tasmanian and British landscapes – the former being generally much more brightly lit in effort to communicate the intensity of a 'hot Antipodean noon'.[43]

Many of the paintings focused on what Glover regarded as the naturally occurring landscape, that is, on the picturesque. Glover, along with many other settlers, failed to recognise that the island's communities had managed the environment in order to create grazing lands. Paintings such as *A View of Mills Plains* were thus actually depictions of the impact of human beings on the land, although they were not recognised as such by the artist or those who viewed his work.[44] Indeed, such landscapes almost invariably contained, self-consciously, traces of the *colonists'* impact on the environment instead, and as such told a quite different story. As was fashionable, almost none of Glover's paintings were pure landscapes;[45] they all featured either people or animals in the foreground – cattle grazing on Mills Plains or women strolling in *Launceston and the River Tamar*. As such, even those paintings that looked to the natural and picturesque provided a narrative of colonists' control of their new environment, their triumph over the wild and untamed landscapes that had been presented in Britain by Lycett a decade before. Glover's paintings thus repeatedly told a story of British conquest.

Although Glover did paint indigenous groups, their absence from the landscape was also noted in his London exhibition. *The Cataract, Two Miles from Launceston, Taken from the Water* was a depiction of a 'spot [formerly] much frequented by the Natives for the purpose of fishing', according to the catalogue, which additionally observed: 'but they are now nearly extirpated.'[46] According to British reviewers, the landscape they had left behind had helped Glover produce a painting of 'extraordinary beauty, grandeur and variety of effect'.[47] No mention was made of the displaced 'Aborigines'.

But indigenous Tasmanians were not entirely absent from Glover's London exhibition. There were several paintings of such groups displayed in Bond Street – and they were subjects he returned to in later painting. In Glover's paintings, unlike his celebrations of colonisation, which were bathed in light, indigenous groups were invariably presented in shade, or gloomy twilight. Perhaps the two most striking of his 'Aboriginal Arcadias' exhibited in London were *A Corrobery of Natives in Mills Plains* (see illustration No. 3), which depicted a dance by firelight in the shadow of a huge and forbidding eucalyptus, and the panoramic *Mount Wellington and Hobart Town from Kangaroo Point* (see illustration No. 4), which features men, women and children dancing and swimming in a shadowed foreground, with Hobart bathed in sunlight behind. Glover was not an ethnographic painter, although the latter work did have an ethnographic purpose according to the catalogue of the 1835 exhibition. It purported to demonstrate that the island's women were very strong swimmers.[48] At the time it was also claimed that the general purpose of the 'Aboriginal Arcadias' exhibited in London was to educate the public about the 'manner and customs of the natives'.[49] Yet Glover was not a realist, determined to represent faithfully a picture of Van Diemen's Land for British audiences. As such, I would argue that his work in general, but particularly his exhibition in London, had a moral and political purpose too.[50]

There exists significant debate about exactly what that purpose was, about what narrative Glover was attempting to communicate to a British audience. Bernard Smith, one of the first art historians to deal seriously with Glover's Australian paintings, suggested he was entirely unsympathetic towards indigenous Tasmanians, indeed that he adopted the attitudes of a crude extirpationist in his paintings. 'Glover's attitude to the Tasmanian native,' Smith wrote,

> is revealed quite clearly in his paintings of them [...] they are represented as small, dark, naked and unattractive little people who dance and leap with quick angular movements

and grotesque gesticulations; he represents them, we might say, as little black devils to be removed from southern paradise.[51]

Certainly, Glover's rendering of indigenous figures was crude, and became cruder as he aged.[52] But this may reflect both a lack of skill and a lack of care. By his own admission his purpose was not to convey any particular likeness, but to reflect *generally* on the nature of traditional society and life before colonisation. In doing so, of course, Glover contributed to the views of that society that abounded in British culture of simple, childlike 'natives' with little or no differentiation between them.

But Glover's focus was really the landscape, and in many ways his paintings of human beings need to be understood in terms of their relationship to the land in which they were represented. The presence of indigenous figures allowed Glover to explore the nature of the landscape *before* colonisation just as the presence of British workers and the harvest allowed him to explore the impact of the British Empire. As Glover acknowledged, indigenous groups were often depicted in a manner which sought to evoke their presence prior to the British invasion, and as such acted as general signifiers of a lost past. He was certainly aware of the fractured reality of life in Van Diemen's Land, and represented that in his paintings in general. He did not attempt to suggest anything other than the transformation of Van Diemen's Land through colonisation, a narrative that of course underpinned the very idea of civilisation and progress through the Empire. Hence his concentration on the (to him) alien eucalyptus in his paintings of the island's original inhabitants, and his rendering of his Tasmanian present as a landscape transformed by European pastoralism.

Glover presented two versions of Van Diemen's Land in his London exhibition, the colonial present and the indigenous past. Of course, such an oppositional view of the colony also contained a deliberate evasion. When Glover arrived in February 1831 the reality of settler–indigenous relations was one of conflict. As he noted there may have been few survivors among the original inhabitants, but the war was not yet over and the summer of that year was a period of renewed violence and panic. When he began painting indigenous subjects they had been defeated, and were being, at best, escorted from the island for their own protection. Yet Glover eschewed the reality of that colonial confrontation. In none of his pictures did he depict the interaction of the colonial and indigenous Van Diemen's Lands: he ignored both the reality of the war and that of the cultural cooperation and exchange that abounded. Indeed, he deliberately avoided the opportunity to depict such a coming together – refusing George Augustus Robinson's invitation to the settlement on Flinders Island.[53]

By evading the historical reality Glover was commemorating the end of indigenous life in Van Diemen's Land. His monumental *Mount Wellington and Hobart Town from Kangaroo Point* was one of the only paintings in which he presented if not the interaction, then the direct juxtaposition, of indigenous and colonial life on the island. Hobart Town was shown from across the water, typically bathed in light – an impressive colonial port. Several boats, large and small, are in the harbour, evoking a sense of an imperial trading centre. Several buildings are clearly visible from across the water, including of course a large church in tribute to the spread not just of civilisation but Christianity too. In an act of immense conceit and self-satisfaction, Glover's own house is clearly visible in the very centre of the painting.[54] If this is a hymn to the imperial future, then the contrast with the figures in the foreground could not be clearer. As ever with Glover's representations of indigenous people, they appear in shade. They are engaged only in the frivolities of a simple life, with most dancing around a fire and some swimming.

The islanders in the painting are a combination of several different groups sketched by Glover between 1831 and 1834, largely on his periodic meetings with Robinson. It is commonly claimed, for example, that it includes the survivors of the Oyster Bay and Big River nations whom Robinson bought to Hobart Town in January 1832.[55] And it certainly includes those individuals whom Glover sketched on a later meeting with Robinson and his followers in 1834. If it is true that it is the Big River and Oyster Bay people represented in the painting, it could be argued that the image represents another evasion, since Glover does not depict them as survivors from battle who had recently negotiated surrender when faced with total annihilation. But as this is a juxtaposition of several different groups, painted at different times, it seems more appropriate to interpret it as Glover's fantasy. By this I do not mean that Glover is not trying to represent something about the reality of colonial Van Diemen's Land, just that the painting needs to be interpreted as a metaphor rather than as a faithful representation. As such Glover seems to have been attempting to represent the final transition from indigenous to colonial Van Diemen's Land. The 'conventionally shadowed foreground of classical landscape' represents a civilisation that is to be displaced by the sunlit uplands of imperial might behind it. If 'Glover's Aboriginals are dancing in the dark', the citizens of imperial Hobart are by contrast walking in the light.[56]

It is important to bear in mind that Glover's paintings of indigenous figures were inherently nostalgic. He last sought out subjects in 1834, but he continued to cast them in paintings until 1847. His enduring fascination with indigenous Tasmanian life, and especially with the corroboree, has led some commentators to speculate that Glover was also articulating in his idealisation of indigenous innocence a kind of envy at the freedom it demonstrated.[57] And the catalogue for his 1835 exhibition in London did include a wistful reference to the gaiety of the island's culture in comparison to the formality of his own. Ian McLean has gone further, suggesting that Glover was articulating a continuing existential guilt in Van Diemen's Land. Glover's 'Aboriginal Arcadias' reflected first the desire for white society to commune with the environment in the manner of their indigenous forebears, in effect an acknowledgement of what they had destroyed. Second, they suggested that for Glover, and for colonial society in general, the displaced communities haunted the land.[58]

Yet mourning the passing of 'Aboriginal' innocence was easy for Glover because, apart from when he produced his very first Tasmanian paintings, he was working at a time when there was no (real or perceived) threat to colonial society from the island's existing inhabitants. As such, he was offering no critique of colonisation in his work, and his celebrations of British Van Diemen's Land seem to confirm that. When one considers also that in paintings such as *Mount Wellington and Hobart Town* and *A Corrobery of Natives in Mills Plains* Glover insisted on representing indigenous Tasmanians in shade or in twilight, it seems that he was attempting to represent their decline to British audiences. As the 1835 exhibition catalogue itself noted the extirpation of indigenous life, it appears that Glover was telling a story about the passing of a people in his paintings. His deliberate choice to present the islanders in semi-darkness was an attempt to articulate a narrative about them and their relationship with colonial society.[59] None of Glover's works presented indigenous peoples in the bright sunshine of a new day.

It is significant that these representations of the indigenous population of the island as belonging to the past, as a memory, were being displayed in London at the same time that the removal of their real-life counterparts from Van Diemen's Land was being completed. Thus Glover seems to have been offering another version of what Patrick Brantlinger would characterise as an extermination discourse. Such ideas were usually accompanied by the rhetoric of Providence and progress, and clearly became a means to rationalise the destructiveness of European colonialism as the century wore on. If John Glover's shadowed indigenous Tasmanians can be understood as the pictorial representation of such a discourse, then it demonstrates that such rhetoric was important for understanding and therefore justifying the ethnic cleansing of Van Diemen's Land as it was being enacted. Therefore such ideas served not just to rationalise the *memory* of genocide, but helped explain genocide to its contemporaries too.

READING GLOVER'S PAINTINGS

Of course, the task of assessing whether or not anyone listened to what Glover was trying to tell them about the fate of Tasmania's

The Last Man

indigenous communities is a difficult one.[60] What is clear, however, is that the exhibition did attract attention, and the idea that Glover had disappeared from the London art scene when he emigrated to Tasmania is an exaggeration.[61] The exhibition was widely reviewed, and attracted largely positive reactions in the press. Sir Thomas Phillips, who purchased one of the 'Aboriginal Arcadias', later suggested that the indigenous presence in the paintings had elicited a negative response from the public – but there is little evidence in the reviews to support this.[62] However, Phillips's claim does suggest that Glover's depiction of indigenous Tasmanians at the very least attracted attention.

However, for the most part the critical response centred on Glover's landscapes, which drew praise – both for the skill of their execution and the beauty of the scenery they represented. He was acknowledged to be a master of his art, who also possessed a scientific eye. As such Glover's paintings were acknowledged as recording a strange reality in the New World, and were not therefore interpreted in allegorical terms at all. Of course, contemporary denial of the ideological content of the paintings does not suggest its absence. That pictures were used and understood as documenting the reality of empire simply demonstrates further the role that art played in making and therefore embedding the ideology of imperialism. The collection of botanical and indeed ethnological information about empire was of course part of the process of gaining mastery over these new environments and Glover's exhibition can be seen in these terms.

Although the landscapes were the primary focus of the critical reaction to Glover's Van Diemen's Land exhibition, there was some discussion of his indigenous figures. First, there was an understanding that Glover's paintings represented the past, part of the 'national history' of Van Diemen's Land.[63] And if Glover's representations were intended to be sympathetic, they were not interpreted as such. The 'grotesque Aborigines' were understood in precisely the manner that Glover presented them – as an unvariegated, 'savage' morass whose lives were dominated by the simple concerns of their apparently childlike state.[64]

Genocide in British Culture

Such a discourse was in many ways an investigation of what it meant to be human. Glover's romanticisation of 'savage' life was confirmed in the exhibition catalogue, which commented on one depiction of a corroboree by saying: 'one seldom sees such gaiety in a ball room as amongst these untaught savages.'[65] Dismissed as silly in the *Literary Gazette*, such apparent celebration of savage life would, according to the review in the *Morning Post*, have 'enraptured Rousseau' in his search for the state of nature. Such abandon was ironically understood to be beyond the reach of the 'Old World'. This 'unequivocal and unsophisticated state of savage existence' was thus implied to be incompatible with modern British, life. As such Glover's critics rejected the humanitarian prescription that indigenous Tasmanians might be redeemed.

Yet what is most striking about the critical reaction to Glover's paintings is the relative lack of attention paid to his indigenous subjects. Not a single review mentioned Glover's observation that the original population of Van Diemen's Land had been all but destroyed. Such silence might be interpreted as a lack of engagement with indigenous Tasmanians' tragedy. But I am not convinced. After all, the exhibition made a clear reference to the 'extirpation' of an entire community. It seems incredible that if such a thing were in any way unknown it would not have aroused comment. Instead, I would interpret this silence as an indication that such news was unremarkable in Britain, that it was commonly understood that indigenous Tasmanians were 'now nearly extirpated'. If Glover's paintings evoked a sense of the inevitable decline of indigenous society in the face of the majesty of empire, then they were telling British audiences nothing that they did not already know.

INDIGENOUS TASMANIANS IN LITERARY CULTURE

Glover's use of indigenous Tasmanians to paint a picture of imperial triumph was not unusual. It was during the 1830s that regional museums in England began to display the ephemera of what they believed to be indigenous Tasmanian culture in a similar fashion. When John Helder Wedge returned from Van Diemen's Land in the mid 1830s in order to nurse his ailing father, he deposited several artefacts in the local Saffron Walden Museum. These included spears and a boomerang – the latter probably having been collected from the people from New South Wales who had been employed by John Batman in Tasmania. Such items appear to have been displayed as the curiosities of an alien culture. As Wedge's father commented when passing on the first of the collections, he could not really understand why a 'naked people of no fixed residence' would need spears and other weapons of war.[66]

This is not to say there were no hopeful narratives that anticipated the 'civilising' of indigenous peoples by the mid nineteenth century. Harriet Martineau's *Dawn Island*, first published in 1845, looked forward to the 'children of nature' being converted by commerce into 'men and Christians' even as the government was losing faith in the transformative impacts of the Empire. But it was widely assumed that for indigenous Tasmanians it was too late. Even the Aborigines' Protection Society by 1847 was referring casually to the 'aboriginal race from the fertile soil of Tasmania' as having been 'blot[ted] out [of] existence'.[67] By then its policy demands of government were to ensure that the same fate did not await other communities.

The primary representation of Van Diemen's Land in mid-nineteenth-century literary culture remained in travel narratives and memoirs, which took the form of either adventure stories in far-off lands or guides for potential emigrants to the reality of the New World. David Burn, for example, wrote a defence of emigration to Van Diemen's Land in 1840 in response to the relatively common charge that other destinations, especially by this stage the new colony of New Zealand, were more attractive because they did not suffer under the burden of the 'moral stain' associated with the penal colonies. Burn's defence of Van Diemen's Land as a 'little commonwealth teeming with industry and prospective wealth' was indignant and passionate. One of the key advantages that Burn pointed to was the absence of the original population. He argued that the island had become 'utterly and for ever free from so dreadful a source of calamity and disquiet' as 'the Aborigines', a distinction that other colonies did not share.[68] The implication, of course, was that the conflict that had tainted the history of Van Diemen's Land would soon be visited on other shores too. For, as John Lort Stokes wrote in his memoir, 'history teaches us that whenever civilised man comes into contact with a savage race, the latter almost inevitably begins to decrease, and to approach by more or less gradual steps towards extinction.'[69]

Memoirists did not simply note the disappearance of indigenous Tasmanians, however; they also sought to explain it in historical terms to their British readers. Such explanations ranged from attributing the disappearance to the bloodthirsty spirit of the 'savages' themselves to an unapologetic celebration of the might of the colonists. Yet what all interpretations shared was an implied defence of the colonial impulse itself, and a belief in the Empire as the embodiment of the march of progress. Perhaps the most strident example of an interpretation based on a belief in the innate savagery of the islanders was that provided by Louisa Anne Meredith. Meredith was the wife of Charles, who had emigrated to Van Diemen's Land in 1820 and under self-government became a member of the representative assembly. Louisa was a writer who regaled British readers with tales of her colonial exile, and particularly the flora and fauna of her Tasmanian Elysium.[70] Her interpretation of conflict between indigenous and settler communities was unapologetic. Responsibility did not lie with the settlers, who, by the time the island was plunged into bloodshed in the 1820s, 'were neither pirates nor robbers [...] but British farmers and country gentlemen', but with the 'fiendish butchery' of the indigenous community.[71]

For the most part, however, the idea that the Risdon Cove massacre was the original offence that inspired vengeance was the most common explanation for the root cause of conflict in Van Diemen's Land and the decline in the indigenous population. Risdon was, in the words of memoirist George Thomas Lloyd, a 'fatal and most unpardonable mistake', a 'cruel and impolitic act' after which the 'link of friendship' between the two communities was rashly severed.[72] The regularity with which such a narrative appeared is easily explained; after all, it combined and projected a number of assumptions about the nature of the Australian colonies. An image of the settlers as convicts and mavericks was confirmed by the idea of their descent into violence, their 'coarse brutality' confirming their status as a 'miserable portion of the European population'.[73] Again we are reminded that the idea of the colonies as in effect a form of anti-society, populated by the dregs of humanity, was an important trope of literary representations of Australia across the nineteenth century.[74]

At the same time, the idea of Australia as Arcadia was also a prominent motif. It was an image bolstered by representations of flora and fauna from the colonies, and was clearly visible in Glover's paintings of Van Diemen's Land. To construct the indigenous community as 'poor ignorant savages' was an important part of this vision. The picture of a community roused to irrational vengeance, of the wild children of nature cast into perpetual conflict, also expressed the disappearance of that community in familiar terms: 'the hostile feeling, once aroused, was never suffered again to sleep.'[75]

Yet, perhaps most importantly, the Risdon Cove fantasy protected the very idea of colonialism, as it had for the government in the 1820s. The extermination or extinction of indigenous peoples had not, according to this reading, been the result of the British presence in Van Diemen's Land in itself, but rather of the actions of those who had betrayed their British heritage and as such the British gift to the world. Thus popular accounts of population decline that relied on the Risdon Cove massacre also contained the last vestiges of the hopeful and humanitarian view that, despite the tragedy of Van Diemen's Land, there could be a better future.

While such narratives fundamentally displayed some sympathy for the indigenous population, they were still rationalisations of a genocidal process. At the same time, they were even malleable enough to accommodate the emerging *Boy's Own* trope of the Empire as a landscape conquered by colonial heroes and strongmen. Such adventure stories became the dominant form of representation of empire towards the end of the century. They told a schizophrenic story about both Britain and its Empire. On the one hand, the Empire could appear almost unfathomably exotic, a 'brilliantly charismatic realm of adventure for white heroes', in the words of Patrick Brantlinger. Yet this was also an adventure free of the complexities and responsibilities of home. These stories were thus a celebration of imperialism, of the manner in which the Empire had conquered the world, while at the same time acknowledging that it was a fantasy – 'daring, distant, charismatic but somehow also irresponsible and immature'.[76] From the 1840s onwards it is possible to detect representations of Van Diemen's Land in this mode.[77] Unlikely as it may seem, George Augustus Robinson was cast as a heroic adventurer in some representations. Louisa Anne Meredith was mystified as to how Robinson had achieved alone what the military might of the government had failed to accomplish.[78] Of course, Meredith could acknowledge no creative role for Robinson's indigenous guides in the process, and portrayed it as a singular and individual achievement in typical adventurer mode. George Thomas Lloyd similarly portrayed Robinson as a 'devoted and courageous adventurer [...] fulfilling his unparalleled mission of mercy and Christian feeling'.[79]

As the century progressed, a *Boy's Own* narrative of imperial responsibility and racial hierarchy was constructed for British schoolchildren. School textbooks tended to represent the Empire as a burden in which the British were responsible for the protection of indigenous peoples.[80] Children's fiction in the shape of the *Boy's Own Paper* and other publications also stressed the missionary responsibilities of empire.[81] There was little doubt that such responsibility was to inferior peoples, who, in the case of Australians, may have been so far down the scale of development that they were doomed to stagnation and indeed destruction.[82] Such publications despaired of the 'stupidity' of indigenous peoples, a fact most obviously displayed by their rejection of settler colonialism.[83] Within such a schema indigenous Tasmanians were simply represented as 'fast fulfilling the destiny that consigns

The Last Man

to decay and extinction all these native races when they come into contact with the civilisation of the white man'.[84]

Similarly, Charles Knight's *Popular History of England* claimed that 'the savage men gradually melted away' in the face of the Empire.[85] Bernard Porter argues that this was an important mechanism by which the British protected themselves from facing the reality of the violence of their colonial conquests.[86] And indeed such articulations of destruction as a natural process were an evasion. Yet I am not convinced that they were enough to disguise the reality of violence in colonial Tasmania.

Within such narratives, Van Diemen's Land, and in particular the settlement at Flinders Island, were fantasy worlds, onto which much wider assumptions about the Empire were projected. For the most part such accounts regretted the inevitability of the racial decline that they recognised. But from the 1850s there also emerged a much harsher, or, in the mindset of the time, much more pragmatic set of explanations for and interpretations of extermination in the Australian colonies more generally. This new narrative, which was in a sense inspired by the experience in Tasmania, asked that the British face up to, and indeed embrace the reality of, their Empire, their occupation of the globe.

'OF THE AUSTRALIAN BLACK MAN WE MAY CERTAINLY SAY HE HAS TO GO'

The radical John Arthur Roebuck wrote unapologetically in his *The Colonies of England* in 1849 that:

> for the sum of human enjoyment to be derived from this globe which God has given us, it is requisite for us to pass over the original tribes that we find existing in the separate lands which we colonise [...] When the European comes into contact with any other type of man, the other type disappears [...] Let us not shade our eyes and pretend not to see this result.[87]

Similarly, in John West's *History of Tasmania*, which was first published in 1852, the author demanded that the British face the consequences of their occupation of Van Diemen's Land – that it had caused the destruction of indigenous society. For West this was a source of regret, and indeed the inevitable consequence of the system of transportation that he opposed. Yet while this was a matter for lament, West also implied that it had been the necessary and worthwhile price of colonial progress:

> the original occupation of this country necessarily involved most of the consequences which followed [...] the right of wandering hordes to engross vast regions – forever to retain exclusive property in the soil, and which would feed millions where hundreds are scattered – can never be maintained.[88]

West's book was published in London and its first edition 'quickly sold out' there.[89]

Such calls for the implications of the colonial project to be more wholeheartedly embraced were the cultural equivalent of the growing distance from the humanitarian version of colonisation in the political sphere. In this new formula, colonies did not need to be justified in terms of the benefits brought to the indigenous populations but in terms of the worth of those colonies in and of themselves. Colonial development was for the benefit of mankind more generally (of course, that general mankind was represented by the British). As West wrote, 'no man can witness the triumph of colonisation, when cities rise in the desert and the wilderness blossoms as the rose, without being gladdened by the change.'[90] While West was prepared to acknowledge that the suffering such change incurred should 'check exultation', it was a short journey from his rhetoric to the more aggressive celebration of the colonial destruction of 'primitive society' that became increasingly evident from the 1850s.

This new discourse was led by figures who have been subsequently adopted into the British literary canon. Samuel Sidney and Charles

The Last Man

Dickens led the way at the end of the 1840s and into the 1850s. Sidney produced a number of influential works on Australia, and wrote regularly on the subject for Dickens's periodical *Household Words*, in which he was scathing about the 'inferiority' of indigenous culture, and especially the idea that settlers should face judicial investigation for violence against indigenous peoples.[91] In essence, Sidney believed that extermination was inevitable, and thus questioned any effort to check this development. Dickens famously attacked what he saw as the humanitarian idealisation of the 'noble savage' in June 1853, in a furious denunciation that amounts, to use modern-day language, to a call for genocide. Dickens wrote:

> I call him a savage, and I call a savage something highly desirable to be civilised off the face of the earth [...] my position is that if we have anything to learn from the Noble Savage, it is what to avoid. His virtues are a fable; his happiness is a delusion; his nobility nonsense. We have no greater justification for being cruel to the miserable object, than for being cruel to a William Shakespeare or an Isaac Newton; but he passes away before an immeasurably better and higher power than ever ran wild in any earthly woods, and the world will be all the better when his place knows him no more.[92]

Twenty years later, Dickens's unapologetically exterminationist rhetoric was repeated by Anthony Trollope. Trollope's guide to emigration, titled *Australia and New Zealand*, was written after his own extensive travels there following a failed bid to win a parliamentary seat in 1868. His Liberal sensibilities included the belief that what he called the 'waters of the world's progress' flowed from Westminster, and the concomitant assumption that no apologies needed to be made for the export of that progress.[93]

Like West, Trollope demanded that his British readers face the logic of their colonial impulses and thus their progress. Colonisation was, in Trollope's estimation, a theft of land, and involved the necessary diminution and then destruction of the original owners of that land. However, he was not prepared to declare this to be morally wrong because it engendered the spread of civilisation and indeed had enabled Europeans to export their surplus population and now increased the wealth of the mother country. That this had been done at the expense of indigenous communities was not for Trollope a matter for regret (and nor was it, he conjectured, in fact a matter of regret for the humanitarian philanthropists he mocked) but simply a matter of reality. His strict sense of racial hierarchy meant that he regarded the replacement of an indigenous population – even the most 'dignified' of whom he characterised as 'sapient monkey[s] imitating the gait and manners of a do-nothing white dandy' – as a positive good.[94] In what again we would have to characterise as a call for genocide, Trollope wrote: 'of the Australian black man we may say certainly that he has to go. That he should perish without unnecessary suffering should be the aim of all who are concerned in this matter.'[95]

While Trollope's rhetoric was extreme, it was simply a development of a progress narrative that celebrated British triumph. It was therefore no coincidence that such rhetoric was articulated by men regarded as radicals and liberals. It was also not a coincidence that it developed out of humanitarian concern. This was just another form of, or perhaps even just a development from, the kind of evangelicalism that saw colonisation as the means to save the 'savage' or to extinguish barbarism. Such language also relied on a celebration of liberal Britain, a sanctification of the British state as the only permissible route to the future. When indigenous Tasmanians appeared, in Britain's own estimation, to have proved that they were unable to accept lessons in civilisation, Trollope's rhetoric of destruction was the inevitable end point. After all, there was little in the discourse of humanitarianism that suggested the possibility of an enduring indigenous culture. As *The Times*'s leader writer wrote in November 1851, the Australian colonies now

> offered the spectacle of savage man cowed and overawed by the influences of a civilisation which he can neither comprehend

nor resist, and awaiting in harmless and listless inaction that speedy extinction to which some untraceable cause has doomed him.[96]

Let us not forget that such rhetoric, such an understanding of the world, began with the indigenous community of Van Diemen's Land. Indigenous Tasmanians and their decline were contributors to a vision of the world that understood that settler colonisation had a 'fatal impact' on indigenous culture. When Tasmanians, and other indigenous communities, failed to accept the worth of that settler civilisation, or when they resisted it, such actions became further evidence of the inevitability of their decline. Such was the starkness of the contrast between the decline of indigenous civilisations and the apparent forward march of Britain that in an entirely self-fulfilling cycle the impact of settler colonies was interpreted as a sign of the essential progress of British culture and society.[97] Such decline itself, then, underpinned a more aggressive vision of the world that saw the eradication of indigenous society itself as a self-evident good. You might say that genocide in Tasmania begat genocide elsewhere in colonial Australia, or at least provided an intellectual justification for it, in that the progress of British society was highlighted by its destructive impact on indigenous Tasmanian society, and that made the destruction of other indigenous societies desirable too.

THE LAST OF THE TASMANIANS

It would be quite wrong, however, to argue that the apparent passing of indigenous Tasmanians did not evoke some disquiet in Britain. Accounts of Tasmanian decline were frequently an exercise in melancholia. *The Times*, for example, declared with a regret tinged with pride that 'we have exterminated the race in Van Diemen's Land'. In doing so the leader comment rejected the idea that the cause of that extermination was some form of inevitable doom, and asked that Britain look again at the nature of its colonisation.[98] James Bonwick's widely publicised account of the destruction of the indigenous Tasmanian community echoed such requests and demanded the reopening of debates on the nature of empire and responsibility for indigenous peoples.[99] As his was the most detailed representation of the destruction of indigenous Tasmanians on offer in mid- to late-nineteenth-century Britain, and because it was a book that provoked some public discussion, it warrants detailed analysis.

Bonwick, a schoolteacher and historian, had emigrated to Hobart in the 1840s. Thereafter he combined teaching with writing and a variety of appointments with colonial governments throughout Australia, but particularly in Victoria. He returned periodically to London, and much of his writing was aimed at the market in that city.[100] Bonwick was an evangelical, who identified with the aims of the Aborigines' Protection Society: his *The Last of the Tasmanians* was part of a reinvigorated campaign throughout the 1870s on the part of the society, who sought in particular to draw attention to the 'extermination' of indigenous peoples in Queensland.[101]

In London, the publication of Bonwick's book was a literary event. As well as being widely reviewed, public readings were staged and in general it caused reflection on the nature of empire. It was published around the time that news of the death of William Lanne reached England, and Bonwick thus seemed to capture the very moment of the Tasmanians' passing. As we have seen, Lanne was survived only by Truganini and Mary Ann Arthur in the Oyster Cove community.

The Last of the Tasmanians brought together many of the fantasies and myths that had surrounded British understanding of the 'extermination' of the indigenous community in Van Diemen's Land during the previous century. And in that sense Bonwick's book was also a product of those cultures of understanding – it was both an anguished cry at indigenous peoples' fate and yet in essence a defence of the colonial idea and the system that had precipitated that destruction. After all, the Aborigines' Protection Society, to which Bonwick subscribed, continued to voice the view that the Empire could bring salvation for indigenous communities, despite grievous errors in Van Diemen's Land.

The Last Man

Bonwick went further than the general discourse in recognising indigenous agency in the 'Black War', referring for example to 'Aboriginal heroism' in the defence of their land. Yet for the most part he relied on traditional narratives. He argued that the Risdon Cove massacre had been the original offence that had precipitated the violence,[102] and that it was the nature of colonial society and the character of the settlers that was the root cause of destruction (rather than the idea of colonisation itself). Van Diemen's Land had become a 'dust-hole for the reception of the moral rubbish and turpitude of Europe' and had been occupied without consideration of the rights of the 'inhabitants of the island'.[103] But the author was also prepared to exonerate the home government from responsibility for violence against indigenous peoples.[104]

Yet while Bonwick's book was outwardly a critique of the nature of the colonisation of Tasmania (if not the colonial idea itself) it also conformed to a familiar imperial discourse too. Bonwick did criticise the agents of destruction in Van Diemen's Land, but he also represented them in a familiar way: the all-powerful men of modernity who were let loose on their helpless and hapless quarry. If Bonwick was ultimately sympathetic to the Tasmanian community and culture, he also conformed to the idea that it had simply been swept away by the might of the British Empire – the 'laughing' children of nature were no match for industrial man. 'We came on them as evil genii,' Bonwick wrote, and 'blasted them with the breath of our presence'.[105] It was common for even those critical of the Empire and its impact on indigenous communities to seek refuge in such imagery, with which the likes of Dickens and Trollope would have also been comfortable. 'English-speaking men are destined to cover the planet,' wrote *The Times* in 1869, 'squeezing other races out of existence [...] the aboriginal Tasmanian has actually vanished.'[106] In this way the celebration of the might of the Empire and mourning for its impacts became melded together.[107]

The reception of Bonwick's book suggests that the reading public may not have shared his angst at the destruction of indigenous

Tasmanian society. More often than not his work was received as a kind of extended colonial curiosity, the literary equivalent of the bones on display in various museums. And the story told in this 'curious work' was certainly understood to conform precisely to the received narrative of Tasmanian extinction or 'the pathetic story of their attempted civilisation and the gradual extinction of their race'.[108] Thus Bonwick was understood to be confirming the wider critique of Australia as a deviant society that strayed from the British purpose in the world – as the *Morning Post* conceded, 'it was a great misfortune to the aborigines of [...] Van Diemen's Land that the men who came to settle among them were chiefly of a class expatriated for their offences against the laws of this country'.[109] Of course, the impact of such rhetoric was to protect the colonial ideal itself and Bonwick's repetition of this well-worn narrative was thus considered little more than a footnote to the more significant history of British expansion. As one reviewer noted of a later edition, Bonwick's was a history of the 'saddest episode in the civilisation of the pacific coasts'. But the reviewer also complained that Bonwick's book was a little too large for the 'relative importance of the story to the vast congress of the British Empire'.[110]

As I have already stated, Bonwick's book was published as news that William Lanne, the so-called 'last man', had died in Hobart in 1869 reached Britain. In the immediate aftermath of his death there was a gruesome struggle for ownership of his remains, which Bonwick reported with some disgust. His body was dismembered, and ultimately his skull appears to have ended up in the collection of the Anatomy department at the University of Edinburgh. Like the remains of many other indigenous Tasmanians, Lanne's skull was analysed as part of an investigation into the relationship between the different 'races of man', an existential discourse into human origins that was one of the most fiercely contested moral, religious and scientific debates of the nineteenth century. That discourse represents perhaps the most significant means of understanding what the destruction of indigenous Tasmanians meant in British culture.

The Last Man

THE DESCENT OF MAN: INDIGENOUS TASMANIANS AND THE SCIENCE OF HUMAN ORIGINS

Collections of human skulls had been commonplace in Britain since the late 1700s, because it was believed that the shape of the cranium provided the means to distinguish between human types.[111] As a consequence, it was thought that the skulls of indigenous Tasmanians would tell scientists much about their role, and indeed that of other 'Aborigines', in the genealogy of mankind, and collecting skulls, as well as other body parts, became a feature of the colonial occupation of Van Diemen's Land from its outset. The body of at least one victim of the massacre at Risdon Cove was preserved in 1804, a practice that continued throughout the century in the name of both science and curiosity.[112]

However, the possession of indigenous remains was never just an exercise in scientific curiosity, but symbolic of the colonial processes of control and exploitation. From the beginning settlers, knowingly or otherwise, asserted their control over local populations by claiming ownership of the dead. Or, to put it another way, collection and control of the dead was an eloquent articulation of the extent of indigenous dispossession. In the case of indigenous Tasmanians, whose varied burial practices largely involved returning the dead to the land, that dispossession involved not only the physical dislocation of the community but the disruption of their spiritual communion too.

Even those most committed to protection were involved in the collection of the dead. George Augustus Robinson originally fought hard to ensure that indigenous people's remains were treated with respect. For the most part that meant allowing the community to dispose of their dead themselves. But unfortunately his respect for the dead and for traditional burial practices was not limitless. First Robinson sought to 'civilise' the disposal of the dead – he described the Flinders Island funeral of one of the former leaders of indigenous resistance, Tongerlongter (known in the settlement as 'King William'), in 1837 as a service that 'would have been thought respectable (if such a term might be applied) by white persons'.[113] But he sought to collect indigenous people's remains too. After the visit of Governor John Franklin to Flinders Island in January 1838, Robinson arranged for Lady Franklin to be given some indigenous curiosities, including the 'skull of an aboriginal'.[114] He also carried several further sets of remains with him when he returned to England in 1851. On his journey home from continental Australia, Robinson stopped off at Oyster Cove. It seems this was not just to bid farewell to his Tasmanian friends, as he made sure to sketch the locations of the graves there before he left.[115]

The impetus for collection did not come from within the colony, however, but from London. The men who sent body parts, skulls and skeletons on the long journey around the world did so in response to requests from metropolitan scientists, sometimes even mediated by the British government. In 1861, for example, the Colonial Office successfully solicited the Tasmanian government for the skulls of 'a male and female native of Tasmania' for what was to become the Pitt-Rivers Museum in Oxford.[116] The instruction from London was that such remains should be gathered without 'injuring in any way the feelings of the few Aboriginal inhabitants who still survive'.[117] That in 1867 the remains of Bessy Clark, one of the Oyster Cove community who had died a few weeks earlier, were disinterred without permission and sent to the Hunterian Museum at the Royal College of Surgeons in London suggests that this instruction was not respected.[118]

Morton Allport, a lawyer and the vice-president of the Royal Society of Tasmania, was responsible for removing Clark from her grave. He sent several full skeletons to Britain in the 1870s, and was just one of several prominent men in Tasmanian society who was also a grave-robber. It does not appear that men like Allport were motivated by monetary profit, as the vast majority of disinterred remains were given as gifts (although the remains of Tasmanians were theoretically valuable). Instead, it seems that what they valued were the connections that such material gave them with learned men and societies at home and the knowledge and material that could then be transferred to the furthest reaches of the Empire. Allport, for example, was sent scientific research materials and publications in return for the remains that he donated to men like William Henry Flower, the conservator of the Royal College of Surgeons.[119]

Allport and the other grave-robbers of Tasmania were equally motivated by the belief that they were engaged in a pan-imperial debate about the origins of the human race, about the very nature of humanity, about who 'we' were, and this became one of the fiercest intellectual conflicts of the day, concerned as it was to establish not only the roots of mankind in the past but whether human beings were equal in the present.

In the biological sciences the declining appeal of the humanitarian vision of empire was reflected in a split between a vision of humanity as a single species (a theory known as monogenesis) and the idea that the 'races' of man were in fact different species, with different origins (a theory known as polygenesis). Self-evidently the latter view had implications for the present and any notion of racial equality or equivalence – although the monogenesis argument did not automatically necessitate a commitment to racial equality either.

So-called polygenists argued that in fact the 'races of men' were distinct species that could, in contravention of the humanitarian ideals of equality, be placed in hierarchical order. Men like Robert Knox, the anatomist who had been the main recipient of the bodies procured by Burke and Hare,[120] offered visions of implacable conflict between different types of men using such a schema. This hypothesis relied in part on the memory of inter-ethnic violence in Tasmania. The 'Black War' became, in what was a self-fulfilling argument, evidence for the idea that different racial types were simply unable to inhabit the same space. According to Knox, the attempt by philanthropists such as those in the Aborigines' Protection Society to suggest otherwise was a 'war against nature'. Knox celebrated the 'clearing out' of 'human aboriginals' as an articulation of the natural law of racial conflict that had also been played out in 'Anglo-Saxon America'.[121] For Knox, in what can now be seen as a Himmlerian rhetorical flourish, it was a necessary, if 'cruel, cold-blooded and heartless deed'.[122] It was also portrayed as the precursor to a much wider racial conflict both in continental Australia and, Knox forebodingly predicted, throughout the colonised world.

Charles Darwin was perhaps the most prominent opponent of polygenists like Knox, and argued that to suggest that there was more than one species of man was to reject the revealed truths of natural selection and evolution.[123] When Darwin had first articulated his theories of evolution in the 1830s it was as a self-conscious liberal humanitarian. His assertion of monogenesis therefore had a clear political and ideological context in the form of the abolition ideal. Yet from the 1850s the political circumstances had changed, and Darwin required a narrative that articulated the new racial realities of the mid century – which included the perceived failure to transform indigenous Tasmanians and their subsequent decline towards extinction.[124] *The Descent of Man* was Darwin's answer to that new political context, in which he asserted that while biologically the human race *was* singular there were in effect cultural differences that allowed for some form of racial hierarchy. The Tasmanians appeared at the bottom of this hierarchy.

In *The Descent of Man* Darwin sought to explain how it was that different racial groups had become extinct over human history, with the recent experience of Tasmania foremost in the equation. His answer, in effect, drew not on biology but on the concept of culture. He argued that when there was contact and competition between racial groups, 'the grade of their civilisation seems to be a most important element in the success of competing nations.'[125] As such, indigenous Tasmanians in Darwin's formulation had been swept aside by a more culturally developed, more civilised people. To use the words of Darwin's contemporary John George Wood in his *The Natural History of Man*, a popular publication that had originally appeared as a weekly serial,

> For the real cause [of indigenous Tasmanians' decline] we must look at the strange but unvariable laws of progression. Whenever a higher race occupies the same grounds as a lower,

the latter perishes, and whether animate or inanimate in nature, the new world is always built on the ruins of the old.[126]

What Darwin did was in effect to turn an observation of what had occurred in Tasmania into a natural law by which we might understand human progress, and of course the triumph of liberal Britain. Darwin wrote:

> when civilised nations come into contact with barbarians the struggle is short [...] of the causes which lead to the victory of civilised nations, some are plain and simple, others complex and obscure. We can see that the cultivation of the land will be fatal in many ways to the savages, for they cannot, or will not, change their habits.[127]

Thus the destruction of indigenous Tasmanian culture itself became evidence for the superiority of civilised man, or for the inferiority of indigenous culture. In this sense, genocide became an important part of an identity in which Britain was imagined to be at the apex of human progress and development. Such an observation bears repeating – the perception of Britain at the apex of human civilisation relied on the memory (and celebration) of genocide.

This debate on human origins also became a historical narrative, in which indigenous Tasmanians and their destruction could again play a very significant role in the formation of identity. If Darwin's narrative created a sense of developmental human progress, from savagery to barbarism, as it were, then it was also an account quite literally of who 'we' as a people were, and where we had come from. Darwin's close associate and fellow liberal John Lubbock is an instructive example here. In 1870 Lubbock published *The Origin of Civilisation and the Primitive Condition of Man*, in which he argued that the British Empire represented a unique scientific opportunity because it encompassed all of developmental human history and 'encompassed races in every stage of civilisation yet attained by man'. By engaging with 'primitive' societies, such as that of Tasmania, Lubbock argued, 'we can even [...] penetrate some of that mist which separates the present from the future.'[128]

Under the influence of this discourse, indigenous Tasmanians were thus rendered representatives of the human past, of Stone Age man – quite literally out of time. In 1893 the department of Anatomy at Cambridge reported excitedly that it had acquired a Tasmanian skull, one of the 'last representatives of Palaeolithic man'.[129] This was a position they continued to occupy in scientific discourse for 50 years or more. Henry Ling Roth's study in 1899 was based on the idea that Tasmanians had enjoyed a culture from the 'remote prehistoric ages'.[130] The Professor of Palaeontology and Geology at the University of Oxford, W.J. Sollas, similarly argued in 1911 that the Tasmanians were survivors of an 'eolithic (pre-Palaeolithic) race'.[131] Sollas acknowledged that it may seem anachronistic to study 'Pleistocene man by an account of a recent race' but claimed that Tasmanians afforded an 'opportunity of interpreting the past by the present'.[132] Indigenous Tasmanians thus played a formative role in the development of the disciplines of anthropology and ethnology – as scientists of natural history took to documenting the varieties of man in the same way that they had documented the variety of animal and plant species discovered in the New World.

Adam Kuper argues that it is difficult to overestimate the role of an imagined Australia, and of Australian peoples, in the development of these human sciences. For the early anthropologists it was as if they had discovered there, and particularly in Tasmania, 'primitive' man himself. This was a consequence of 'the seductive analogy of Darwin's explorations, which had shown that isolated island populations were particularly instructive, sometimes nourishing primitive biological forms which had died out elsewhere'. Under such an illusion, the declining Tasmanian population appeared to be 'cultural dinosaurs',[133] survivors from an earlier stage of evolution, 'not from the Stone Age in general but from the earliest stages of the Stone Age',[134] who were capable of 'giv[ing] us some idea of the conditions of the early prehistoric tribes of the Old World'.[135] This scientific discourse often lamented the passing of such an 'interesting' people as the Tasmanians, if not always in strictly moral terms then as a loss to human science. Yet it also continually proffered a justification for genocide, and indeed required the disappearance of an indigenous population to function. The Tasmanians were a people of the past, a cultural hangover whose time was up – what more evidence did one need than their rapid exit from history itself? As George W. Stocking has written: 'extinction was simply a matter of straightening out the scale and placing the Tasmanians back into the dead prehistoric world where they belonged.'[136] Or, as Professor Sollas argued, the destruction of Tasmanians, their society and their culture was 'a sad story, [but] we can only hope that the replacement of a people with a cranial capacity of only about 1,200 cc by one with a capacity one-third greater may prove ultimately of advantage in the evolution of mankind.'[137]

Such interest in the apparent wiping out of indigenous Tasmanians often created new accounts of their demise. For Darwin, an apparent reproductive failure was the key – with the allegation that the island's women had been rendered infertile by contact with European men.[138] This perception of infertility became embedded in nearly all anthropological investigations. Others postulated the centrality of disease, arguing that indigenous peoples were unable to cope with imported Western maladies. Such a narrative conveniently naturalised the causes of population decline, but still had a powerful sense of racial hierarchy about it. For James Erskine Calder, writing in the leading anthropological journal in the 1870s, indigenous Tasmanians were almost responsible for their own demise – which Patrick Brantlinger has described as a fantasy of 'auto-genocide'.[139] For Calder, the primary causes of extermination were inter-'tribal' conflict, and a primitive response to European disease: 'unlike the European he [the indigenous Tasmanian] knew no remedy'. Indeed, such was the destructive nature of indigenous Tasmanians' response to lung disease that Calder could assert: 'I quite believe that the original cause of their decay lay in their own imprudence.'[140] In such a formula the islanders were declared

Genocide in British Culture

to be so out of step with the modern world that they had essentially committed a kind of collective suicide. Of course, modernity only intruded onto Van Diemen's Land when the British arrived.

'KING BILLY'S SKULL': THE BONES OF INDIGENOUS
TASMANIANS IN BRITISH CULTURE

It was because of this existential discussion that William Lanne's body was fought over in such a gruesome manner in the aftermath of his death. The corpse became the site of a struggle for control of scientific knowledge between colonial Tasmania and metropolitan Britain. As 'desperate men' of 'personal ambition', representatives of the Royal Society of Tasmania and great British scientific institutions plundered his remains.[141] William Lodewyk Crowther, a local doctor and politician, removed Lanne's skull from his body in the immediate aftermath of his death on 5 March 1869 in response to a request from the Royal College of Surgeons in London. But knowing that the Royal Society of Tasmania also assumed ownership of Lanne's skeleton and planned to disinter him after burial, Crowther attempted to disguise his activities by replacing the skull with that of a recently deceased teacher who was also lying in the Hobart hospital morgue.[142]

This grisly tale of the disrespect shown to Lanne's remains did not end with Crowther's theft of 'King Billy's skull'. George Stokell, the 'recently appointed house surgeon' in Hobart, had been charged with the responsibility of protecting Lanne from mutilation by the Royal Society. Although he failed to prevent the removal of his skull, he decided that in order to prevent further desecration he would cut off the hands and feet.[143] Although Lanne was afforded the respect of a burial, his grave was undisturbed only for a few hours – after which his body was removed and subsequently disappeared.

Immediately, Lanne's death was characterised, in London and Hobart, as the passing of 'the last man'. As a consequence, and under the influence of the debate on human origins, Lanne represented almost an instantaneous fossil, the last representative of a past people

The Last Man

whom the British Empire had replaced. As such he appeared to Britons imbued with a sense of their own supremacy as symbolic of both his own people's innate inferiority and British majesty and might. As a consequence, both in Tasmania and in Britain, Lanne's remains were a prize worth fighting over.

But Lanne's mutilation actually became the source of much local and indeed international scandal. In Tasmania, respectable Hobart society was outraged at the treatment of the corpse. Lanne had in some ways been regarded as a part of the European community. He had become a mariner at the age of 14 and spent much of his life at sea as a whaler. He 'appears to have found greater acceptance from his sea-faring mates than any of his compatriots' did in colonial society.[144] Added to this was the fact that the dismemberment of his corpse was inextricably linked with the vandalism of another – white – corpse. As a result, the matter prompted angst regarding the limits of scientific investigation of the body.[145] There was also a fear that, in the rest of the British world, the treatment of Lanne's corpse would further debase the name of Tasmania – already associated with a brutal colonial history.[146] From the manner in which the affair was reported in London, for example in Bonwick's *The Last of the Tasmanians*, it is clear that such fears were not without foundation. Yet while clearly repulsed by the chaotic and violent treatment of Lanne's body, Bonwick's chief concern was that the remains of 'the last man' had been lost to science.[147] An orderly and clinical preservation of Lanne's remains was, Bonwick argued, the ideal – not their respectful disposal in line with either his or his community's wishes. It is notable that Lanne's acceptance into the white community did not extend to Britain, where he was simply caricatured as 'the last man'.

Of course, Bonwick's desire to recover Lanne's skeleton was based on a belief that it might underpin an intervention in the great debate of the age. For all the melancholy with which Victorian scientists viewed the 'extinction' of the 'Tasmanian race', there was a revelling in that destruction too. This was 'the most interesting event in the history of Tasmania, after its discovery', precisely because of what it revealed about the nature of mankind.¹⁴⁸ Indeed, William Lodewyk Crowther later advised William Henry Flower that Lanne's skull was a physical riposte to the polygenists who assumed that indigenous Tasmanians' position in the evolutionary ladder was fixed. According to Crowther, because Lanne had lived much of his life among the European community, his cranium exhibited physical changes and illustrated 'to a most striking degree the improvement that takes place in the lower race when subjected to the effects of education and civilisation.'¹⁴⁹

Crowther's observation of Lanne's development betrayed an assumption about Tasmanian racial inferiority that itself drove the desire to collect Tasmanian remains as the 'best example of a truly primitive race'.¹⁵⁰ In a bizarrely circular fashion, the apparent fact of Tasmanian extermination itself was taken as confirmation of that racial inferiority, which further motivated the desire to collect the bones of the dead.¹⁵¹ As it was argued in an essay published as part of Henry Ling Roth's turn-of-the-century summation of scholarship around indigenous Tasmanians, 'it was only very shortly before the Tasmanians became extinct that the importance of preserving their osteological remains seems to have been recognised.'¹⁵²

And of course assumptions about Tasmanian inferiority also betrayed a sense of British or European racial superiority. Crowther's analysis of Lanne's development was based on the belief that his interaction with 'higher races' had transformed him. As such both polygenists and monogenists fixed Tasmanians at the bottom of a racial hierarchy that placed Anglo-Saxons at the top of the scale. The examination of the remains of Tasmanians was therefore both a product and a symptom of the denigration of indigenous life and culture that was at the centre of the colonial endeavour. Furthermore, it was an exercise in self-worship too, producing a vision of the world that fixed race as a biological category – whether capable of evolution and transformation or not.

But what happened to Lanne's body? Of the rest of the skeleton it is impossible to say. Of the skull there are several reported possibilities. It was still in Crowther's possession in the 1870s, and the assumption is that it was ultimately sent to Britain. One version has it being disposed of overboard during the journey. Perhaps more likely is the suggestion that it was ultimately donated, via Crowther's son, Edward, to the Anatomy department at the University of Edinburgh – where Edward had studied.[153] Certainly, throughout the twentieth century the British museum community believed that 'King Billy's skull' was in Edinburgh.[154] In the 1990s the Tasmanian Aboriginal Centre requested the return of Lanne's remains along with others still held in the collection in Edinburgh. That return was ultimately negotiated, although the university officially disputed that the remains they returned included those of 'the last man'.

That 'King Billy's skull' was just one of many sets of Tasmanian human remains that were returned from Edinburgh is evidence that the tale of Lanne's dismemberment is only the most lurid among many. Cressida Fforde argues that human-origins debates at the turn of the century relied on a 'metric torrent' – largely through the measurement of skulls – based on what were in effect stolen remains. In 1898 it was reported that the Royal College of Surgeons had two complete Tasmanian skeletons and 17 skulls, and that the Natural History Museum had a further complete skeleton. The University of Oxford's collection of Tasmanian remains included seven skulls, and there were two more in Cambridge and in the museum of Netley Hospital in Southampton.[155] The collection of the Royal College of Surgeons was largely destroyed during World War II, but at the beginning of the twenty-first century fully 18 institutions in Britain still reported holding the remains of indigenous Tasmanians.[156]

DISPLAYING THE DEAD

Scientific discussions of the 'extermination' of the Tasmanians, its causes and its implications for understanding the human condition were not confined to the pages of learned journals. Nor was the harvesting of the bodies of the dead a process that was in any way obscured from a wider public in Britain. Indeed, as the example of

James Bonwick demonstrates, we should not interpret revulsion at the treatment of Lanne's corpse as a general objection to the practice of collecting and experimenting on indigenous peoples. Additions to university collections of human remains were frequently reported in the press,[157] and as such the status of indigenous peoples and particularly Tasmanians was a matter for much wider public discussion. Skulls from Arthur Keith's collection in the Royal College of Surgeons were used to illustrate public lectures in the 1908, for example.[158] As has already been noted, the relics of the lost Tasmanians had been displayed in museums since the 1830s. And when the idea that the islanders were disappearing became embedded, alongside the idea that they represented some kind of cultural and historic curiosity, then human remains from Tasmania were also placed on permanent display.

By 1900 visitors could see the remains of Tasmanians in the Pitt-Rivers Museum in Oxford, the Hunterian Museum of the Royal College of Surgeons and the Natural History Museum in London. The last of these in particular had an important cultural presence and it commanded over 400,000 visitors a year.[159] From the 1880s visitors to the museum would have been able to see 'a selection of skulls, showing the different modifications of the cranial and facial bones in the various races of mankind'.[160] These modifications were hierarchically compared with one another. The Tasmanians, stated the 1885 guide to the mammalian galleries, 'have a very small brain cavity', which was 'strongly contrasting [...] with the skull of the European'. The capacity of the brain cavity was assumed to be directly related to intelligence: 'those races of mankind which have [...] small brain cases are of a lower type.'[161]

While the Natural History Museum adopted what was essentially a monogenist interpretation of human variation in their displays, their presentation of remains did not suggest that indigenous Tasmanians were fully human. The provenance of remains was, for example, documented only in terms of who had been involved in their transfer to the museum. No attempt was made to identify where in Tasmania the remains had been collected from – let alone the identities of the individuals concerned. Again, this was a sense of hierarchy informed by an understanding of genocide. The museum's visitors were made explicitly aware that Tasmanians had been 'exterminated'. While this was acknowledged as 'unfortunate', the institution also attempted to explain their demise without reference to the violence of the 'higher races' that their racial classification implicitly celebrated. Indeed, the 'extinction' of the lower races of man was presented, in keeping with the general extermination discourse, as the outcome of a *natural* process – bound up with perceptions of, and indeed understood as evidence of, Tasmanian inferiority.[162]

It is worth reiterating that the concomitant to the identification of Tasmanians, and indeed other indigenous peoples, as 'lower' races was the self-identification of European or indeed British racial superiority. It is also worth pausing to consider the relationship between this perceived superiority, the narcissism and self-worship evident in museum displays, and 'extermination' or, as we might term it, genocide. The existence of genocide was referred to and thus implicitly celebrated – the skulls of Tasmanians were displayed as evidence of this extermination, which in turn demonstrated indigenous Tasmanians' inferiority. Therefore genocide, or extermination, was an important idea in the racialised constructions of self offered in the Natural History Museum, and more generally in British culture.

Ironically, of course, the 'metric torrent' unleashed by the collection of human remains in the later nineteenth and early twentieth centuries rather undermined the attempt to measure racial difference. Repeated skull measurements demonstrated, for example, the differences within rather than between assumed racial groups, and by the 1920s it could no longer be demonstrated that 'race was an empirical reality'.[163] However, indigenous Tasmanians remained a touchstone in conceptions of race, a kind of cultural shorthand for racial inferiority. In part this was because this was still the manner in which the remains of the dead were displayed in British museums. But it was also the result of the enduring fixation with the idea that

Genocide in British Culture

Tasmanians had been entirely exterminated, which extends to the present day. The implications of the endurance of that idea will be discussed the final chapter.

For now, it is perhaps worth considering what the implications of colonial collection and display are for our understanding of the role that genocide played in British culture. On one level, what we have seen are repeated examples of the acknowledgement of genocide and the degree to which the extermination of indigenous Tasmanians had been assimilated. As a result, I am confident that British culture across the nineteenth century contained consistent confrontations with the idea of racial extermination in the British Empire. Responses to the reality of that destruction varied greatly, from despair to celebration. Some of the meanings attached to it were means of evading its moral implications. In the main the destruction of the indigenous islanders remained fixed around the idea of the 'dying race'. At the very least this was a concept that removed any sense of British responsibility, as it was latched onto a biological theory of racial differentiation. Added to this, the implication of the 'dying race' theory was further to embed a sense of racial hierarchy – and as such further to consign the 'Stone Age' Tasmanians to the bottom of an order that the British were at the top of. In this sense, genocide in Tasmania became within British culture a further indication of imperial British glory and majesty. What better indication of British might than the destruction of an entire race? I am reminded again of the words of *The Times* in July 1869: 'English-speaking men are destined to cover the planet [...] so the race goes on spreading, digging and planting, and squeezing other races out of existence, until the Red Indian promises to disappear and the aboriginal Tasmanian has actually vanished.'[164]

SIX

Coming to Terms with the Past?

If indigenous Tasmanians and their destruction have had a deep-rooted presence in British culture since the 1820s, then there has been, at least since the beginning of the twentieth century, a parallel process in Britain by which attempts have been made to confront the legacy of colonial genocide. Yet these discourses (which in Holocaust studies would be described as attempts to come to terms with the past) have, paradoxically, often served only to reveal how deep-rooted colonial assumptions about the now 'extinct', 'Stone Age', Tasmanians are in British history and culture.

In analysing the attempts to account for and indeed live with the idea of genocide in Tasmania in twentieth-century Britain, I am, however, confronted with an uncomfortable contradiction. This chapter will argue that genocide in Tasmania has not been forgotten. On the contrary, we will see how consistently genocide is referred to – first in critical discourse about the Empire and then in the debate about the return of human remains stored and displayed in museums. Indeed, I hope to show how the idea of destruction remains an important part of some accounts of British superiority. And it is here that I am confronted with the uncomfortable possibility that this book is part of that colonial discourse that emphasises British power. After all, this is a book that identifies *British* genocide in Tasmania. Might this also be interpreted as an attempt to claim the history of violence in the British Empire as evidence of British power?

The account of British involvement in the destruction of indigenous

The Last Man

Tasmanians provided in the previous chapters might for example be criticised as going rather against the grain of the post-colonial turn in historiography. Unlike much of the new imperial history, I have made no effort 'escape the metropolitan gaze'[1] and have concentrated firmly on the history of the British and their attempt to impose themselves on Van Diemen's Land. If post-colonial studies sought (and continues to seek) to re-empower the colonised, to demonstrate that indigenous peoples were agents in their own history and had a past independent of their colonisers, then my emphasis on the destructive contribution of the British themselves does not conform to that.[2] Indeed, in emphasising that genocide occurred in *British* Tasmania, it could be argued that I am falling into the trap of reinforcing the notions of the colonial strongman and the weak, oppressed and victimised indigenous Tasmanians.

In mitigation I would argue that post-colonial studies is also concerned with identifying the manner in which colonial societies domesticated their empires within their own cultures, with uncovering the various ways in which they exerted power over those territories and peoples that that they controlled. Indeed post-colonialism is concerned to demonstrate how total the colonisers' control of the colonised really was, by revealing the extent to which the perceived superiority of imperial societies was anchored in culture, and ultimately in the colonisers' understanding of themselves. The previous chapter began the task of investigating this in relation to genocide in Tasmania, and the present chapter seeks to understand how that genocide is interpreted up to the present day in Britain. In doing so I make no claims to be comprehensive; instead I explore a series of moments at which genocide in Tasmania has appeared in public discourse in Britain throughout the twentieth century and consider their implications. This particularly British focus is important: I do not discuss Australian renderings of the story that have had little impact in the United Kingdom. In so doing, I will argue that some ideas about the meaning of genocide first articulated in the 1800s survive in public conversation in Britain to this day. It is ultimately for readers

Coming to Terms with the Past?

to decide whether or not my own narrative is just a perpetuation of the kinds of thinking that I have identified here.

The chapter will begin with a discussion of the shape of the genocide in Tasmania as represented in anti-imperial histories across the twentieth century, before continuing with an in-depth discussion of the most prominent public discourse concerning this subject: the discussion of the return by British museums of the remains of indigenous Tasmanians and other cultural property, which took place from the 1950s but crystallised in the 1990s.

THE SHAME OF EMPIRE

I will consider first how genocide in Tasmania has been utilised in the literary and scholarly critique of colonialism. Concurrent with a museum and scientific culture that appeared to revel in colonial violence, from the beginning of the twentieth century genocide in Tasmania was also employed for what on the face of it appears to be the opposite political purpose. For all the imperial fawning in local museums locked into a colonial culture, there has been a consistent strain of anti-imperial politics and scholarship in Britain that has used genocide in Tasmania to highlight the iniquities or indeed the lie of British imperial progress.

This is not to say that the narratives identified in the previous chapter did not live on. Particularly in the 1920s, around the Empire Exhibition in 1924 for example, we can see repetitions of the 'dying race' idea that deliberately appeared to evade the violence of the Tasmanian frontier.[3] And the representations constructed in museum displays of the dead endured well into the twentieth century. Indeed, even the most critical perspectives on the Empire from the end of the nineteenth century onwards betrayed the legacy of assumptions of the racial inferiority of indigenous Tasmanians.

The most famous example is H.G. Wells's reference to Tasmania in the preface to *The War of the Worlds*, first published in 1898. Wells compared his Martian invasion to the British treatment of the 'inferior races': 'The Tasmanians, in spite of their human likeness, were entirely swept out of existence in a war of extermination waged by European immigrants.'[4] In citing the experience of Tasmanians in this manner, Wells drew on a tradition of colonial critique that had been first established by abolitionists in the nineteenth century, ultimately embodied in the Aborigines' Protection Society.

Yet, as in the case of that society, Wells's example suggests that we ought not to be too sentimental about the characterisations of genocide constructed by the critics of empire. Whatever the force of his critique, he seems to have accepted the veracity of the idea of racial inferiority specifically in relation to Tasmanians. In his *The Outline of History* (1919) Wells described indigenous Tasmanians as 'Palaeolithic', adopting the language of scientific racism. And the idea of Tasmanians' 'human likeness' in *The War of the Worlds* seems to demonstrate, at the very least, some ambivalence about indigenous peoples' role in human genealogy.[5] Indeed, Wells used, in *The War of the Worlds*, the idea of genocide as an indicator of the Tasmanians' inferiority – that they had been 'swept' from existence confirmed their status in a racial hierarchy. As such Wells was operating a very similar sense of the implications of genocide in Tasmania for the understanding of race and racial differentiation to that employed by those much more sympathetic to the imperial project.[6] Indeed, the very imagery of 'sweeping' away conformed to a progress mantra that saw the British as the masters of history.

Yet from Wells onwards, the genocide of Tasmanians holds a consistent place as a rhetorical weapon in the critique of British imperialism across the twentieth century. Consider this example, which is suggestive of the role that an understanding of genocide in Tasmania played in the formation, for example, of post-colonial liberation movements and ideologies, or at least attempts to imagine them. Douglas Duff, who served for the British in Palestine, reported overhearing the speech in Jerusalem of a man attempting to stir up Palestinian resistance to British rule in the 1930s. This unnamed agitator used the example of Tasmania as evidence of British brutality. He told his crowd that the Tasmanians were 'completely extinguished [...] by bullets and bayonets and unjust laws, by English hatred and greed'. Not only did genocide in Tasmania in this formulation provide evidence of the brutality of British rule, but the 'bones of the last Tasmanians' were a 'solemn warning to all we men of Arab blood'.[7] Even if we don't accept this account at face value, and think Duff's character a fantasy, it is nevertheless evidence that in the 1930s the experience of indigenous Tasmanians remained important in the imagination of empire. For Duff at least, writing from his home in Dorset, the destruction of indigenous Tasmanians had become a shorthand for the critique of British colonialism.

In the aftermath of World War II, and in the era of decolonisation, the idea of genocide in Tasmania continued to be a kind of rhetorical fail-safe in the critique of empire. The novelist Sebastian Faulks suggests that it became a ritual of anti-imperial discourse. In his novel *Engleby*, Faulks imagines a conversation with Ken Livingstone in which the former Labour Party politician states: 'it is impossible not to feel some sort of crude stirring when you hear "Land of Hope and Glory", but you have to set that against the systematic slaughter of the Tasmanian Aborigines.'[8] Michael Rothberg has argued that the memory of colonial genocide and the Holocaust should not be seen as competitive but complementary, and certainly, in relation to Tasmania, it appears that the horrors of the Final Solution did prompt reappraisals of the colonial past. For example, *Black War* by Tasmanian journalist Clive Turnbull, first published in 1948, offers a searing critique of white atrocities in the author's homeland that is clearly informed by more contemporary atrocities in Nazi Europe. Turnbull compares the experience of indigenous Tasmanians to other 'non-Aryan' peoples.[9] He also considers the story of indigenous extermination in Tasmania as symbolic of the 'story of all peoples dispossessed by conquerors' and thus as an indictment of all forms of imperialism.[10]

In Britain itself, V.G. Kiernan's *The Lords of Human Kind*, published in 1972, placed the experience of indigenous Tasmanians within both a general history of colonial dispossession and the history of genocide, understood explicitly in the context of the Holocaust. Kiernan described British policy in Tasmania as both an 'extermination' and a '*final solution*'.[11] This emphasis appears in the original and seems a clear attempt to link the Holocaust and colonial genocide. Kiernan's description of the Tasmanians' extermination is intriguing, and not just for its rhetorical allusions to the Holocaust. He repeats the allegation that indigenous Tasmanians were survivors of the Stone Age, and the idea that indigenous violence in the 'Black War' was not a rational response to invasion but some kind of vengeful spasm in which 'Tasmanians were turned against all white men'.[12] Again, therefore, we are faced with the limits of this kind of critique of British imperialism, in that it appeared still to be located in a sense of indigenous Tasmanian inferiority. Such a discourse has continued into the twenty-first century. As an example, Jeremy Paxman's recent *Empire* comments that the 'unfortunate people' of Van Diemen's Land were unable to survive a trial of strength with 'the most technologically advanced nation on earth'.[13]

In 2000 Matthew Kneale depicted indigenous Tasmanians' extermination and representation in science in the post-colonial novel *English Passengers*. Kneale's portrayal is ironic: he mocks both the scientific discourse on human origins that sought to collect corporeal remains and Robinson's efforts to save indigenous souls. The novel alone is evidence of the enduring power of the idea that the Empire had destroyed indigenous Tasmanian communities as a critique of the British Empire. Tasmania therefore continued to represent the 'Heart of Darkness' of Britain's imperial past.[14] Reviews also noted that the novel was based on 'one of the most shameful events in the history of the British Empire, the wholesale extermination of the people of Van Diemen's Land'.[15] As Kneale himself suggested, however, that idea of extermination was itself used as evidence of Tasmanian inferiority: 'how else could they have so foolishly permitted themselves to be exterminated?'[16]

Coming to Terms with the Past?

THE MYTH OF EXTINCTION

The idea of extermination often interacted with the idea that the *entire* indigenous Tasmanian population had been destroyed, down as it were to 'the last man'. This is a particularly tenacious myth. In the late 1970s Tom Haydon and Rhys Jones's film about Truganini, *The Last Tasmanian*, was broadcast on British television.[17] The film was controversial in Tasmania because it implied that Truganini had indeed been the 'last' Tasmanian, and as such denied the Aboriginality of the contemporary Tasmanian Aboriginal community. In Britain, such a response was absent. One letter writer to the *Radio Times* described his reaction: 'I am ashamed to be British and Christian. In comparative terms it [*The Last Tasmanian*] made Hitler's extermination programme seem small-time as the *entire* Aboriginal population was annihilated in the most despicable way.'[18] Newspapers, television and radio would continue to repeat the idea that in Tasmania, under the British flag, 'the colonists went on man-hunting safaris till there were no Tasmanians left.'[19] Examples that rely on the idea of complete extermination can be found up to the beginning of the twenty-first century too. Ian Hernon labelled the 'Black War' one of *Britain's Forgotten Wars* in a narrative that ended: 'in barely seventy years an *entire* race has been driven to extinction. It is a stain which has never been removed from the banners of the British Empire.'[20]

The idea of total extermination not only fixed a version of genocide in an understanding of racial identities, it also relied on and articulated an understanding of race as an immutable and biological characteristic. After all, from the first declarations of Tasmanian extinction onwards it was also accepted that there was an enduring 'Aboriginal' community in Tasmania, but that these people were not 'Tasmanian Aborigines', as it were. The presence of communities on Cape Barren Island, one of the Furneaux Group off the north-east coast of Tasmania, was for example regularly reported in the British press or in travel accounts.[21] And indeed the 'Aboriginality' of individual Tasmanians was discussed in scientific literature at the end of the nineteenth century. In particular, there was an extensive debate as to whether in fact Truganini was the 'last Tasmanian' at all. It was suggested that perhaps Fanny Cochrane Smith was a surviving indigenous Tasmanian. Smith was ultimately declared not to be *racially* Tasmanian because she was, like the Cape Barren communities, understood to be of 'mixed blood'.[22]

The idea of 'Aboriginal' extinction was also a common trope of accounts of Tasmania in travel literature in the first half of the twentieth century – just as narratives of conflict were important in the émigré literature of the early colonial period. The absence of Tasmania's indigenous population was routinely referred to in these travelogues – as if it somehow added to the exotic allure of this remote location.[23] Yet if racial conflict was a way of confirming the otherness of Tasmania, the absence of indigenous Tasmanians was also used to suggest the similarities between Tasmania and Britain and as such the completeness of the colonial victory over the island's wilderness. George Porter's *Wanderings in Tasmania* reflected, for example, on the success with which the colonists had transplanted British culture, while marvelling at the 'careless' extermination of the 'amazingly primitive and pathetic' Tasmanians. Again, the idea of extermination was used to construct a sense of racial hierarchy – one culture had been destroyed, while another had successfully replaced it on the other side of the world.[24]

Belief in the 'complete' extermination of indigenous Tasmanians was in part based on a racialised understanding of the world. As in the 1800s, it was often accompanied by the idea that that extermination was the result of some kind of natural process. In the 1930s, for example, the myth of indigenous Tasmanians' total extermination began to be harnessed in a British critique of contemporary Australian treatment of indigenous populations. The idea that all such populations were slated for extinction had, in Australia at least, actually begun to lose force by this point. This was in part because of the obdurate survival and indeed reversal of the demographic decline in indigenous communities there. As a consequence, a variety of pressure groups began to campaign for indigenous rights, including William Cooper's Australian Aborigines' League, which was given public attention in Britain.

Cooper, from the Yorta Yorta people, had emerged as representative of indigenous communities in New South Wales and Victoria in the 1930s. In 1937 he attempted to submit a petition of several thousand signatures to King George VI demanding intervention for the care of indigenous communities, not least through their representation in the Australian parliament.[25]

Unlike the Tasmanian petition of the 1840s, Cooper's demands never officially reached the monarch. But they were reported in the British press, something that occasioned much reflection on extermination in Tasmania as the historical background to Cooper's protests. Although the petition appears now to be a rather obvious articulation of 'Aboriginal' agency, Cooper had invited the king to 'prevent the extinction of the Aboriginal race' and as such it fed into the still prevalent extinction discourse in Britain. *The Times* cited the example of Tasmania to agree that Cooper's fear of extinction 'is only too well founded' because of a process of 'tribal decay and racial decline'. Ironically, the paper printed in the same edition the judgement of the anatomist Frederic Wood Jones that the 'dying race' thesis was 'humbug' which had 'gilded' the colonial 'extermination of the natives'.[26] But Wood Jones's new narrative was not allowed to undermine the overall impression of natural decline that had become so fixed.

As we can see, references to the extinction, or extermination, of indigenous Tasmanians remained a fact of British culture throughout the twentieth century. The skulls of indigenous Tasmanians remained on display in the Natural History Museum until at least the 1950s.[27] Lyndall Ryan claims that 'King Billy's skull' was on display in Edinburgh until the 1980s.[28] Regional museums too contained the scattered ephemera of indigenous Tasmania, usually displayed without context.[29] As well as the collection of material held in Saffron Walden that was donated by John Helder Wedge in the 1830s and displayed periodically until the 1990s, other examples include the bust of Woorraddy displayed in Swindon Museum and Art Gallery – without 'cultural context' – until the 1990s.[30] In the Royal Albert Memorial Museum

The Last Man

in Exeter a shell necklace purportedly belonging to Truganini was displayed until 1997 (see illustration No. 5).

We cannot know exactly how these items were displayed, and certainly not how they were understood. It seems likely that all were in some way related to the 'dying race' theory – because that was simply the way in which colonial Tasmania was understood. Indeed, what is striking about the examples that we can identify with any precision is how little the meanings attached to objects changed over the twentieth century. When Truganini's necklace was first displayed in Exeter in 1933, for example, it was reported in a local newspaper to be a 'pathetic relic of a vanished people', who were in the 'same condition as the European men of the older Stone Age'.[31] When it was finally removed from display in 1997 (in order to be returned into the care of the Tasmanian Aboriginal Centre) the display 'remembered' Truganini as a 'spirited and able woman' but commented (in a way that demonstrates both the long roots of the extermination discourse of the nineteenth century and the way that that could lead to obfuscation and denial) that 'the natives were unable to comprehend new European values [after the invasion]. They could neither oppose nor conform, and they drifted into listless serfdom. It is not hard to see why Aboriginal culture is now the province of history.'[32] So we can see that, at the beginning of the twenty-first century, just as at the end of the nineteenth, the idea that indigenous Tasmanians were somehow doomed to extinction could still be found publicly articulated in museum displays across Britain.

THE RETURN OF HUMAN REMAINS

Throughout the postwar era, and especially since the 1980s, there has been a debate in Britain (and throughout the West) about whether the former trophies of empire should be returned to the lands and peoples that they originated from. This debate has been concerned with a great deal of material including a wide variety of cultural property. But, especially in relation to human remains, extensive public discussions of the issue were in the first instance related to the return of indigenous Tasmanian remains to the contemporary Tasmanian Aboriginal community. It is a discourse that appears to represent both a genuine effort to atone for colonial atrocities and a perpetuation of colonial ideologies – including the myth of Tasmanian extinction. Indigenous Tasmanians, and assumptions about them, are so central to this debate that an extended discussion is required.

In the late 1940s the relationship between the presence of human remains in museum collections and efforts to confront the injustices of the colonial past became a public issue in Tasmania and has remained so ever since. Some 40 or 50 years later Britain would also be forced to confront the legacy of colonial genocide because of its collections of Tasmanian (and other) remains and begin a (still ongoing) process of coming to terms with the imperial past. That process was largely set in motion because of the activism of the Tasmanian Aboriginal Centre and a community that many in Britain assumed to be 'extinct'. Responses to that campaign, for example from the institutions that held indigenous Tasmanian remains, also offer eloquent examples of the degree to which colonial attitudes remained embedded in British culture.

In 1947 the Anglican archdeacon of Hobart discovered among his father's papers a request from Truganini that her remains not be subjected to the same indignities as William Lanne's. That request, which had been made several times prior to her death in 1876, had been ignored. Indeed, Truganini's skeleton had been put on public display in the Tasmanian Museum and Art Gallery in Hobart in 1904. Like those in Britain, her remains were presented as a 'trophy of white settler triumphalism', evidence of the failure of this inferior people's ability to come to terms with the arrival of the modern world in colonial Van Diemen's Land.[33] As a consequence of the rediscovery of Truganini's wishes, the Anglican Church authorities in Tasmania sought to persuade the Tasmanian Museum to destroy the remains as an act of atonement for the crimes of the colonial past, and in accordance with her desire to be cremated and scattered at sea.

The Tasmanian Museum refused the request in the name of 'science', concluding in 1951 that it should retain the remains. This was a judgement for which the museum sought confirmation from the scientific community, soliciting expert opinion from a number of locations, including institutions in Britain that also held remains. This scholarly community articulated a consistent view that Truganini's skeleton was of particular anthropological and biological value – as she had been the 'last Tasmanian'. Such responses begin to highlight the complexity of the idea of genocide in relation to such remains, in that an assumption of extinction, the idea of a successful genocide, was used to deny the rights of a living community in the present. Submissions to the museum also suggested that to destroy the remains would have been a 'stupid piece of sentimentality' and a 'scientific crime of the worst order'. Crucially, it was argued that this was not the way to 'atone for the original crimes committed against living Tasmanians […] it is bad enough for us, the white race, to have destroyed the Tasmanians, but it is still worse for us to commit such an act of ignorant vandalism.'[34] This argument was proposed despite Truganini's remains not having been used in any major published research.

But the 'scientific' case for retention was not just wrong on its own terms – it also displayed how scientific attitudes could *themselves* reflect colonial attitudes and their curious interaction with the genocidal past. The idea of returning remains was constructed as a sentimental or irrational exercise – such an act of fundamental sympathy with a community presumed destroyed was seen as the opposite of the enlightened reason of the (implicitly white and European) scientific community. This is reminiscent of attempts to explain conflict between indigenous and settler communities in the previous century as being the result of the irrational will to vengeance of a population blind to the advances of civilisation. In John Cove's words: 'scientists defined their interests in Truganini's remains as a self-evident good located within a unified and global pursuit of knowledge beneficial to all humankind.'[35] At the same time, the incantation of the destructive power of the 'white race' was articulated with a familiar combination of regret and awe.

Coming to Terms with the Past?

In the middle of the twentieth century the assumption that remains were of scientific value, or at least that they might be in the future, was not just applied to extant collections. Although the Natural History Museum in London might have ceased to display the remains of Tasmanians as an exemplar of racial hierarchy in the 1950s, it continued to solicit additions to its research collections. In 1955 and 1956, for example, the museum worked hard to obtain further human remains from the estate of William Crowther, who had of course been responsible for the removal of William Lanne's skull.[36] While the postwar world might have reluctantly accepted that the idea of race was largely a construction, this did not prevent institutions like the Natural History Museum from continuing to explore, through the documentation of remains, what they understood as the physical differences between racial communities.[37]

The idea that the entire indigenous Tasmanian community had been destroyed was so embedded in Britain that debates about what should be done with remains from Tasmania did not have to confront the issue of what harm the retention of remains might do to indigenous communities *in the present day*, since it was assumed that no such communities existed. In Australia no such assumption could be made, of course, and from the early 1970s there was a gradual change in attitudes to human remains, largely as a result of political campaigns by indigenous groups. In Tasmania, grouped around what would become the Tasmanian Aboriginal Centre, the indigenous community were becoming increasingly assertive in the 1970s. This assertiveness centred on campaigns for land rights, and crucially for the return of human remains to the communities from which they had been stolen.

Since the end of the 1960s the Tasmanian Museum and Art Gallery had been the subject of public and private protest about the return of Truganini. The museum did not avoid dialogue over the issue, but by 1974 was still unable to sanction the return of the skeleton because of its apparent scientific importance. Demonstrating the degree to which it was swimming against the tide of political and increasingly scholarly opinion in Australia, however, the museum was ultimately ordered to return the remains to the Tasmanian state government in line with the recommendation of the Australian Institute of Aboriginal Studies, which was also brokering the return of remains elsewhere in Australia. On 1 May 1876, a century after she had died, Truganini's remains were cremated and scattered at sea.

Why was the issue of returning remains so important to indigenous communities? In part it was simply about recognising the iniquity of the circumstances of collection – at best, remains from Tasmania had been stolen from graves. Thus, refusing to return them was a perpetuation of the gross power disparities that ensured that it was possible for museum collections to hold remains in the first instance. But, more than just reflecting the power relations at the heart of the colonial exercise, both the act of collecting skulls and skeletons and the work that had been carried out on them were part of the expression of that power. The ransacking of graves had been based on and further entrenched the view that indigenous peoples were inferior, and therefore to return remains – especially to empowered indigenous community groups who were asserting themselves politically – was to reject the idea of inferiority and begin to overturn the ideological basis of colonialism itself. If the collection of remains had been used to construct one narrative of 'Aboriginality', their return was part of a new narrative constructed by indigenous communities themselves. In the words of the Aboriginal and Torres Strait Islander Commission in 2001: 'the removal of human remains strongly contributed towards an overall feeling of dispossession amongst indigenous peoples of Australia.'[38] The return of remains was therefore the beginning of an attempt to overcome that dispossession.

That feeling of dispossession was not just about the politics of power and representation. It was also concerned with the spiritual life of indigenous peoples, and calls for return were also demands that their cosmologies be respected. The remains held in Western museums had by definition been disrupted and removed from their spiritual communities. For many indigenous peoples the dead were understood as an enduring part of the extant community who should be returned to

Coming to Terms with the Past?

the land from which they came, and therefore their removal from that land was the cause of a profound spiritual disruption, a rupture in the 'wholeness' of the community.[39] As representatives of the Tasmanian Aboriginal Centre put it to the Museums Association of the United Kingdom in 1997:

> as a matter of religion and practice any human remains are automatically returned to their original tribal lands and their people. The whole point of reclaiming such remains is so we are able at last to put to rest in a traditional ceremony conducted by Aboriginal people the spirits of our ancestors who were disinterred from burial grounds or killed in the bush.[40]

In Tasmania the return of Truganini's remains had a further important, symbolic dimension. As the 'last Tasmanian', Truganini embodied the idea that the entirety of the indigenous Tasmanian community had been destroyed. The return of her remains to the living descendants of that community also significantly ruptured that extinction myth and declared loudly, 'We are alive.'[41] Although, as we have already seen, that message was not really heard in Britain.

After the Tasmanian Aboriginal Centre had secured an agreement for the return of all skeletal remains held in Tasmania – including, in 1984, the collection established by William Crowther – its attention turned to remains held outside Australia – chiefly (but not exclusively) in Britain. If Truganini's remains had been the most symbolic in Tasmania, then the skull of William Lanne was the most resonant of any held elsewhere. Because he was 'the last man' and because of the famously gruesome treatment of his corpse, 'King Billy's skull' held an important communal and propaganda value. The Tasmanian Aboriginal Centre first approached the University of Edinburgh for a return in 1982, and by 1990 negotiations were concluded successfully.[42] After a wide consultation that included consideration of the academic as well as political issues involved, the university authorities, supported by the wider academic community, decided not just to return remains to Tasmania but that the 'university should adopt a policy of returning all human remains, when so requested, to appropriate representatives of cultures in which such remains have particular significance'.[43]

In returning remains, the University of Edinburgh reflected a growing consensus in favour of repatriation internationally. As well as the Tasmanian Aboriginal Centre's victories in Australia, between 1985 and 1994 the United Nations worked towards a declaration on the rights of indigenous peoples that stated *explicitly* that remains, and indeed cultural property, should be returned to indigenous communities. These rights were, the declaration suggested, entirely intertwined with the cultural autonomy of indigenous communities. The declaration thus understood the return of remains as an important part of the abandonment of the forced assimilation that had defined the colonial era, and an additional protection for indigenous communities to that provided by the genocide convention.[44] The World Archaeological Congress adopted a policy that called for the 'express recognition that the concerns of various ethnic groups [...] are legitimate'. Although it also requested that the demands of the scientific community be respected, the 'Vermillion Accord' (as the declaration is known) asked that agreements over the return of remains be negotiated. Perhaps most significantly of all, in 1990 the United States passed the Native American Graves Protection and Repatriation Act, 'the first time anywhere in the world a nation's indigenous population(s) have been recognised as the rightful owners of their ancestors remains'.[45] In 1993 Museums Australia adopted 'Previous Possessions, New Obligations', a policy document that looked towards the return of remains and other cultural property as an act of reconciliation in the new, culturally diverse Australia.[46]

This was not, however, a consensus that had spread as far as the United Kingdom. Up until the end of the twentieth century many British institutions refused to engage with indigenous communities over the issue of return. National organisations such as the Natural History Museum simply claimed that they were legally unable to return any property under the auspices of the British Museum Act

1963, which, representatives of the Tasmanian Aboriginal Centre commented, museums clung to 'as more binding than an act of God'.[47] The Royal College of Surgeons, the Natural History Museum and the University of Cambridge all refused requests for return with reference to this legislation.[48]

Institutions in Scotland were not covered by the British Museum Act, and as such were legally free to return remains. The University of Edinburgh's decision to do so thus set a precedent in Britain, and was therefore perhaps the first act in the 'decolonisation' of British museum collections. The commitment to return came after significant debate, and as such confirmed that the moral, political arguments in favour of doing so and the recognition of the cultural rights of indigenous peoples held sway. The university decided not just to return remains to the Tasmanian Aboriginal Centre – who had mounted a very effective and very public campaign for them – but to adopt a general policy which favoured return. The changes in attitudes in Australia and the United States had thus gained their first significant foothold in the United Kingdom.

In many ways, what followed the University of Edinburgh's decision could be portrayed as a developing movement in favour of repatriation, and thus a rapid acceptance on behalf of many institutions in Britain – from government to the museum community – of the harm done, both in the past and the present, by their collection and then retention of human remains and indigenous cultural property. In relation to Tasmania, it could be argued that this movement was a recognition of the moral need to atone for the crimes of the imperial past, and indeed to acknowledge that Britain, and British institutions, had been and continued to be implicated in the genocidal consequences of the colonial occupation of Van Diemen's Land. In July 2000 the British government – in a joint statement by the then prime ministers of the United Kingdom and Australia, Tony Blair and John Howard – recognised the moral imperative behind the return of remains and pledged to work towards that goal, acknowledging the 'special connection that indigenous people have with ancestral remains'.[49] The British government then established the Human Remains Working Group under the auspices of the Department for Culture, Media and Sport, which issued an authoritative report, based on expert consultation, in November 2003.[50] That report, although it did not explicitly suggest all institutions should return all remains, clearly prioritised the case for repatriation. In 2005, after further consultation, the department issued a guidance policy that suggested that all institutions needed to work cooperatively with indigenous communities.[51] That cooperation ultimately envisaged the return of all remains to their spiritual origins. As a consequence of those developments, institutions such as the Royal College of Surgeons, the Natural History Museum, the Pitt-Rivers Museum and the University of Cambridge all have policies that recognise the importance of indigenous rights to the remains of their ancestors.[52] Following the original decision of the University of Edinburgh in 1990, at the time of writing, some 23 years later, virtually all Tasmanian remains in British institutions have been returned.

There were other examples of cooperation between museums in Britain and the Tasmanian Aboriginal community that appear to point to an acknowledgement of past suffering and to the desire for atonement in the present. In 1997 the Royal Albert Memorial Museum, for example, returned Truganini's necklace and bracelet to representatives of the Tasmanian Aboriginal Centre. In 1994 the necklace had been seen on display in the museum by a former resident of Hobart then living in Britain, Marion Tewkesbury, who wrote to a Hobart newspaper and to the Tasmanian Aboriginal Centre suggesting that the necklace should be returned, as she put it in correspondence with the Exeter museum, 'in recognition of ethnic Tasmanians' tragedy'.[53] While the presence of the necklace in Exeter had been documented in Australia some 30 years previously,[54] this public intervention appeared to galvanise a campaign for return. Michael Mansell, de facto leader of the community, set out the Tasmanian Aboriginal Centre's fundamental position in June 1994 when he declared that the necklace had been 'effectively stolen' and thus should be returned. The necklace was important because it was the product of traditional practices that the colonists had sought to destroy. More than this, though, as negotiators explained to the Exeter museum, because it had been made by Truganini herself it had an even greater cultural significance. Truganini had 'continued her cultural practices throughout her life, often under great persecution' and as such the necklace represented Tasmanian resistance and survival.[55]

The negotiations for the return of the necklace were difficult and at the beginning of the process were challenged by the depth of emotion that the issue evoked. When the museum authorities replied to the Tasmanian Aboriginal Centre's original request that they were sympathetic to the idea of a return but needed to enquire as to the storage arrangements for the necklaces in Tasmania,[56] they were undoubtedly taken aback at the ferocity of the response – largely because the museum was not able to recognise its own articulation of colonial ideologies and assumptions. In the words of John Wells of the Tasmanian Aboriginal Centre:

> We have resisted the temptation to take offence at your comments about the safe storage of Truganini's possessions. We can assure you that we regard the items as highly as does your institution and we would certainly not do anything to jeopardise their safekeeping. We note with sadness that the very institutions which have kept our cultural property from us all these years now regard it as their responsibility to protect our cultural items from our negligence.[57]

Finally, however, such barriers were overcome and the necklace was returned in a public ceremony in November 1997, the outcome of a cooperative process that according to the Tasmanian Aboriginal Centre itself set 'a courageous example' to the museum profession in the United Kingdom. In exchange for the necklace and bracelet the museum was presented with some traditionally made baskets from the Tasmanian Aboriginal community. Since 1999 these have been displayed in the museum's 'world cultures' gallery with an explanation of the repatriation process and some reflection on the institution's status as a repository of 'contested objects'.[58]

OUR COLONIAL PRESENT

As I have said, this narrative *could* be understood as evidence of a progressive effort in Britain to come to terms with and overcome the colonial past – to atone and look to a cooperative future. The return of remains *could* be interpreted as the post-colonialisation of Britain. Yet the story of the return of Truganini's necklace hints at the degree to which British connections with the country's genocidal history are not being fully confronted.

When the Leisure Committee of Exeter City Council met on 14 March 1995, its major item for discussion was Truganini – a clear indication of the degree to which the past could emerge into the present in the most surprising of venues. Yet the minutes of that meeting also suggest a level of evasion too – in that although it was noted that the necklace was of 'outstanding spiritual importance' to the 'surviving Tasmanian Aboriginal community' the committee's members were not invited to reflect on *why* that might be.[59] Equally, one of the serendipitous consequences of repatriation was a flurry of correspondence to the Royal Albert Memorial Museum from private individuals who also held necklaces like Truganini's. Often the writers were seeking a valuation for their property. Of course, these bracelets may not have been stolen property at all – they were manufactured for sale in Tasmania into the 1930s – but they offer an intriguing indication of the degree to which Britain could be connected to its colonial past in ways that ordinarily would not be visible. Indeed, some letters suggested that Britons had developed cultural practices that could accommodate Tasmanian indigenous artefacts, the relics of a destroyed culture. One family from Cornwall, for example, reported that it was tradition for women in their family to wear their shell necklace and bracelet on their wedding day.[60] Of course, we cannot know how these individuals understood the artefacts that they were wearing, or the significance that they attached to them. Yet assuming family weddings were not occasions to reflect on genocide, we might conclude that they are an intriguing example of how Britain's dark past could be both present and ignored right up until the end of the twentieth century.

The debate that preceded the University of Edinburgh's unprecedented decision to return 'King Billy's skull' might also be interpreted as emphasising the enduring colonial discourse at play in British institutions and the enduring complexity of efforts to escape such assumptions. This decision was not reached easily. At first, the request was refused.[61] Vigorous arguments against return were proposed within the university community throughout the period under which the proposal was being considered. For example, the university's briefing paper on 'the arguments' constructed a binary opposition between what it described as the 'moral, political and cultural' case for return and the 'scientific' arguments against. In doing so it perpetuated the characterisation of indigenous populations as irrational in comparison to the rational, enlightened and scientific West.[62]

At the same time, efforts to wrestle with contemporary Aboriginal identity relied on an essentially biological view of race when they referred to the 'genetic extinction' of the indigenous Tasmanian population.[63] Earlier recommendations from the senior management of the university had cautioned that it needed to be 'borne in mind that the Tasmanian Aboriginals were now extinct' in the context of a discussion about whether there was in fact a legitimate representative organisation to whom the remains could be returned.[64] Arguments for retention suggested that the material had been collected in a valid attempt to study human origins, but ignored entirely the role that such studies had had in embedding and perpetuating ideas of race, and indeed racial hierarchy, in Western culture. One of the last acts of the scientific community that argued against return was to declare that 'King Billy's skull' held by Edinburgh was not in fact William Lanne – something that could be interpreted as an apparently desperate final attempt to assert the certainty and superiority of Western science over indigenous Tasmanian faith.[65]

The Last Man

Cressida Fforde has argued persuasively that we should not characterise the fraught discourse over the return of colonial-era remains as divided between indigenous communities on one side and Western scientists on the other – precisely because it conforms to the stereotype that represents indigenous communities as irrational and in opposition to the enlightened West. It also does not reflect the reality – for example, clearly the majority of museum professionals in Britain now favour return, which they regard not as a loss to science or to their museum collections but as an opportunity to develop knowledge about other cultures. Equally, the British government's response, the Human Remains Working Group, largely pointed towards a cooperative future, envisaging that institutions that held remains would work together with indigenous communities to organise and learn from the return in a 'spirit of collaboration'.[66] It took evidence from professionals who testified to the benefits of working in cooperation with indigenous communities, and within a framework that allowed communities to control access to and share research on archaeological remains.[67] But it stopped short of mandating that all remains be returned by law to indigenous communities – a move that would have reflected the letter of some submissions to the group on behalf of those communities.[68]

But despite this desire to emphasise collaboration and compromise, there is little doubt that the debate did, and indeed does, remain essentially polarised between on the one hand those who recognised an ethical imperative to return remains and on the other those who recognised an alternative ethical imperative to retain them, in order that remains might be scientifically studied. For example, the Human Remains Working Group itself essentially accepted the recommendations of the Aboriginal and Torres Strait Islander Commission that the only ethical position was in favour of return, and indeed specifically recommended that 'where there is reason to believe the original removal of remains occurred without consent' those remains should not be retained. This effectively meant that all colonial-era remains, which had necessarily been removed *without* consent, should be returned. Yet the representative of the Natural History Museum who sat on the Human Remains Working Group, Neil Chalmers, issued a dissenting judgement – precisely because he rejected the ethics of that position. What is more, when the debate was and is represented to a wider public it is certainly presented in those Manichean terms.[69]

It is difficult to find a neutral position in a debate in which one of the sources of cultural disconnection is a conflicting conception of the very nature of time. Those who favour retention, who tend to think of time in terms of linear progression, cannot understand how indigenous communities can feel a connection with those from whom they are separated by several generations and hundreds of years. But, for indigenous communities, 'time is circular. Those ancestors who may have died hundreds of years ago are [...] still members of the group of living people today.'[70] Thus it is a fundamental disagreement about the nature of knowledge itself, the manner in which we can know the world in which we live. Those who favour retention proclaim that they are engaged in scientific research that will benefit all humanity; indigenous groups, however, deny the right of Western scientists to speak on their behalf. As indigenous-rights campaigner Rodney Dillon said in the aftermath of the Blair–Howard declaration, 'Aborigines were not put on this earth for British scientists to do research on.'[71]

Those who campaigned vigorously for retention, like the representatives of the Natural History Museum or the University of Cambridge, effectively adopted the Enlightenment position (as articulated by their forebears in the nineteenth century) that they were carrying out research for the benefit of all humanity. In the words of Robert Foley (director of the Leverhulme Centre for Human Evolutionary Studies at the University of Cambridge): 'these skeletons are an irreplaceable record not just of particular cultures and populations, but of humanity as a whole.' Foley also claimed that the descendants of those people in the present demanding return would themselves prefer to see such remains retained by museums as 'part of global heritage, and as a source of historical and scientific ideas and discoveries'.[72] Similarly, Neil Chalmers, in his dissent from the working group report of 2003, declared that he could not consent to the idea that only an ethical case could be made for repatriation because that ignored the universally conceived 'public benefits' of scientific research into remains.[73]

This conception of the universal benefits of science, and indeed the presumption that scientists can speak for all humanity, both now and in the future, gives some indication of the *colonial* nature of the debate about remains in the public sphere. It was a debate between – in the words of Kenan Malik, who argued against return – 'those who believe in the possibility of universal human knowledge and those who view the truth as culturally constrained'. Malik continues in a manner that eloquently demonstrates the assumption that Western scientists were able to speak *for* indigenous communities: 'the destruction of such material through repatriation damages *our* ability to understand *our* past.'[74] Consider also Robert Foley's argument that indigenous communities themselves should want remains to be retained for 'science'. Foley suggested in a 2003 debate, quite rightly, that the desire to return remains was historically contingent – a post-colonial articulation of identity which sought to right the wrongs of colonial injustice:

> I think you should also remember that in the future, future generations both of ourselves and indigenous communities may well look back if all this material has all disappeared and wonder what has happened to their history […] As they're hopefully given greater access to education and the wealth that goes with development then they will want to see this preserved in the same way […] that we enjoy discovering about our pasts through television programmes and going to museums.[75]

Foley's claims are suffused with colonial assumptions that would not have been out of place during the original exploitation of Van Diemen's Land. He not only represents Western science as the natural outcome of human progress, but assumes that all other peoples will, through 'development', become, in effect, like 'us'. Thus the (self-declared) scientific perspective on the return of remains was an argument for an ongoing colonisation.

Coming to Terms with the Past?

It is not just in these assumptions that arguments in favour of retention appeared to reflect some colonial positions. Consistently, debates about the return of remains in the United Kingdom have returned to the idea that indigenous Tasmanians had been entirely destroyed. It was present in the University of Edinburgh's discussions about 'King Billy's skull', and is invariably part of debates on the subject in the public sphere. Robert Foley argued in 2003 that the University of Cambridge was unable to return any of its three Tasmanian skulls because there was no genetic community to which they could be returned: 'the Tasmanians no longer exist, and can have no descendants.'[76] A group of British museums raised the idea of extermination as a practical barrier to return in their submission to the government's working group of the early 2000s:

> A further problem has been the possible lack of mandate vested in those individuals representing repatriation. In particular, to remove particular genotypes from the possibility of scientific investigation is akin to a form of racism if not genocide, because those genotypes would be excluded from important ways in which we may continue to investigate or define our species.[77]

So much for the claim that the myth of indigenous Tasmanian extinction had been 'consigned to the flames' in the cremation of Truganini's remains.[78]

As I have already stated, subscribing to the extinction myth is to operate an entirely biological or genetic understanding of the idea of race. Its survival suggests that claims of the death of race science have been somewhat exaggerated. Furthermore, such arguments from the British science community repeat the assumptions of the Aborigines' Protection Society that only they could offer protection to (in this case the genetic material of) indigenous Tasmanians. Indeed another submission to the working group argued that although the circumstances of the collection of remains were unacceptable, we should acknowledge and indeed celebrate the fact that such material was saved: 'had our predecessors not been so inquisitive and so organised, then this material [...] would have been lost forever.'[79]

Not only do such arguments deny the existence of a contemporary indigenous community in Tasmania, they suggest that 'we' are the beneficiaries of genocide, that the alleged completeness of extermination absolves institutions of any responsibility to consider the contemporary impact of their holding such remains. One is forced to recall Darwin's claim that Van Diemen's Land had the advantage of having destroyed the indigenous population. It is also difficult to escape the conclusion that such statements implied the same wonder at the apparent power that the idea of extermination bestowed on the colonists themselves. One group of scientists is quoted in the working group's report as stating:

> the extermination of the Aboriginal Tasmanians (genocide) is an appalling crime and amongst the worst atrocities of colonialism. Ironically, in this case, the facts render demands for the repatriation of remains of Tasmanian origin empty. Strictly speaking the Tasmanians were a geographical isolate and have no descendants to claim their relatives.[80]

The logic of such claims was clear: 'we' (that is, Western scientists) won the right to control of these remains through 'our' wholesale destruction of the indigenous community.

The response of the Tasmanian Aboriginal Centre to such attempts to use the genocidal past to deny their existence in the present was predictably angry. They asserted that the issue was the right of Aboriginal peoples *now* to control access to the remains of *their* ancestors – that there was no universal scientific right of access but a need to respect indigenous peoples *today*. They regretted the use of language and challenged the conceptualisation of race at work in the scientific community, stating: 'we are not animals to be described as "pure" or "spoiled" by intermarriage. The use of such language reminds us of the Nazi era.'[81]

Coming to Terms with the Past?

Ultimately, of course, the Human Remains Working Group did agree that the only ethical response was to return remains to their communities of origin, and slowly institutions have also adopted policies reflecting that basic assumption. However, the journey each institution has made to a policy favouring return has been tortuous –representing a process of working through the colonial past that has further revealed both the deep roots of colonial thinking and, in the case of Tasmania, the degree to which a specific interpretation of genocide has been entrenched.

Consider, for example, the decision to return remains to Tasmania by the Natural History Museum, which was finally taken in 2006. The Tasmanian Aboriginal Centre's request for material in that year, after it had failed to gain access to remains on at least three previous occasions, was uncompromising. In October it demanded that the Natural History Museum return all Tasmanian human material without condition. Indeed, it pre-empted any attempt to impose conditions (for example of access to the remains) as 'perpetuating the same imbalance of power which framed the circumstances of the original collection'. It made clear that requests for return were motivated by a desire both to effect restitution for previous crimes and to restore existing communities today, and as such that any retention of remains did not just fail to atone for the past but would do harm *in the present*. Finally, it decried any further research in the following and very powerful terms:

> Considered from the time of first contact as scientific curiosities, Tasmanian Aboriginal people both living and dead have been subject for generations to invasive scrutiny by scientists of all kinds [...] this objectivising of a people in the name of a people is dehumanising and racist.[82]

However, the museum continued to resist the return of material – and to base that opposition on, in effect, reiterations of the kind of assumptions that had been made across the previous two centuries. Whatever the outcome, the museum recommended to trustees that all remains needed to be accessible to 'qualified scientists and historians'. It repeated the allegation that indigenous Tasmanians were in effect a Stone Age relic, arguing that the Natural History Museum's collection of nineteenth-century skulls, which included the one given by Robinson to Lady Franklin, represented a sample of '*ancient* human material'. And they echoed previous ideas that *they* represented the best hope of preventing and protecting the Tasmanian material and preventing Tasmanian disappearance from 'future analysis of human diversity and evolution'.[83] Such a formulation appeared to suggest that the request for the return of remains was indigenous Tasmanians' last act in their two-century-long auto-genocide. It also repeated the so often articulated assumption that it was the colonial or imperial institutions such as the Natural History Museum that were the best guardians of knowledge. If, in Kenan Malik's words, these were debates about 'who owns knowledge' then the answer from many quarters seemed to remain: 'We do,' or at any rate: 'We should.'

In the event the trustees did agree to return, which finally took place in May 2007. This was only after a protracted legal process had prevented the Natural History Museum carrying out further tests on the indigenous human material, which the trustees had recommended come before their being given back.[84] The Tasmanian Aboriginal Centre agreed not to destroy the remains in order to preserve their DNA, but retained control over their use. Although other processes of return and repatriation had been mutually beneficial, this exchange was marked by mutual hostility and distrust. It was also represented within the British popular press using familiar tropes that suggested that the scientists had been forced to bow to the pressures of irrational superstition and faith: it was, for example, reported in *The Times* under the headline 'Museum surrenders vital clues to human evolution'.[85]

The vast majority of Tasmanian human material held in museums in Britain, which was largely stolen from graves during the nineteenth century, has now been returned to the care of the Tasmanian Aboriginal community. But this does not mean that the traces of indigenous Tasmanians, and indeed of their destruction at British hands, have been *entirely* expunged from British culture. Some material possessions are still held in British museums. In Saffron Walden the spears and waddies that John Helder Wedge collected in Tasmania – although probably from those indigenous people who had been brought from New South Wales and who worked for John Batman – are still on show. When Wedge collected them, he intended to display them as examples of the 'primitive' cultures that he experienced in the New World. From what we can tell from sketches of the museum collection that survive, they were originally displayed in this manner – or simply allowed to 'speak for themselves [...] as objects of wonder' in a collection of colonial treasures and curiosities. In the twenty-first century, and in keeping with quite different ethics of display, they are contained in an exhibition on the very nature of colonial collection. Under the banner 'What are these objects doing here?' visitors are invited to think about the connections between a small market town in Essex and the colonised world – a context that more adequately articulates the 'contract of trust between the curator as the guardian of the collections and [their] originating community'.[86]

Other museums continue to hold material relating to the indigenous Tasmanian community – but no longer display it. In Swindon Museum and Art Gallery the bust of Woorraddy lies in its archive, removed from display in 2000. In travel guides to Tasmania, if the dark colonial past features at all it is much more likely to be in relation to convicts than to genocide – to 'white slaves' rather than the 'Black War', as it were.[87] However, in addition to the debates concerning human remains, reflection on the fate of indigenous Tasmanians in the colonial era does periodically puncture the British present. The 'Port Arthur massacre' of April 1995, when a lone gunman killed 35 people and wounded many others at the convict tourist site, was inevitably reported with reference to Tasmania's dark and violent past, as in the following from the *Independent*: 'other than the island's nineteenth-century colonial massacres of Aborigines, yesterday's tragedy was easily Australia's worst killing of recent times.'[88]

From the mid nineteenth century onwards the idea that indigenous Tasmanians had been exterminated has underpinned a variety of articulations of British superiority. This chapter has shown that such discourses endure into, at the very least, the recent past. This is neatly summarised by the words of former editor of *The Times* and bastion of the Tory establishment William Rees-Mogg in 1998: 'the genocide of the Tasmanian Aboriginals [...] was also part of an historic record which brought the benefits of civilisation to a quarter of the world.'[89]

CONCLUSION

A British Genocide in Tasmania

In all its forms the tragedy unleashed on indigenous Tasmanians was a *British* genocide. Violence was carried out by British men in order to expand and then to defend a British colony. The legal justification of that action was explicitly provided by the British government: indeed the instructions of the Colonial Office stated that the colonial government was obliged to defend the colony with force against indigenous resistance. Furthermore, that resistance was itself a response to an impulse for colonial development that came from London and was sustained by massively increased emigration from Britain at the beginning of the 1820s. Throughout the period of violence the British Colonial Office maintained a commitment to the relentless pursuit of colonial development that was in many ways its cause. The new frontiers were to be defended by force. The British government approved every measure taken by George Arthur's colonial administration in Hobart. It approved the original effort to seek a territorial solution to the enmity between indigenous and settler communities by confining the former to a specific portion of the island; it approved the move to martial law to enforce that proclamation; and it approved 'the Line', an action that was at the very least framed in apocalyptic language and whose participants believed it to be a campaign of extermination.

This is not to say that the Colonial Office did not regret or even abhor the brutality that helped reduce the indigenous population by 90 per cent between first contact and 1830. They did, but were powerless to do anything about it. That powerlessness resulted not from the distances of the early-nineteenth-century Empire, but from the refusal of the British government to face the logic of its own policies. The Colonial Office consistently believed that colonial development was the means of saving indigenous peoples, when it was actually the root of their dislocation and destruction. Indeed, it was in fact widely assumed that if the intentions of British colonialism had been maintained indigenous peoples would have thrived under the 'amity and kindness' of benign imperial rule. Instead they were mistreated by a settler population that, according to the British narrative, were themselves made up of the criminal and the deviant and thus betrayed their British heritage. This was just one of the interpretations of violence in Tasmania that the British constructed in order to protect the idea of colonialism itself.

The destruction wreaked in Van Diemen's Land was reported to the reading public in Britain in a variety of forms. It was consistently referred to in emigration propaganda – both in the press and in the many émigré publications that were designed to lure new emigrants to the English Elysium in Van Diemen's Land. It was commonly believed that the indigenous population was engaged in an irrational vengeful spasm motivated by the memory of the massacre at Risdon Cove and other atrocities. Such a belief maintained a faith in the purity of the British colonial endeavour and betrayed a series of racialised assumptions about the nature of indigenous society and culture.

Indigenous Tasmanians were believed to be 'children of nature', out of step with the modern world. As early as the mid 1820s, the idea that, accordingly, indigenous Tasmanians were doomed to be wiped from the face of the earth was widespread in Britain. Such an extermination discourse was a means of rationalising the genocidal relations between settler and indigenous communities. It was a colonial fantasy that explained away a war for the control of the land as the inevitable clash between the all-powerful British and the helpless 'natives'. Furthermore, the idea that indigenous Tasmanians were being somehow swept away itself became further evidence for Tasmanian inferiority and British majesty. Indeed, such a view was much more

Conclusion

widely entrenched in Britain that it was in the colony itself – where it was understood that what was occurring between 1824 and 1831 was a war for control of the land.

Not that extermination discourse was universal in Britain. Humanitarian voices, often emanating from the abolition movement, rejected the notion that indigenous peoples were necessarily doomed. Instead they argued consistently that colonialism needed to be conducted in the correct spirit in order that it might benefit indigenous populations too. Yet such a vision of the benefit that the colony might bring was itself a vision of destruction, in that it involved the abandonment of all vestiges of indigenous culture. Across the entire political and cultural spectrum, those concerned with colonialism looked forward to a future when indigenous Tasmanian culture was just a memory. I have labelled this a genocidal consensus.

When the attempt to defeat indigenous resistance in Tasmania by force failed, the colonial government turned to a more vigorous attempt at conciliation and made efforts to implement the humanitarian vision in a practical policy. This was enthusiastically supported in Britain. The government absolutely approved of George Robinson's 'Friendly Mission', and colluded in transforming that mission into a campaign of ethnic cleansing from 1832 onwards. That ethnic cleansing was couched in terms of protection – indigenous Tasmanians were moved away from Van Diemen's Land to protect them from the settlers who wished to exterminate them. But they were also moved away to protect them from themselves. Once on Flinders Island, indigenous peoples were to be transformed into a European peasantry. They were to be taught to farm the land like Europeans, to worship God like Europeans. Ultimately, the majority also died from European diseases. The campaign of transformation enacted on Flinders Island amounted to cultural genocide.

If that was a cultural genocide shaped in Hobart, it was enthusiastically received in London. Indeed, the Colonial Office was so taken with Flinders Island as a model of how to deal with indigenous populations that it adopted it as the blueprint for the rest of the Australian colonies. George Augustus Robinson's appointment as chief protector of Aborigines was negotiated through London, and he was charged with responsibility for in effect performing British policy in his new role. That policy was to sedentarise indigenous populations and confine them to small reservations of land. In doing so, those populations would be protected, and more importantly their territory could be developed. Their culture, and the basis of their communal life to date, however, would be destroyed.

The failure of Flinders Island, and of Robinson's efforts at 'protection' on continental Australia, ensured that from the end of the 1830s faith in the possibilities of humanitarian colonial policy declined. Levels of mortality on Flinders Island in particular convinced officials in the Colonial Office that their faith in Robinson's civilising mission had been misplaced. Yet the Colonial Office did not, as a consequence, investigate new policies towards indigenous peoples in Australia. Instead it assumed simply that nothing could be done. The decline of indigenous Tasmanians despite efforts to protect and to save was taken as evidence that such communities were beyond hope. It was believed that they were somehow out of time, and that they could not be reconciled to the modern world. The Colonial Office transferred all responsibility for supervising indigenous peoples' exit from the stage of history to the colonies themselves. The genocidal decline that the British had both caused and presided over then became evidence for the inevitability of indigenous Tasmanians' doom.

In London this new pessimism was reflected in a wider culture. Discourse surrounding indigenous peoples became much more hard-edged from the 1840s onwards and the idea that their decline was unavoidable and preordained became much more firmly fixed in British culture. At its root this idea of inevitability was a means of explaining what we would call genocide today – albeit one that avoided reflection on the inherent violence of the colonial project. But, more than that, it was an articulation of British identity. The inevitable-decline thesis assumed the inferiority of indigenous cultures and therefore the superiority of British culture – indeed the very fact of indigenous

Conclusion

extermination and decline became evidence for this racialised vision of the world.

In the human sciences this idea of extermination was important in a discourse about human origins – to which indigenous Tasmanians and the idea that they had been exterminated were crucial. For those who believed that the 'races of man' were distinct species, catastrophic population decline in Tasmania was evidence for that contention. For those who believed that man was a single species, it became evidence of the cultural differences between different peoples. Furthermore, the sense that Tasmanians had been an isolated population group suggested that they could be understood as a people apart, somehow lost to human development. The idea that Tasmanians allowed scientists direct access to the 'Stone Age' was common. All of these ideas themselves were supported by the idea of genocide – the destruction of Tasmanians was evidence for all of these assumptions. As such, genocide in Tasmania became harnessed within discourses fundamentally concerned with identity – questions of who we are. And because this was such a firmly hierarchical vision of the world, it was not just a question about indigenous peoples' identities, but about ideas of Western, European and British identity too.

This was not only a learned discourse, but one that was spread across much wider culture. It reached its widest audiences through museum display. The skulls and skeletons of indigenous Tasmanians and other peoples were exhibited in museums across Britain. Visitors were invited to look at them and see not only the past but themselves in the present. The 'inferiority' of exterminated Tasmanians spoke to the superiority of Western, European cultures. The very fact of extermination was again used as evidence of that vision of superiority and inferiority. What more indication was needed of the primitiveness of indigenous culture than the fact that the Tasmanians had been exterminated by modern, Western, British man? Thus the idea of extermination was important in underpinning a sense of progress.

These visions of identity and its relation to extermination have been proposed up to the present day. Museum displays continued to contain indigenous Tasmanian remains until very recently, and still exhibit the ephemera of indigenous culture. In debates about the return of indigenous remains from Western institutions many of the assumptions embedded in the nineteenth-century discourse on human origins were (and continue to be) repeated. The idea that indigenous Tasmanians' remains from the 1860s represent some fossils of Stone Age man can be heard often, as can the idea that indigenous Tasmanians had been permanently expunged from the earth, and the human gene pool. Thus, at the beginning of the twenty-first century it appears that understandings of race as a genuinely physical and biological characteristic endure. What is more, the colonial assumption that Western scientists have something more universally important to say than irrational indigenous cultures was also often made in debates about the return of indigenous remains, implying that the discourses that justified the collection of remains in the first instance, and the grotesque power disparities they represented, endure into the present. The idea of extermination remains important in this discourse; moreover, the colonial ideologies that underpinned the destruction in the first instance are shown to survive.

This project began, as I stated at the beginning of the book, with Holocaust studies. In my own wrestling with the legacy of the Holocaust I became concerned that the modern memory culture surrounding the genocide of the Jews had become ritualised and safe, that it did not compel us to ask awkward and searching questions of the British past, but allowed us to dwell in the easy assumptions of British moral and ethical superiority. As a result, I wished to discover for myself some of the brutalities of the British past. What I have found is that the offence of racial extermination is not something just perpetrated by others in the name of maniacal ideologies that are so very different to our own. Genocide does not rely only on assumptions that are very different from those on which our own worlds are based. Genocide

Conclusion

occurred in the British past, and moreover was related to ideas, like the concept of progress, that are familiar to us today. Indeed it is an idea that still underpins some thinking about the British Empire. If this book has a contemporary relevance it is to say that when we think about the British Empire we should remember the violence on which it was based, and when we think about genocide we should remember that it is part of our world too.

Furthermore, genocide in Tasmania is physically present in Britain today – traces of the depopulation of Van Diemen's Land are even embedded in the English landscape. If you walk out of the city of Bath and up the hill towards Widcombe, for example, you will soon come to Bath Abbey cemetery, where if you look closely you will find the ghosts of genocide on the other side of the world. It is an extraordinarily *English* scene, a bucolic landscape with a horizon dotted with Victorian villas built from Bath limestone. In the graveyard set in this English garden you will find the grave of George Augustus Robinson, who died in 1866 (see illustration No. 6). It is an unremarkable tomb, and the engraving upon it has been obscured. But if you look very closely you can clearly make out the remarkable description of Robinson as the 'Pacificator of the Tasmanian Aborigines'. The cemetery guidebook explains with a familiar combination of wonder and despair that Robinson emigrated to Hobart in the 1820s and became 'an intermediary with the natives [...] [he] gained their confidence and convinced them all – the whole Tasmanian population, *an entire race of human beings*' to accompany him off Tasmania to the outlying Flinders Island where he 'presided over their decay'.[1]

Robinson's grave seems thus to represent rather well the somewhat shadowed presence of the destruction of indigenous Tasmanians in both the British past and the British present. The grave is obscured by undergrowth, its inscription difficult to discern. It is therefore both present and almost not, both there and not there, almost consumed by the land in which it lies. In that sense, although it can't always be seen, it has become part of the nation itself. In a variety of ways – not all of which are palatable – it is indeed a part of who 'we' are.

NOTES

INTRODUCTION

1   For a discussion of the development of British Holocaust memory see Andy Pearce, 'The development of Holocaust consciousness in contemporary Britain, 1979–2001', *Holocaust Studies: A Journal of Culture and History* xiv/2 (2008), pp. 71–94.
2   See for example Tony Blair's autobiography, in which he describes the evolution of his thinking on foreign policy, which was framed through an understanding of the Holocaust and genocide in Rwanda as examples of the failure of non-intervention. Tony Blair, *A Journey* (London: Hutchinson, 2010), p. 63.
3   Tom Lawson and James Jordan (eds), *The Memory of the Holocaust in Australia* (London: Vallentine Mitchell, 2008).
4   Of course, this interaction has been considered by other scholars. See: Neil Levi, '"No sensible comparison"? The place of the Holocaust in Australia's history wars', *History and Memory* xix/1 (2007), pp. 124–56; A. Dirk Moses, 'Genocide and Holocaust consciousness in Australia', *History Compass* i/1 (2003), pp. 1–11.
5   When referring to the original inhabitants of the island known as Tasmania I have used the phrase '*indigenous* Tasmanians', in order to reflect the fact that the term 'Tasmanians' on its own acknowledges no differentiation and is entirely imposed. However, the qualifying 'indigenous' is sometimes dropped when I am referring to and exploring the ideas of others, because that term was used in the past.
6   The Secretary of State for the Colonies was also referred to as the 'Colonial Secretary'. However, the same term was used for an official based in Hobart who was involved in the administration of the colony. To avoid confusion, in this book the term 'Colonial Secretary' is only ever used to refer to the latter. The British government minister is referred to as 'the Secretary of State for the Colonies', or 'the Secretary of State' for short.
7   George Murray to George Arthur, 5 November 1830, in A.G.L. Shaw (ed.), *Van Diemen's Land: Copies of All Correspondence between Lieutenant Governor Arthur and His Majesty's Secretary of State for the Colonies, on the Subject of the Military Operations Lately Carried Out against the Aboriginal Inhabitants of Van Diemen's Land* (originally published by the House of Commons, 23 September 1831; facs. ed., Hobart, Tas.: Tasmanian Historical Association, 1971), p. 55.

8   Henry Reynolds, *An Indelible Stain? The Question of Genocide in Australia's History* (Ringwood, Vic.: Penguin Australia, 2001), p. 4 (emphasis added).
9   See Damien Short, 'Australia: A continuing genocide?', *Journal of Genocide Research* xii/1–2 (2010), pp. 45–68.

ONE · DEFINING TERMS

1   Henry Reynolds, *A History of Tasmania* (Melbourne, Vic.: Cambridge University Press, 2012), p. 5.
2   Van Diemen's Land was the name given to the territory proclaimed as part of the British Empire from 1803. In the first instance this was not a separate colony but part of the larger colony of New South Wales. In 1825 Van Diemen's Land became an independent colony. In 1856 it was awarded self-government and renamed Tasmania. Throughout this book, for reasons of style more than anything else, the terms will be used interchangeably.
3   Where I have named individuals from the indigenous communities in Tasmania, I have tried to use the names by which, as far as we can tell, those people identified themselves, or at least by which they were most familiarly known. Of course, by doing this it may be that I inadvertently repeat one of the means by which settler colonialism deprived indigenous peoples of their identity. For the most part I have followed the names used in Lyndall Ryan, *Tasmanian Aborigines: A History Since 1803* (Sydney, NSW: Allen & Unwin, 2012).
4   For a history of one enduring indigenous Tasmanian community see Rebe Taylor, *Unearthed: The Aboriginal Tasmanians of Kangaroo Island* (Kent Town, SA: Wakefield Press, 2002).
5   James Boyce, *Van Diemen's Land* (Melbourne, Vic.: Black, Inc., 2010), p. 4. See elsewhere in Boyce's book for a detailed discussion of the Tasmanian environment and its impact on the history of the colony.
6   For a detailed history of how indigenous Australians, including Tasmanians, managed their environment, see Bill Gammage, *The Biggest Estate on Earth: How Aborigines Made Australia* (Sydney, NSW: Allen & Unwin, 2011), especially pp. 157–86 on the use of fire to dictate land use.
7   A quotation from Jacques Labillardière, a naturalist accompanying d'Entrecasteaux, found in John West, *The History of Tasmania, Vol. II* (1852; Launceston, Tas.: J.S. Waddell, 1966), p. 4.
8   See the description repeated in James Bonwick, *The Last of the Tasmanians, or, The Black War of Van Diemen's Land* (London: Sampson Low, Son & Marston, 1870), p. 23.
9   For descriptions of the indigenous population by the first British settlers, such as they are, see Lyndall Ryan, *The Aboriginal Tasmanians* (Sydney, NSW: Allen & Unwin, 1996), p. 75.

Notes

10 Henry Reynolds, *Fate of a Free People* (Camberwell, Vic.: Penguin Australia, 2004), p. 87.
11 For discussions of the development and application of the concept of *Terra nullius* in Australia, see: Henry Reynolds, *The Law of the Land* (Ringwood, Vic.: Penguin Australia, 1992), p. 32; Andrew Fitzmaurice, 'The genealogy of *Terra nullius*', *Australian Historical Studies* xxxviii/129 (2007), pp. 1-15.
12 Ryan, *Tasmanian Aborigines*, pp. 8-14.
13 Ibid., p. 42.
14 Ibid., p. 13. It is difficult to establish the European population of Van Diemen's Land at this point too. Although we can say with certainty for example that there were 49 individuals involved in the establishment of the settlement at Risdon Cove, there was also a sizeable group on Tasmania's outlying islands who might be described as being involved in an informal colonisation. See Boyce, *Van Diemen's Land*, pp. 15-20.
15 Reynolds, *History*, p. 14.
16 Ryan, *Tasmanian Aborigines*, p. 49.
17 Boyce, *Van Diemen's Land*, p. 59.
18 West, *History* (1966), p. 14.
19 Ryan, *Tasmanian Aborigines*, p. 57.
20 Ibid., p. 59.
21 Ibid., pp. 58-68.
22 West, *History* (1966), p. 11.
23 The Colonial Secretary's Office in Hobart, especially after 1826, collected all of the correspondence that passed through it in relation to the 'Aboriginals'. The first volume of this documentary collection contains over 1,000 pages of letters describing attacks on settlers and their property. This correspondence includes threats to abandon the frontier if the government does not provide protection, such as the memorial dated 24 September 1827 sent by the 'land and stock holders and free inhabitants of the county of Cornwall', which threatened the 'abandonment' of properties on the frontier. See AOT CSO 1/316/7578/1, ff. 75-8.
24 Previously Ryan had identified 700 deaths: see John Connor, *The Australian Frontier Wars 1788-1838* (Sydney, NSW: University of New South Wales Press, 2002), p. 87. Recently, however, she has revised that to a figure of 878. See Ryan, *Tasmanian Aborigines*, p. 143.
25 For the difficulty of documenting with precision indigenous deaths see Graeme Calder, *Levee, Line and Martial Law: A History of the Dispossession of the Mairremmener People of Van Diemen's Land* (Launceston, Tas.: Fullers Bookshop, 2010), p. 174.
26 Flinders Island is compared to a gulag in Benjamin Madley, 'Patterns of frontier genocide', *Journal of Genocide Research* vi/2 (2004), pp. 167-92.
27 Henry Melville, *The History of the Island of Van Diemen's Land: From the Year 1824 to 1835* (London: Smith, Elder & Co., 1835), pp. 83-4.

28 West, *History* (1966), p. 16.
29 Ibid., p. 96.
30 Clive Turnbull, *Black War: The Extermination of the Tasmanian Aborigines* (Melbourne, Vic.: Cheshire-Lansdown, 1948), p. 3.
31 V.G. Kiernan, *The Lords of Human Kind: European Attitudes to the Outside World in the Imperial Age* (London: Penguin, 1972), p. 277.
32 For one of the most recent see Ben Kiernan, *Blood and Soil: A World History of Genocide and Extermination from Sparta to Darfur* (New Haven, CT: Yale University Press, 2009), pp. 263–80.
33 Henry Reynolds, *An Indelible Stain? The Question of Genocide in Australia's History* (Ringwood, Vic.: Penguin Australia, 2001), p. 51. Reynolds is particularly critical of Frank Chalk and Kurt Jonassohn (eds), *The History and Sociology of Genocide* (New Haven, CT: Yale University Press, 1990).
34 Reynolds, *Indelible Stain*, p. 77.
35 Bain Attwood, *Telling the Truth about Aboriginal History* (Crows Nest, NSW: Allen & Unwin, 2005), p. 42.
36 Boyce, *Van Diemen's Land*, p. 3.
37 Ryan, *Tasmanian Aborigines*, p. 58.
38 See: Calder, *Levee, Line and Martial Law*; Ian McFarlane, *Beyond Awakening: The Aboriginal Tribes of North West Tasmania* (Launceston, Tas.: Fullers Bookshop, 2008).
39 See for example Cassandra Pybus, *Community of Thieves* (Port Melbourne, Vic.: Minerva Australia, 1992).
40 Boyce, *Van Diemen's Land*, p. 272.
41 Ryan, *Tasmanian Aborigines*, p. 103.
42 Neville Meaney, '"In history's page": Identity and myth', in Deryck M. Schreuder and Stuart Ward (eds), *Australia's Empire* (Oxford: Oxford University Press, 2009), p. 386.
43 Reynolds, *Fate of a Free People*, p. 87. See also Henry Reynolds, 'Genocide in Tasmania', in A. Dirk Moses (ed.), *Genocide and Settler Society: Frontier Violence and Stolen Indigenous Children in Australian History* (New York, NY: Berghahn, 2004), p. 139.
44 Niall Ferguson, *Empire: How Britain Made the Modern World* (London: Penguin, 2003), p. 108.
45 Bonwick, *Last of the Tasmanians*, p. 31.
46 Hannah Arendt, *The Origins of Totalitarianism* (New York, NY: Schocken Books, 2004), pp. 242–86.
47 West, *History* (1966), p. 95.
48 See for example: Kiernan, *Lords of Human Kind*; Turnbull, *Black War*.
49 Stuart Macintyre and Anna Clark, *The History Wars* (Melbourne, Vic.: Melbourne University Press, 2003), p. 124.
50 Ryan, *The Aboriginal Tasmanians*, p. 103.
51 Reynolds, *Indelible Stain*, p. 73.

Notes

52 For a discussion of the issue of intent with relation to Australia and Tasmania see ibid., p. 27. For a critique of Reynolds's approach to the question of genocide see John Docker, 'The "great Australian silence" and the "indelible stain": Genocide denial, historical consciousness, and the honour of nations and empires' (forthcoming).
53 National Inquiry into the Separation of Aboriginal and Torres Strait Islander Children from Their Families, *Bringing Them Home* (1997), p. 190.
54 A term coined by historian Geoffrey Blainey in 1993 to refer to overly critical accounts of Australian history.
55 See Macintyre and Clark, *History Wars*. For a specific rebuttal of Windschuttle's thesis, see Robert Manne (ed.), *Whitewash: On Keith Windschuttle's Fabrication of Aboriginal History* (Melbourne, Vic.: Black, Inc., 2003).
56 Quoted in Neil Levi, '"No sensible comparison"? The place of the Holocaust in Australia's history wars', *History and Memory* xix/1 (2007), p. 140.
57 Inga Clendinnen, *Dancing with Strangers: The True History of the Meeting of the British First Fleet and the Aboriginal Australians, 1788* (London: Canongate, 2005).
58 Attwood, *Telling the Truth*, p. 103.
59 Quoted in ibid., p. 88.
60 Mark Levene, *Genocide in the Age of the Nation State, Vol. II: The Rise of the West and the Coming of Genocide* (London: I.B.Tauris, 2005), p. 13.
61 A. Dirk Moses, 'An Antipodean genocide? The origins of the genocidal moment in the colonization of Australia', *Journal of Genocide Research* ii/1 (2000), pp. 89–106.
62 Alison Palmer, *Colonial Genocide* (Adelaide, SA: Crawford House Publishing, 2000), p. 51.
63 For the genocidal history of the Van Diemen's Land Company see McFarlane, *Beyond Awakening*.
64 For example, in June 1838 a group of men, women and children from the Weraerai people were killed in what is known as the 'Myall Creek massacre'. Uniquely, seven of the perpetrators were identified and hanged for their crimes.
65 Colin Tatz, 'Genocide in Australia', *Journal of Genocide Research* i/3 (1999), p. 318. See also Colin Tatz, 'Genocide in Australia: By accident or design?', *Indigenous Human Rights and History: Occasional Papers* i/1 (2011).
66 Levene, *Rise of the West*, p. 21. Levene discusses the work of Dirk Moses here.
67 Palmer, *Colonial Genocide*, p. 35.
68 Attwood, *Telling the Truth*, p. 91. See also p. 220, n. 1.
69 Quoted in A. Dirk Moses, 'Empire, colony, genocide: Keywords and the philosophy of history', in A. Dirk Moses (ed.), *Empire, Colony, Genocide: Conquest, Occupation, and Subaltern Resistance in World History* (New York, NY: Berghahn, 2010), p. 9.

70 Bain Attwood, in *Telling the Truth about Aboriginal History*, suggests that genocide is not necessary for this conceptualisation of the indigenous experience of settler colonialism, but he does not offer an adequate account of what might (in conceptual terms) replace it.

71 Norbert Finzsch, '"...Extirpate or remove that vermine": Genocide, biological warfare, and settler imperialism in the eighteenth and early nineteenth century', *Journal of Genocide Research* x/2 (2008), pp. 215–32.

72 This was a thesis put forward in N.G. Butlin, *Our Original Aggression: Aboriginal Populations of Southeastern Australia 1788–1850* (Sydney, NSW: Allen & Unwin, 1983), and subsequently rejected in Judy Campbell, *Invisible Invaders: Smallpox and Other Diseases in Aboriginal Australia 1780–1880* (Melbourne, Vic.: Melbourne University Press, 2002). More recently Campbell's thesis has been called into question. See Craig Mear, 'The origin of the smallpox outbreak in Sydney in 1789', *Journal of the Royal Australian Historical Society* xciv/1 (2008), pp. 1–14.

73 Tony Barta, 'Relations of genocide: Land and lives in the colonization of Australia', in Isidor Wallimann and Michael N. Dobkowski (eds), *Genocide and the Modern Age: Etiology and Case Studies of Mass Death* (Westport, CT: Greenwood Press, 1987), pp. 237–51. Barta also notes that the imperial British government understood the destructiveness of their policies in Tony Barta, '"They appear actually to vanish from the face of the earth." Aborigines and the European project in Australia Felix', *Journal of Genocide Research* x/4 (2008), pp. 519–39.

74 See Patrick Brantlinger, *Dark Vanishings: Discourse on the Extinction of Primitive Races 1800–1930* (Ithaca, NY: Cornell University Press, 2003).

75 See for example Linda Melvern, *A People Betrayed: The Role of the West in Rwanda's Genocide* (London: Zed Books, 2000). See pp. 230–1 for a discussion of the British Foreign Office's reluctance to use the term genocide.

76 Donald Bloxham, *The Great Game of Genocide: Imperialism, Nationalism and the Destruction of the Ottoman Armenians* (Oxford: Oxford University Press, 2005), pp. 207–34.

77 Quoted in Reynolds, *Indelible Stain*, p. 11.

78 For a similar discussion see Tatz, 'Genocide in Australia', p. 316.

79 For an example of the possibilities of this project see Wendy Lower, *Nazi Empire-Building and the Holocaust in the Ukraine* (Chapel Hill, NC: University of North Carolina Press, 2005).

80 See Tom Lawson, *Debates on the Holocaust* (Manchester: Manchester University Press, 2010).

81 This articulation owes much to Bob Chase, 'History and poststructuralism: Hayden White and Fredric Jameson', in Bill Schwarz (ed.), *The Expansion of England: Race, Ethnicity and Cultural History* (London: Routledge, 1996), pp. 61–91.

Notes

82 Deryck M. Schreuder and Stuart Ward, 'Introduction: What became of Australia's empire?', in Deryck M. Schreuder and Stuart Ward (eds), *Australia's Empire* (Oxford: Oxford University Press, 2009), p. 22.

TWO · GENOCIDE IN VAN DIEMEN'S LAND

1 Henry Reynolds, *Fate of a Free People* (Camberwell, Vic.: Penguin Australia, 2004), p. 87. See also Henry Reynolds, 'Genocide in Tasmania', in A. Dirk Moses (ed.), *Genocide and Settler Society: Frontier Violence and Stolen Indigenous Children in Australian History* (New York, NY: Berghahn, 2004), p. 139.
2 John West, *The History of Tasmania, Vol. II* (1852; Launceston, Tas.: J.S. Waddell, 1966), p. 96.
3 James Boyce, *Van Diemen's Land* (Melbourne, Vic.: Black, Inc., 2010), pp. 35–6.
4 Knopwood's diary entry, 28 November 1806, in Robert Knopwood, *The Diary of the Reverend Robert Knopwood 1803–1838*, ed. Mary Nicholls (Hobart, Tas.: Tasmanian Historical Research Association, 1977), p. 126.
5 James Boyce, *God's Own Country? The Anglican Church and Tasmanian Aborigines* (Hobart, Tas.: Social Action and Research Centre, 2001), p. 1.
6 Lyndall Ryan, *Tasmanian Aborigines: A History Since 1803* (Sydney, NSW: Allen & Unwin, 2012), p. 48.
7 According to the testimony of Edward White, a convict, to the Aborigines Committee in March 1830. See A.G.L. Shaw (ed.), *Van Diemen's Land: Copies of All Correspondence between Lieutenant Governor Arthur and His Majesty's Secretary of State for the Colonies, on the Subject of the Military Operations Lately Carried Out against the Aboriginal Inhabitants of Van Diemen's Land* (originally published by the House of Commons, 23 September 1831; facs. ed., Hobart, Tas.: Tasmanian Historical Association, 1971), p. 53.
8 The original eyewitness testimony was from Lieutenant Moore, who sent a letter to Governor Collins reporting the violence. See Graeme Calder, *Levee, Line and Martial Law: A History of the Dispossession of the Mairremmener People of Van Diemen's Land* (Launceston, Tas.: Fullers Bookshop, 2010), p. 233.
9 Knopwood's diary entry, 3 May 1804, in Knopwood, *Diary*, p. 51.
10 Knopwood's statement, 'Minutes of evidence taken before the Committee for the Affairs of the Aborigines, 11 March 1830', in Shaw (ed.), *Van Diemen's Land*, pp. 52–3.
11 Edward White's testimony, 'Minutes of evidence taken before the Committee for the Affairs of the Aborigines, 16 March 1830', in Shaw (ed.), *Van Diemen's Land*, pp. 53–4.
12 Quoted in Sharon Morgan, *Land Settlement in Early Tasmania: Creating an Antipodean England* (Cambridge: Cambridge University Press, 1992), p. 145.

13 John Thomas Bigge, *Report of the Commissioner of Inquiry on the State of Agriculture and Trade in the Colony of New South Wales* (1823), p. 83.
14 'Report of the Aborigines Committee, 19 March 1830', in Shaw (ed.), *Van Diemen's Land*, p. 38.
15 George Murray to George Arthur, 5 November 1830, in Shaw (ed.), *Van Diemen's Land*, pp. 55–6.
16 See Robinson's diary entry, 29 November 1829, in N.J.B. Plomley (ed.), *Friendly Mission: The Tasmanian Journals and Papers of George Augustus Robinson 1829–1934* (2nd ed., Hobart, Tas.: Queen Victoria Museum and Art Gallery and Quintus Publishing, 2008), pp. 99–100.
17 Cassandra Pybus makes a similar interpretation in *Community of Thieves* (Port Melbourne, Vic.: Minerva Australia, 1992), p. 38.
18 See Henry Reynolds, *The Law of the Land* (Ringwood, Vic.: Penguin Australia, 1992), p. 13, and Reynolds, *Fate of a Free People*, p. 125.
19 Reynolds, *Fate of a Free People*, p. 88.
20 Boyce, *Van Diemen's Land*, p. 63.
21 Knopwood's diary entry, 19 May 1807, in Knopwood, *Diary*, p. 132.
22 James Bonwick, *The Last of the Tasmanians, or, The Black War of Van Diemen's Land* (London: Sampson Low, Son & Marston, 1870), p. 44.
23 Boyce, *Van Diemen's Land*, p. 84.
24 For a summary of a number of reported acts of violence see Lyndall Ryan, 'List of multiple killings of Aborigines in Tasmania: 1804–35', *Online Encyclopedia of Mass Violence*. Available at http://www.massviolence.org/List-of-multiple-killings-of-Aborigines-in-Tasmania-1804?cs=print (accessed 29 August 2013).
25 Bonwick, *Last of the Tasmanians*, pp. 39–40.
26 Quoted in 'Report of the Aborigines Committee, 19 March 1830', in Shaw (ed.), *Van Diemen's Land*, p. 36.
27 'Report of the Aborigines Committee, 19 March 1830', in Shaw (ed.), *Van Diemen's Land*, p. 36.
28 Knopwood's diary entry, 15 November 1815, in Knopwood, *Diary*, p. 217.
29 John Connor, *The Australian Frontier Wars 1788–1838* (Sydney, NSW: University of New South Wales Press, 2002), p. 85.
30 Ryan, *Tasmanian Aborigines*, p. 61.
31 Lyndall Ryan, *The Aboriginal Tasmanians* (Sydney, NSW: Allen & Unwin, 1996), p. 79.
32 *Morning Post*, 14 November 1821.
33 George William Evans, *History and Description of the Present State of Van Diemen's Land, Containing Important Hints to Emigrants* (London: John Souter, 1824), p. 25.
34 Bigge, *Report of the Commissioner*, p. 25.
35 Ryan, *Tasmanian Aborigines*, p. 25.
36 West, *History* (1966), p. 12.

37 Bigge, *Report of the Commissioner*, p. 18.
38 Eric Richards, *Britannia's Children: Emigration from England, Scotland, Wales and Ireland since 1600* (London: Hambledon Press, 2004), pp. 85–6.
39 A.G.L. Shaw, 'British attitudes to the colonies', *Journal of British Studies* ix/1 (1969), p. 86.
40 John Helder Wedge, *The Diaries of John Helder Wedge*, eds Justice Crawford, W.F. Ellis and G.H. Stancombe (Hobart, Tas.: Royal Society of Tasmania, 1962), p. xiv.
41 See for instance the *Lancaster Gazette*, 13 November 1819.
42 *Hampshire Telegraph*, 29 December 1823.
43 Edward Curr, *An Account of the Colony of Van Diemen's Land* (London: George Cowie & Co., 1824), p. 11.
44 *The Times*, 5 October 1824.
45 If the emigrants' guides of the 1820s were aimed at men, by the 1830s there was a clear sense that young women were needed in the colony. See James Bischoff, *Sketch of the History of Van Diemen's Land and an Account of the Van Diemen's Land Company* (London: John Richardson, 1832), p. 90.
46 Charles Jeffreys, *Van Diemen's Land: Geographical and Descriptive Delineations of the Island* (London: J.M. Richardson, 1820), p. v.
47 Mrs Augustus Prinsep, *The Journal of a Voyage from Calcutta to Van Diemen's Land, Comprising a Description of That Colony During a Six Months' Residence* (London: Smith, Elder & Co., 1833), p. 54.
48 See for instance Curr, *Account of the Colony*.
49 Jeffreys, *Van Diemen's Land*, p. 67.
50 Morgan, *Land Settlement*, p. 163.
51 Evans, *History and Description*, p. 25.
52 Prinsep, *The Journal of a Voyage*, p. 79.
53 *Hampshire Telegraph*, 29 December 1823.
54 Charles Darwin, *The Descent of Man and Selection in Relation to Sex* (1871; London: Penguin, 2004), pp. 212–21.
55 Henry Reynolds, *An Indelible Stain? The Question of Genocide in Australia's History* (Ringwood, Vic.: Penguin Australia, 2001), p. 144.
56 See Patrick Brantlinger, *Dark Vanishings: Discourse on the Extinction of Primitive Races 1800–1930* (Ithaca, NY: Cornell University Press, 2003) for a brilliant discussion of these discourses in their later form.
57 Ryan, *The Aboriginal Tasmanians*, p. 88.
58 Robert Hughes describes Arthur's Van Diemen's Land as the 'closest thing to a totalitarian society that would ever exist in the British Empire'. His words are quoted in Piers Brendon, *The Decline and Fall of the British Empire* (London: Vintage, 2008), p. 68.
59 Peter Chapman, 'Introduction', in Peter Chapman (ed.), *Historical Records of Australia, Resumed Series III, Despatches and Papers Relating to the*

History of Tasmania, Volume VII, January to December 1828 (Canberra, ACT: Commonwealth Parliamentary Library, 1997), p. 1.
60 William Sorell to the Colonial Office, 3 May 1817, ML CY 2343.
61 James Stephen to George Arthur, n.d. [1824], ML CYA 2164.
62 James Stephen to George Arthur, 31 July 1824, ML CYA 2164.
63 Paul Knaplund, *James Stephen and the British Colonial System 1813–1847* (Madison, WI: University of Wisconsin Press, 1953), p. 25.
64 These figures are contained in the report sent on George Arthur's departure from Van Diemen's Land. See House of Commons, *Copy of a Despatch from Colonel Arthur to Lord Glenelg Dated the 29th October 1836* (1837), p. 22.
65 Morgan, *Land Settlement*, p. 19.
66 House of Commons, *Copy of a Despatch*, p. 25.
67 Morgan, *Land Settlement*, p. 59.
68 Robert Montgomery Martin, *History of the Colonies of the British Empire in the West Indies, South America, North America, Asia, Australasia, Africa and Europe* (London: W.H. Allen & Co., 1843), p. 453.
69 Ryan, *Tasmanian Aborigines*, p. 79.
70 Reynolds, *Fate of a Free People*, p. 90.
71 Henry Bathurst to Ralph Darling, 14 July 1825, in Chapman (ed.), *Historical Records*, p. 21 (emphasis added). This instruction was first passed to Governor Ralph Darling of New South Wales and then relayed to Governor Arthur in Hobart.
72 Connor, *Australian Frontier Wars*, p. 65.
73 Reynolds, *Fate of a Free People*, p. 92.
74 Morgan, *Land Settlement*, p. 154.
75 For an account of this see Ryan, *Tasmanian Aborigines*, pp. 77–8.
76 Statistics quoted in Connor, *Australian Frontier Wars*, p. 85.
77 AOT CSO 1/316/7578/1, f. 48.
78 Gilbert Robertson's testimony, 'Minutes of evidence taken before the Committee for the Affairs of the Aborigines, 3 March 1830', in Shaw (ed.), *Van Diemen's Land*, pp. 47–8.
79 Morgan, *Land Settlement*, p. 148.
80 See for example Robinson's diary entry, 16 June 1830, in Plomley (ed.), *Friendly Mission*, p. 206.
81 Reynolds, *Fate of a Free People*, p. 97.
82 Colin Tatz, 'Genocide in Australia: By accident or design?', *Indigenous Human Rights and History: Occasional Papers* i/1 (2011).
83 Reynolds, *Fate of a Free People*, p. 98.
84 Ibid., p. 100.
85 Ryan, *Tasmanian Aborigines*, p. 96.
86 Government notice, 29 November 1827, in Shaw (ed.), *Van Diemen's Land*, p. 21.
87 George Arthur to Viscount Goderich, 10 January 1828, in Shaw (ed.), *Van Diemen's Land*, p. 3.

Notes

88 Ryan, *The Aboriginal Tasmanians*, p. 103.
89 See 'Proclamation, 15 April 1828, by His Excellency, Colonel George Arthur', in Shaw (ed.), *Van Diemen's Land*, pp. 23–4.
90 See George Arthur to William Huskisson, 17 April 1828, quoted in Reynolds, 'Genocide in Tasmania', p. 134.
91 'Proclamation, 15 April 1828, by His Excellency, Colonel George Arthur', in Shaw (ed.), *Van Diemen's Land*, pp. 23–4.
92 William Huskisson to George Arthur, 6 May 1828, TNA: PRO CO 408/5.
93 George Murray to George Arthur, 29 August 1828, TNA: PRO CO 408/5.
94 George Murray to George Arthur, 20 February 1829, in Shaw (ed.), *Van Diemen's Land*, p. 8.
95 Reynolds, *Fate of a Free People*, p. 111.
96 This is the phrase used by Thomas Anstey, police magistrate, in communication with George Arthur, 30 June 1829, AOT CSO 1/316/7578/7 (no folio No.).
97 'Report of the Aborigines Committee, 19 March 1830', in Shaw (ed.), *Van Diemen's Land*, p. 45.
98 'Instructions from Arthur to brigade commanders on the establishment of martial law, 3 November 1828. Contained in despatch sent to the Colonial Office in March 1830', TNA: PRO CO 280/24 (emphasis added).
99 See Jorgenson's report, 18 June 1829, AOT CSO 1/316/7578/7, f. 275 (emphasis added).
100 'Report of the proceedings of a journey of observation by five armed prisoners of the crown forming a party for the pursuit and capture of the Aboriginal tribes, under the charge of Constable George James and accompanied by Jorgen Jorgenson', AOT CSO 1/316/7578/7, f. 279.
101 Batman's report, 7 September 1828, AOT CSO 1/316/7578/7, ff. 142–5. It is also quoted in Alastair H. Campbell, *John Batman and the Aborigines* (Malmsbury, Vic.: Kibble Books, 1987), p. 31.
102 George Murray to George Arthur, 25 August 1829, in Shaw (ed.), *Van Diemen's Land*, p. 14.
103 Ibid.
104 Clive Turnbull, *Black War: The Extermination of the Tasmanian Aborigines* (Melbourne, Vic.: Cheshire-Lansdown, 1948), p. 87.
105 See 'Report of the Aborigines Committee, 19 March 1830', in Shaw (ed.), *Van Diemen's Land*, p. 42.
106 Peter Chapman, 'Introduction', in Chapman (ed.), *Historical Records*, p. xxxvii.
107 Henry Melville, *The History of the Island of Van Diemen's Land: From the Year 1824 to 1835* (London: Smith, Elder & Co., 1835), p. 26.
108 George Arthur to George Murray, 15 April 1830, in Shaw (ed.), *Van Diemen's Land*, pp. 15–17.
109 'Report of the Aborigines Committee, 19 March 1830', in Shaw (ed.), *Van Diemen's Land*, p. 42.

110 George Murray to George Arthur, 5 November 1830, in Shaw (ed.), *Van Diemen's Land*, p. 55.
111 Ibid.
112 Arthur wrote to Murray on 20 November 1830, for example, explaining the necessity in his eyes of the introduction of 'the Line'. He describes his personal disappointment, or sense of betrayal, at the absconding of Umarrah (whom Arthur referred to as 'Eummarrah'), who had been held by the colonial authorities for the previous two years. Arthur explained his personal belief that 'Eummarrah' *'understood* that the wishes of the government were those of kindness and benevolence towards his race' and yet still he escaped (emphasis added). For Arthur this was confirmation of the essentially 'treacherous character of these savages'. See Shaw (ed.), *Van Diemen's Land*, p. 59.
113 Reynolds, *Fate of a Free People*, p. 117.
114 For example, Jorgenson urged throughout the period of the roving parties that more coordinated action was required. See Jorgenson's report, 29 July 1829, AOT CSO 1/316/7578/7, ff. 319–21.
115 Melville, *History of the Island*, p. 99.
116 Bonwick, *Last of the Tasmanians*, p. 137.
117 *Hobart Town Gazette*, 10 September 1830.
118 Knopwood's diary entry, 25 October 1830, in Knopwood, *Diary*, p. 562.
119 See George Arthur to George Murray, 20 November 1830, in Shaw (ed.), *Van Diemen's Land*, p. 59.
120 Knopwood's diary entry, 25 October 1830, in Knopwood, *Diary*, p. 566.
121 George Arthur to Viscount Goderich, 27 August 1831, TNA: PRO CO 280/29.
122 N.J.B. Plomley, *Jorgen Jorgenson and the Aborigines of Van Diemen's Land* (Hobart, Tas.: Blubber Head Press, 1991), p. 99.
123 Reynolds, *Fate of a Free People*, p. 112.
124 For details of the correspondence between George Murray and George Arthur, 23 April 1830, and for this interpretation, see Reynolds, *Fate of a Free People*, pp. 115–16.
125 George Murray's successor at the Colonial Office was Frederick John Robinson, 1st Viscount Goderich, the former prime minister.
126 Indeed, James Stephen testified that he had never heard any Secretary of State criticise Arthur's handling of Van Diemen's Land. See James Stephen to George Arthur, 8 July 1835, ML CYA 2164.
127 Ian McFarlane, *Beyond Awakening: The Aboriginal Tribes of North West Tasmania* (Launceston, Tas.: Fullers Bookshop, 2008), p. 65.
128 James Bischoff, *A Comprehensive History of the Woollen and Worsted Manufactures and the Natural and Commercial History of Sheep* (London: Smith, Elder & Co., 1842), p. 92.
129 Curr, *Account of the Colony*.

Notes

130 Details of the terms in which the company was established are outlined in Henry Bathurst to Edward Curr, 15 April 1825, in Henry Bathurst and House of Commons, *Van Diemens Land: Return to an Address of the Honourable House of Commons, Dated 10th May 1825; for Minutes of the Intended Arrangements between Earl Bathurst... and the Proposed Van Diemens Land Company* (1825).
131 See for example Annual Report of the Van Diemen's Land Company, 1826, ML FM 4/1564.
132 Edward Curr argued that the lands were uninhabited in his correspondence with Bathurst. See Edward Curr to Henry Bathurst, 22 March 1835, in Bathurst and House of Commons, *Van Diemens Land*, p. 1. See also McFarlane, *Beyond Awakening*, p. 70, for a discussion.
133 Quoted in McFarlane, *Beyond Awakening*, p. 77.
134 Boyce, *Van Diemen's Land*, p. 202.
135 Kerry Pink, *Winds of Change: A History of Woolnorth* (Timaru, New Zealand: Van Diemen's Land Company, 2003), p. 26. For a narrative of the massacre see also Ryan, *Tasmanian Aborigines*, p. 167.
136 See Robinson's diary entry, 10 August 1830, in Plomley (ed.), *Friendly Mission*, p. 230.
137 Pybus, *Community of Thieves*, p. 39.
138 See McFarlane, *Beyond Awakening*, p. 101, where McFarlane argues that Edward Curr was at odds with company policy.
139 Directors of the Van Diemen's Land Company to Edward Curr, 11 April 1829, ML FM 4/1567 (despatch No. 93).
140 'Mr Goldie's letter', 23 February 1830, AOT CSO 1/316/7578/17, f. 115.
141 Annual report of the Van Diemen's Land Company, 1831, ML FM 4/1564.
142 Pybus, *Community of Thieves*, p. 38.
143 Directors of the Van Diemen's Land Company to Edward Curr, 2 June 1831, ML FM 4/1567 (despatch No. 14).
144 Viscount Goderich to George Arthur, 17 June 1831, TNA: PRO CO 408/7.
145 Of course, many settlers were from other parts of Britain.
146 Quoted in Gwyneth and Hume Dow, *Landfall in Van Diemen's Land: The Steels' Quest for Greener Pastures* (Footscray, Vic.: Footprint, 1990), p. 44.
147 Letter of 21 February 1827, quoted in Dow and Dow, *Landfall*, p. 45.
148 Wedge, *Diaries*, pp. 39, 48, 55, 57, 62.
149 Ryan, *Tasmanian Aborigines*, p. 66.
150 John Helder Wedge to the Colonial Secretary, 30 August 1830, AOT CSO 1/316/7578/17, f. 151.
151 John Helder Wedge to the Colonial Secretary, 30 January 1834, AOT CSO 1/316/7578/17, f. 315.
152 Viscount Goderich to George Arthur, 17 June 1831, TNA: PRO CO 408/7.

THREE · ETHNIC CLEANSING

1. James Boyce, *Van Diemen's Land* (Melbourne, Vic.: Black, Inc., 2010), p. 278.
2. Lyndall Ryan, *The Aboriginal Tasmanians* (Sydney, NSW: Allen & Unwin, 1996), p. 124.
3. Indeed, Henry Reynolds argues that Robinson was really the conduit for an indigenous political action in which people like Truganini recognised that he represented the only hope for the survival of their peoples and negotiated accordingly. See Henry Reynolds, *Fate of a Free People* (Camberwell, Vic.: Penguin Australia, 2004), pp. 136–42.
4. For details of Robinson's life in Britain and his first years in Van Diemen's Land see Vivienne Rae-Ellis, *Black Robinson: Protector of the Aborigines* (Melbourne, Vic.: Melbourne University Press, 1996), pp. 3–18.
5. Quotation from Robinson's proposed book on his experiences in Tasmania, quoted in N.J.B. Plomley (ed.), *Friendly Mission: The Tasmanian Journals and Papers of George Augustus Robinson 1829–1934* (2nd ed., Hobart, Tas.: Queen Victoria Museum and Art Gallery and Quintus Publishing, 2008), p. 51.
6. Robinson's motivations have been the subject of some controversy. Historians such as N.J.B. Plomley and Lyndall Ryan urge that we must take seriously his desires to save and that he was motivated by philanthropy. Plomley argues that he 'deserves our remembrance for what he did'. See Plomley (ed.), *Friendly Mission*, p. 11. Ryan cannot understand why he is so often condemned. See Lyndall Ryan, 'Historians, friendly mission and the contest for Robinson and Trukanini', in Anna Johnston and Mitchell Rolls (eds), *Reading Robinson: Companion Essays to Friendly Mission* (Hobart, Tas.: Quintus Publishing, 2008), p. 158. Others, such as Vivienne Rae-Ellis in a now rather discredited biography, have suggested that he was motivated only by vanity and greed. See Rae-Ellis, *Black Robinson*. As we shall see, both interpretations have their merits at various times in his career.
7. See Robinson's plan for the settlement at Bruny Island, 15 April 1829, in Plomley (ed.), *Friendly Mission*, p. 57.
8. Reynolds, *Fate of a Free People*, p. 132.
9. Robinson's diary entry, 15 November 1830, in Plomley (ed.), *Friendly Mission*, p. 310. See also the entry for 11 October 1829, p. 91, in which he compares the situation in Van Diemen's Land to a 'slave trade in miniature'.
10. See Plomley (ed.), *Friendly Mission, passim*. See in particular entry for 8 August 1830, p. 229, which describes a service. See also: 1 November 1830, p. 296, when Robinson comments that he is 'confident it was the work of God' that he was kept safe; 17 December 1830, p. 326, when he confides that he has 'reason to know that the work which I am engaged in is the work of God'.
11. George Arthur to Viscount Goderich, 10 January 1828, in A.G.L. Shaw (ed.), *Van Diemen's Land: Copies of All Correspondence between Lieutenant*

Notes

Governor Arthur and His Majesty's Secretary of State for the Colonies, on the Subject of the Military Operations Lately Carried Out against the Aboriginal Inhabitants of Van Diemen's Land (originally published by the House of Commons, 23 September 1831; facs. ed., Hobart, Tas.: Tasmanian Historical Association, 1971), p. 4.

12 Lyndall Ryan, *Tasmanian Aborigines: A History Since 1803* (Sydney, NSW: Allen & Unwin, 2012), p. 157.
13 Quoted in Plomley (ed.), *Friendly Mission*, p. 65.
14 Robinson's diary entry, 31 May 1829, in Plomley (ed.), *Friendly Mission*, p. 61.
15 See Robinson's diary entry, 9 July 1829, in Plomley (ed.), *Friendly Mission*, p. 69.
16 See for example Robinson's diary entry, 6 December 1829, in Plomley (ed.), *Friendly Mission*, p. 103.
17 Robinson's diary entry, 14 July 1830, in Plomley (ed.), *Friendly Mission*, p. 220.
18 George Murray to George Arthur, 5 November 1830, TNA: PRO CO 408/7, reproduced in Shaw (ed.), *Van Diemen's Land*, pp. 55–7.
19 See for example directors of the Van Diemen's Land Company to Edward Curr, 23 February 1831, ML FM 4/1567 (despatch No. 5).
20 Robinson described his pleasure at being the first person to lead a Christian service on this portion of the island in August 1830. See Robinson's diary entry, 8 August 1830, in Plomley (ed.), *Friendly Mission*, p. 229.
21 Ryan, *The Aboriginal Tasmanians*, p. 143.
22 See Robinson's diary for the period, in Plomley (ed.), *Friendly Mission*, pp. 296–330. Robinson wrote to Arthur from Swan Island during November 1830, and thus during 'the Line', to report that 'a successful intercourse has been effected among the sanguinary tribes of natives, who have for so great a period infected the settled districts and known as the Oyster Bay, Little swan port, Ben Lomond, Cape Portland and Pipers River aborigines'. George Augustus Robinson to George Arthur, 20 November 1830, AOT CSO 1/316/7578/2, f. 216.
23 George Augustus Robinson to George Arthur, 1 November 1830, AOT CSO 1/316/7578/4, ff. 38–9.
24 Robinson's diary entry, 15 November 1830, in Plomley (ed.), *Friendly Mission*, p. 313.
25 Robert Hughes described Robinson as an 'evangelical pied piper'. Quoted in Reynolds, *Fate of a Free People*, p. 135.
26 Reynolds, *Fate of a Free People*, pp. 135–43.
27 Robinson's diary entry, 10 November 1830, in Plomley (ed.), *Friendly Mission*, p. 305.
28 Robinson's diary entry, 1 November 1830, in Plomley (ed.), *Friendly Mission*, p. 296.

29 Robinson's diary entry, 2 November 1830, in Plomley (ed.), *Friendly Mission*, p. 300.
30 George Augustus Robinson to George Arthur, 20 November 1830, AOT CSO 1/316/7578/2, f. 216.
31 George Arthur to George Murray, 4 April 1831, TNA: PRO CO 280/28.
32 'Extract from the minutes of the executive council of Van Diemen's Land, 23 February 1831', TNA: PRO CO 280/28 (emphasis added).
33 George Arthur to George Murray, 4 April 1830, TNA: PRO CO 280/28.
34 Viscount Goderich to George Arthur, 19 October 1831, TNA: PRO CO 408/7.
35 Viscount Goderich to George Arthur, 5 May 1832, TNA: PRO CO 408/9.
36 George Arthur to Viscount Goderich, 25 October 1831, TNA: PRO CO 280/30. News of Thomas's murder was first communicated in G.A. Abbot to George Arthur, 17 September 1831, AOT CSO 1/316/7578/1, f. 961.
37 Report of the Aborigines Committee, 24 October 1831, TNA: PRO CO 280/30.
38 George Arthur to Viscount Goderich, 25 October 1831, TNA: PRO CO 280/30.
39 Ryan, *Tasmanian Aborigines*, p, 192; Boyce, *Van Diemen's Land*, p. 290.
40 For Arthur's account of the meeting, see TNA: PRO CO 280/30.
41 Robinson's diary entry, 21 October 1831, in Plomley (ed.), *Friendly Mission*, p. 522.
42 References from Plomley (ed.), *Friendly Mission*, pp. 523, 526.
43 Robinson's official report on the agreement, 30 January 1832, AOT CSO 1/316/7578/4, ff. 143–73. It is also reproduced in Plomley (ed.), *Friendly Mission*, p. 601.
44 See Robinson's diary entry, 14 December 1831, in Plomley (ed.), *Friendly Mission*, p. 585.
45 Reynolds, *Fate of a Free People*, p. 142.
46 From the petition to Queen Victoria that was received in London in March 1847, reproduced in Reynolds, *Fate of a Free People*, p. 7.
47 George Augustus Robinson to George Arthur, 5 January 1832, AOT CSO 1/316/7578/4, ff. 128–33.
48 George Arthur to George Murray, 4 April 1831, TNA: PRO CO 280/28.
49 Viscount Goderich to George Arthur, 21 June 1832, TNA: PRO CO 408/9.
50 George Arthur to the Colonial Secretary, 15 January 1832, in Plomley (ed.), *Friendly Mission*, p. 620.
51 Ryan, *The Aboriginal Tasmanians*, p. 162.
52 Robinson regularly communicated his movements to George Arthur. The fourth volume of the Colonial Secretary's Office Papers on the Aboriginals is dedicated to his reports in 'pursuit' of the natives. See AOT CSO 1/316/7578/4.
53 George Arthur to Viscount Goderich, 14 April 1832, TNA: PRO CO 280/34.

Notes

54 George Arthur to Viscount Goderich, 18 March 1833, TNA: PRO CO 280/41 (emphasis added). This letter included minutes of the Van Diemen's Land Executive Council discussions of Robinson's activities.
55 Robinson's diary entry, 3 September 1832, in Plomley (ed.), *Friendly Mission*, p. 682.
56 Robinson's diary entry, 16 July 1832, in Plomley (ed.), *Friendly Mission*, p. 665; Ryan, *Tasmanian Aborigines*, p. 205.
57 Robinson's diary entry, 18 September 1832, in Plomley (ed.), *Friendly Mission*, p. 693.
58 Ryan, *Tasmanian Aborigines*, p. 205.
59 Ibid., p. 206.
60 Robinson's diary entry, 21 May 1833, in Plomley (ed.), *Friendly Mission*, p. 762.
61 Robinson's diary entry, 3 August 1833, in Plomley (ed.), *Friendly Mission*, p. 811.
62 See for example his 'reflections' on 8 March 1834, in Plomley (ed.), *Friendly Mission*, p. 891.
63 Charles Darwin, *The Voyage of the Beagle: A Naturalist's Voyage around the World* (1839; London: John Murray, 1913), p. 475.
64 George Augustus Robinson to George Arthur, 17 October 1833, AOT CSO 1/316/7578/4, ff. 277–94.
65 Charles James Napier, *Colonization, Particularly in Southern Australia, with Some Remarks on Small Farms and Over-Population* (London: T. & W. Boone, 1835), p. 104.
66 George Arthur to Lord Glenelg, 22 July 1837, quoted in Henry Reynolds, *The Law of the Land* (Ringwood, Vic.: Penguin Australia, 1992), p. 94.
67 Robert Montgomery Martin, *History of the Colonies of the British Empire in the West Indies, South America, North America, Asia, Australasia, Africa and Europe* (London: W.H. Allen & Co., 1843), p. 450. Revenue from the sale of Crown lands was £1,979 in 1831 and £26,176 in 1836.
68 Plomley (ed.), *Friendly Mission*, p. 605, records a *Hobart Town Courier* report from 14 January 1832 welcoming the removal of the 'Aborigines'.
69 Martin, *History of the Colonies*, p. 453. There were 682,128 sheep in the colony in 1831, and 906,813 in 1836.
70 Lord Glenelg to John Franklin, 11 May 1837, TNA: PRO CO 408/14.
71 Rae-Ellis, *Black Robinson, passim*.
72 See Robinson's diary entry, 28 September 1836, in which he complains that 'the immense revenue arising from the sale of lands consequent on the increased value by the removal of the aborigines' counts for 'nothing', in N.J.B. Plomley (ed.), *Weep in Silence: A History of the Flinders Island Aboriginal Settlement* (Hobart, Tas.: Blubber Head Press, 1987), pp. 384–5.

FOUR · CULTURAL GENOCIDE

1   Henry Reynolds, *The Law of the Land* (Ringwood, Vic.: Penguin Australia, 1992), pp. 88–9.
2   Hodgkin's evidence to the select committee, in House of Commons, *Report from the Select Committee on Aborigines (British Settlements) with Minutes of Evidence, Appendix and Index* (1836), p. 455.
3   Zoe Laidlaw, '"Aunt Anna's report": The Buxton women and the Aborigines Select Committee, 1835–37', *Journal of Imperial and Commonwealth History* xxxii/1 (2004), p. 4.
4   James Stephen to Thomas Fowell Buxton, n.d. [1837], in Caroline Emilia Stephen, *The Right Honourable Sir James Stephen: Letters with Biographical Notes* (London: John Bellows, 1906).
5   *Morning Chronicle*, 2 July 1834.
6   House of Commons, *Report from the Select Committee* (1836), p. 508.
7   House of Commons, *Report of the Parliamentary Select Committee on Aboriginal Tribes (British Settlements)* (1837), p. vi, quoted in James Heartfield, *The Aborigines' Protection Society: Humanitarian Imperialism in Australia, New Zealand, Fiji, Canada, South Africa and the Congo, 1836–1909* (New York, NY: Columbia University Press, 2011), p. 9.
8   James Backhouse, *A Narrative of a Visit to the Australian Colonies* (London: Hamilton Adams, 1843), p. 174.
9   See 'Backhouse and Walker's report summer 1833–4', in N.J.B. Plomley (ed.), *Weep in Silence: A History of the Flinders Island Aboriginal Settlement* (Hobart, Tas.: Blubber Head Press, 1987), p. 269.
10   Alan Lester, 'Humanitarians and white settlers in the nineteenth century', in Norman Etherington (ed.), *Missions and Empire* (Oxford: Oxford University Press, 2005), p. 73.
11   See for example Dr John Philip to Thomas Fowell Buxton, 10 February 1843, RHL MSS Brit. Emp. s444, vol. 20a, pp. 355–7.
12   James Backhouse to Thomas Fowell Buxton, dated only 'the early part' of 1835, RHL MSS Brit. Emp. s444, vol. 13, pp. 411–12.
13   Ibid.
14   George Arthur to Thomas Fowell Buxton, 18 September 1834, RHL MSS Brit. Emp. s444, vol. 13, pp. 356–60.
15   House of Commons, *Report from the Select Committee* (1836), p. 24.
16   Ibid., p. 639.
17   Heartfield, *The Aborigines' Protection Society*, p. 20.
18   House of Commons, *Report of the Parliamentary Select Committee on Aboriginal Tribes (British Settlements)* (1837), p. vii.
19   See: Lester, 'Humanitarians and white settlers', p. 70; Patrick Brantlinger, *Dark Vanishings: Discourse on the Extinction of Primitive Races 1800–1930* (Ithaca, NY: Cornell University Press, 2003), p. 74.

20 Elizabeth Elbourne, 'The sin of the settler: The 1835–36 select committee on aborigines and debates over virtue and conquest in the early nineteenth-century British white settler empire', *Journal of Colonialism and Colonial History* iv/3 (2003).
21 Henry Fox Bourne, *The Aborigines' Protection Society: Chapters in Its History* (London: P.S. King, 1899), p. 60.
22 For a discussion of imperialist ideology see Patrick Brantlinger, *Rule of Darkness: British Literature and Imperialism 1830–1914* (Ithaca, NY: Cornell University Press, 1988), p. 3.
23 Reynolds, *The Law of the Land*, p. 80.
24 House of Commons, *Report of the Parliamentary Select Committee* (1837), p. 4.
25 Ibid., p. 2.
26 Ibid., p. vii.
27 Ibid.
28 Standish Motte, *Outline of a System of Legislation for Securing Protection to the Aboriginal Inhabitants of All Countries Colonised by Great Britain* (London: John Murray, 1840), p. 11.
29 John Docker, *The Origins of Violence: Religion, History and Genocide* (London: Pluto Press, 2008).
30 Aborigines' Protection Society, *The First Annual Report of the Aborigines' Protection Society* (London, 1838).
31 Lord Glenelg to Richard Bourke, 26 July 1837, in House of Commons, *Australian Aborigines: Copies or Extracts of Despatches Relative to the Massacre of Various Aborigines, in the Year 1838 and Respecting the Trial of Their Murderers* (1839), p. 3.
32 For Colonial Office support of the idea of a trial see Lord Glenelg to George Gipps, 16 November 1838, in House of Commons, *Australian Aborigines*, p. 26.
33 Lord Glenelg to George Gipps, 21 December 1838, in House of Commons, *Australian Aborigines*, p. 33 (emphasis added).
34 A.G.L. Shaw, 'British policy towards the Australian Aborigines, 1830–1850', *Australian Historical Studies* xxv/99 (1992), p. 272.
35 See George Arthur to Thomas Spring-Rice, 27 January 1835, TNA: PRO CO 280/55.
36 Lord Glenelg to George Arthur, 20 October 1835, TNA: PRO CO 408/12.
37 Lyndall Ryan, *Tasmanian Aborigines: A History Since 1803* (Sydney, NSW: Allen & Unwin, 2012), pp. 229–32.
38 Henry Reynolds, *Fate of a Free People* (Camberwell, Vic.: Penguin Australia, 2004), pp. 183–6.
39 Robinson's diary entry, 25 December 1835, in Plomley (ed.), *Weep in Silence*, p. 329.
40 Robinson's diary entry, 21 December 1835, in Plomley (ed.), *Weep in Silence*, p. 326.

41 Reynolds, *Fate of a Free People*, p. 166.
42 Ibid.
43 James Boyce, *God's Own Country? The Anglican Church and Tasmanian Aborigines* (Hobart, Tas.: Social Action and Research Centre, 2001), p. 37.
44 Robinson's 'Report on the Aboriginal establishments at Flinders Island, 24 June 1837', in House of Commons, *Australian Aborigines*, pp. 6–20.
45 Robinson described how he provided locks for cupboards in order to give a sense of individual ownership. See ibid.
46 Ibid.
47 Ibid.
48 House of Commons, *Report of the Parliamentary Select Committee* (1837), p. 84.
49 Vivienne Rae-Ellis, *Black Robinson: Protector of the Aborigines* (Melbourne, Vic.: Melbourne University Press, 1996), p. 164.
50 Reynolds, *Fate of a Free People*, p. 166.
51 See for example Robinson's diary entry, 22 February 1837, in which he reflects on the Big River people's ability to sing hymns in English, in Plomley (ed.), *Weep in Silence*, p. 426.
52 See Lord Glenelg to John Franklin, 8 January 1838, TNA: PRO CO 408/14 (despatch No. 241).
53 Lord Glenelg to George Gipps, 31 January 1838, in House of Commons, *Australian Aborigines*, pp. 4–5.
54 'The education of native races in British colonies', *Aborigines' Friend and Colonial Intelligencer*, January 1877.
55 Rae-Ellis, *Black Robinson*, p. 149. For correspondence between London and Hobart in which Robinson's appointment is discussed see James Stephen to George Arthur, 20 July 1837, in which Stephen enquires as to whether Robinson is still 'in full possession of his energies' for the task. ML CY 1025.
56 All of this is outlined in Lord Glenelg to George Gipps, 31 January 1838, in House of Commons, *Australian Aborigines*, pp. 4–5.
57 See George Gipps to Lord John Russell, 19 July 1841, in House of Commons, *Australian Aborigines*, p. 126.
58 Lord John Russell to George Gipps, 21 December 1839, in House of Commons, *Aborigines (Australian Colonies): Copies or Extracts from the Despatches of the Governors of the Australian Colonies, with the Reports of the Protectors of Aborigines, and Any Other Correspondence to Illustrate the Condition of the Aboriginal Population of the Said Colonies* (1844), p. 25.
59 Lord John Russell to George Gipps, 25 August 1840, in House of Commons, *Aborigines (Australian Colonies)*, p. 73.
60 Lord John Russell to George Gipps, 8 October 1840, in House of Commons, *Aborigines (Australian Colonies)*, p. 104.
61 Brantlinger, *Dark Vanishings*, p. 93.

Notes

62 Heartfield, *The Aborigines' Protection Society*, pp. 115–20. For a discussion of the idea of 'protection' in twentieth-century Australia, see Stephen Gray, *The Protectors: A Journey through Whitefella Past* (Sydney, NSW: Allen & Unwin, 2011).
63 *Aborigines' Friend and Colonial Intelligencer*, February 1875.
64 Alison Palmer, *Colonial Genocide* (Adelaide, SA: Crawford House Publishing, 2000), p. 49.
65 Lester, 'Humanitarians and white settlers', p. 80.
66 Shaw, 'British policy', p. 276.
67 Catherine Hall, *Civilising Subjects: Metropole and Colony in the English Imagination 1830–67* (Cambridge: Polity Press, 2002), p. 21, quoted in Alan Lester, 'Humanitarians and white settlers in the nineteenth century', in Norman Etherington (ed.), *Missions and Empire* (Oxford: Oxford University Press, 2005), p. 80.
68 Aborigines' Protection Society, *Seventh Annual Report of the Aborigines' Protection Society* (London: Smith, Elder & Co., 1844), p. 21.
69 John Franklin to Lord Glenelg, 3 August 1837, TNA: PRO CO 280/77 (despatch No. 83).
70 Quoted in Shaw, 'British policy', p. 275.
71 From an article in the *Monthly Chronicle* in June 1841, syndicated in the regional press. See for example the *Bury and Norwich Post*, 18 June 1841.
72 John Lort Stokes, *Discoveries in Australia* (London: T. & W. Boone, 1846), p. 470.
73 *Morning Post*, 30 May 1845.
74 John Dixon, *Condition and Capabilities of Van Diemen's Land as a Place of Emigration: Being the Experience of Nearly Ten Years' Residence in the Colony* (London: Smith, Elder & Co., 1839), p. 24.
75 See for example Lord Glenelg to John Franklin, 1 February 1838, TNA: PRO CO 408/14 (despatch No. 250).
76 Ryan, *Tasmanian Aborigines*, p. 237.
77 Rae-Ellis, *Black Robinson*, pp. 180–219.
78 Ryan, *Tasmanian Aborigines*, p. 244.
79 See for example George Gipps to Lord John Russell, 3 February 1841, in House of Commons, *Aborigines (Australian Colonies)*, p. 85, which contains reports of violence from the new colony.
80 George Augustus Robinson to Charles Joseph La Trobe, 20 August 1841, in House of Commons, *Aborigines (Australian Colonies)*, p. 132.
81 Quoted in Shaw, 'British policy', p. 280.
82 Lord Stanley to George Gipps, 20 December 1842, in House of Commons, *Aborigines (Australian Colonies)*, p. 221.
83 See for example the *Aborigines' Friend and Colonial Intelligencer*, May/June 1848.
84 Plomley (ed.), *Weep in Silence*, pp. 110–32.

85 Lyndall Ryan, *The Aboriginal Tasmanians* (Sydney, NSW: Allen & Unwin, 1996), p. 196.
86 Plomley (ed.), *Weep in Silence*, p. 134.
87 Ibid., p. 140.
88 Quoted in Nicholas Cree, *Oyster Cove: Last Home of the Tasmanian Aboriginal* (Latrobe, Vic.: Geneva Press, 1979), p. 34.
89 After he had been permanently removed from Flinders Island Jeanneret returned to England, where during the 1850s he launched a campaign aimed at exonerating his name. He wrote letters to the press (see the *Daily News*, 14 March 1853) and published several pamphlets. See for example Henry Jeanneret, *The Vindication of a Colonial Magistrate* (London: Hope & Co., 1854).
90 This is an extract from a report on Flinders Island written by Jeanneret in 1847, reproduced in Jeanneret, *Vindication*, p. 63.
91 For correspondence relating to the Jeanneret case see TNA: PRO CO 408/24, including Lord Stanley to John Eardley-Wilmot, 24 September 1844, and William Ewart Gladstone to John Eardley-Wilmot, 11 August 1845, in which Gladstone regretfully asks that Jeanneret be reinstated because he had not received proper hearing or been given the opportunity to answer allegations against him.
92 Reynolds, *Fate of a Free People*, p. 7.
93 Ryan, *Tasmanian Aborigines*, p. 247.
94 Reynolds, *Fate of a Free People*, p. 16.
95 Quoted in Ryan, *Tasmanian Aborigines*, p. 247.
96 Henry Grey to William Denison, 1 April 1847, TNA: PRO CO 408/28.
97 Henry Reynolds, *An Indelible Stain? The Question of Genocide in Australia's History* (Ringwood, Vic.: Penguin Australia, 2001), p. 101.
98 Cassandra Pybus, *Community of Thieves* (Port Melbourne, Vic.: Minerva Australia, 1992), p. 161.
99 Shaw, 'British policy', p. 283.
100 Ibid., p. 284.
101 Ryan, *The Aboriginal Tasmanians*, p. 205.
102 Plomley (ed.), *Weep in Silence*, p. 179.
103 *Aborigines' Friend and Colonial Intelligencer*, March 1850.
104 George W. Stocking, *Victorian Anthropology* (New York, NY: The Free Press, 1987), p. 275.
105 David Sampson, 'Strangers in a strange land: The 1868 Aborigines cricket tour and other indigenous performers in mid-Victorian Britain', PhD thesis, University of Technology, Sydney, 2000, p. 87.
106 See for example *The Times*, 5 February 1861.
107 This headline appeared in *The Times*, 28 December 1864.
108 A large report appeared for example in the *Illustrated London News*, 7 January 1865. Similar reports appeared in *Lloyds Weekly Newspaper*, 1 January 1865, and the *Royal Cornwall Gazette*, 6 January 1865.

Notes

109 Ryan, *Tasmanian Aborigines*, p. 267.
110 Robert Hughes, *The Fatal Shore: A History of the Transportation of Convicts to Australia 1787–1868* (London: Vintage, 2003), p. 641.
111 See the *Daily News*, 19 November 1869.
112 J.A. Langford, 'Truganini', *Gentleman's Magazine*, October 1876.
113 See for instance the *Ipswich Journal*, 10 October 1876.
114 In May 1834 Robinson reports a conversation with a group including Truganini about the indigenous Tasmanians accompanying him to England. He wrote: 'Some of them said how long should they remain, three moons?, when they were immediately checked by TRUGERNANNA who said that they were evidently under a mistake and that England was not like Flinders Island, they would have to remain a good many warm weathers. Others said they would be frightened.' See Robinson's diary entry, 20 May 1834, in N.J.B. Plomley (ed.), *Friendly Mission: The Tasmanian Journals and Papers of George Augustus Robinson 1829–1934* (2nd ed., Hobart, Tas.: Queen Victoria Museum and Art Gallery and Quintus Publishing, 2008), p. 914.
115 Ryan, *Tasmanian Aborigines*, p. 269.
116 *The Times*, 6 July 1876.

FIVE · GENOCIDE IN BRITISH CULTURE

1 *Independent on Sunday*, 19 April 2009 (emphasis added).
2 Bernard Porter, *The Absent-Minded Imperialists: What the British Really Thought about Empire* (Oxford: Oxford University Press, 2004). Porter's book is aimed at historians and especially literary scholars who assert the constancy of the presence of empire.
3 Bernard Porter, 'Further thoughts on imperial absent-mindedness', *Journal of Imperial and Commonwealth History* xxxvi/1 (2008), pp. 101–17.
4 Ibid., p. 110.
5 *Jackson's Oxford Journal*, 8 January 1825.
6 *The Examiner*, 17 October 1824. See also the *Morning Chronicle*, 20 September 1826.
7 *The Standard*, 5 August 1829.
8 'Another attack by the natives', shouted the headline in the *Morning Chronicle*, 25 May 1825.
9 See for example the *Morning Post*, 24 January 1824.
10 *Morning Chronicle*, 28 March 1829.
11 *Caledonian Mercury*, 20 April 1829.
12 *Morning Chronicle*, 23 April 1829.
13 *Berrow's Worcester Journal*, 19 May 1831.
14 *Royal Cornwall Gazette*, 28 April 1832.
15 See George Arthur to George Murray, 20 November 1830, in A.G.L. Shaw

(ed.), *Van Diemen's Land: Copies of All Correspondence between Lieutenant Governor Arthur and His Majesty's Secretary of State for the Colonies, on the Subject of the Military Operations Lately Carried Out against the Aboriginal Inhabitants of Van Diemen's Land* (originally published by the House of Commons, 23 September 1831; facs. ed., Hobart, Tas.: Tasmanian Historical Association, 1971), pp. 57–61.

16 *The Examiner*, 18 May 1831.
17 Anna Johnston, 'George Augustus Robinson, the "Great Conciliator": Colonial celebrity and its postcolonial aftermath', *Postcolonial Studies* xii/2 (2009), pp. 153–72.
18 *Caledonian Mercurcy*, 23 July 1832.
19 Johnston, 'George Augustus Robinson', p. 156.
20 *Morning Post*, 16 June 1834.
21 As a further example, in July 1835 the *Caledonian Mercury* reported the 'capture of the last native inhabitants' of Van Diemen's Land. See the *Caledonian Mercury*, 13 July 1835.
22 William Thomas Moncrieff, *Van Diemen's Land: An Operatic Drama in Three Acts* (London: Thomas Richardson, 1831).
23 David Sampson, 'Strangers in a strange land: The 1868 Aborigines cricket tour and other indigenous performers in mid-Victorian Britain', PhD thesis, University of Technology, Sydney, 2000, p. 72.
24 Moncrieff, *Van Diemen's Land*, p. 37.
25 John Heaviside Clark, *Field Sports of the Native Inhabitants of New South Wales* (London: Edward Orme, 1813).
26 Penelope Edmonds, '"Failing in every endeavour to conciliate": Governor Arthur's proclamation boards to the Aborigines, Australian conciliation narratives and their transnational connections', *Journal of Australian Studies* xxxv/2 (2011), pp. 201–18.
27 Tim Bonyhady, *The Colonial Image: Australian Painting 1800–1880* (Sydney, NSW: Australian National Gallery and Ellsyd Press, 1987), pp. 14–15.
28 Joseph Lycett, *Views in Australia or New South Wales and Van Diemen's Land* (London: John Souter, 1824).
29 Tim Bonyhady, *Images in Opposition: Australian Landscape Painting 1801–1890* (Melbourne, Vic.: Oxford University Press, 1985), p. 33.
30 Glover relayed to Robinson his disquiet about the relationship between a convict employed in a roving party and an indigenous women (Karnebutcher) in August 1831. See Robinson's diary entry, 12 December 1831, in which he reflects on the August meeting with Glover, in N.J.B. Plomley (ed.), *Friendly Mission: The Tasmanian Journals and Papers of George Augustus Robinson 1829–1934* (2nd ed., Hobart, Tas.: Queen Victoria Museum and Art Gallery and Quintus Publishing, 2008), p. 582.
31 See Robinson's diary entry, 5 January 1834, in Plomley (ed.), *Friendly Mission*, p. 868.

Notes

32   Robinson's diary entry, 22 March 1836, in N.J.B. Plomley (ed.), *Weep in Silence: A History of the Flinders Island Aboriginal Settlement* (Hobart, Tas.: Blubber Head Press, 1987), pp. 349–50.
33   Jeanette Hoorn, *Australian Pastoral: The Making of a White Landscape* (Fremantle, WA: Fremantle Press, 2007), p. 84.
34   From a letter John Glover to George Augustus Robinson, 16 July 1835, an extract from which is printed in Plomley (ed.), *Friendly Mission*, p. 971, n. 5.
35   Alan Lester, 'George Augustus Robinson and imperial networks', in Anna Johnston and Mitchell Rolls (eds), *Reading Robinson: Companion Essays to Friendly Mission* (Hobart, Tas.: Quintus Publishing, 2008), p. 27.
36   David Hansen (ed.), *John Glover and the Colonial Picturesque* (Hobart, Tas.: Tasmanian Museum and Art Gallery, 2003), pp. 71–2.
37   Two paintings are reported as being exhibited in July 1832. The *Morning Chronicle*, 26 July 1832, ran an article that briefly described them under the headline 'Fine arts in Van Diemen's Land'.
38   Hoorn, *Australian Pastoral*, p. 72.
39   Bonyhady, *Images in Opposition*, p. 28.
40   Ian McLean, 'Figuring nature: Painting the indigenous landscape', in David Hansen (ed.), *John Glover and the Colonial Picturesque* (Hobart, Tas.: Tasmanian Museum and Art Gallery, 2003), p. 125.
41   Ibid.
42   John Glover, *A Catalogue of Pictures Descriptive of the Scenery and Customs of the Inhabitants of Van Diemen's Land, Together with Views in England and Italy Painted by John Glover Esq.* (London, 1835).
43   Hansen (ed.), *John Glover*, p. 98.
44   Bill Gammage, *The Biggest Estate on Earth: How Aborigines Made Australia* (Sydney, NSW: Allen & Unwin, 2011), p. 19.
45   David Hansen, 'The picturesque and the Palawa: John Glover's *Mount Wellington and Hobart Town from Kangaroo Point*', in Timothy Barringer, Geoff Quilley and Douglas Fordham (eds), *Art and the British Empire* (Manchester: Manchester University Press, 2007), p. 46.
46   Glover, *Catalogue of Pictures*, picture No. 33.
47   *Court Journal: Gazette of the Fashionable World*, 27 June 1835.
48   Glover, *Catalogue of Pictures*, picture No. 45.
49   Ibid.
50   Ian McLean, *White Aborigines: Identity Politics in Australian Art* (Melbourne, Vic.: Cambridge University Press, 1998), pp. 40–2.
51   Bernard Smith, *European Vision and the South Pacific 1768–1850: A Study in the History of Art and Ideas* (Oxford: Clarendon Press, 1960), p. 483.
52   For example, Glover's last watercolour, *Corroboree of Natives in Van Diemen's Land* (1846), is particularly crude. See Hansen (ed.), *John Glover*, p. 241.
53   Nicholas Thomas, *Possessions: Indigenous Art / Colonial Culture* (London: Thames & Hudson, 1999), pp. 69–70.

54 Hansen (ed.), *John Glover*, p. 211.
55 Ibid., p. 102.
56 Hansen, 'The picturesque and the Palawa', p. 51.
57 Bonyhady, *Images in Opposition*, p. 24.
58 McLean, *White Aborigines*, p. 50 and *passim*.
59 McLean, 'Figuring nature', p. 128.
60 Bonyhady, *Images in Opposition*, p. 25.
61 Michael Rosenthal, 'Lost in the new world', *Guardian*, 27 March 2004.
62 Hansen (ed.), *John Glover*, p. 102.
63 *Court Journal: Gazette of the Fashionable World*, 27 June 1835.
64 *Morning Post*, 4 July 1835.
65 *Literary Gazette*, 4 July 1835.
66 Charles Wedge to the Saffron Walden Natural History Museum, 23 March 1835. Copy of letter held by Saffron Walden Museum.
67 *Aborigines' Friend and Colonial Intelligencer*, March 1847.
68 David Burn, *A Picture of Van Diemen's Land* (originally published in the *Colonial Magazine*, 1840–1; facs. ed., Hobart, Tas.: Cat and Fiddle Press, 1973).
69 John Lort Stokes, *Discoveries in Australia* (London: T. & W. Boone, 1846), p. 463.
70 See for example Louisa Anne Meredith, *Some of My Bush Friends in Tasmania: Native Flowers, Berries and Insects* (London: Day & Son, 1860).
71 Louisa Anne Meredith, *My Home in Tasmania: During a Residence of Nine Years* (London: John Murray, 1852), pp. 191, 212.
72 George Thomas Lloyd, *Thirty-Three Years in Tasmania and Victoria* (London: Houlston & Wright, 1862), pp. 54–5.
73 Francis R. Nixon, *The Cruise of the Beacon: A Narrative of a Visit to the Islands in Bass's Straits* (London: Bell & Daldy, 1857), p. 19.
74 Patrick Brantlinger, *Rule of Darkness: British Literature and Imperialism 1830–1914* (Ithaca, NY: Cornell University Press, 1988), pp. 127–9.
75 Nixon, *Cruise of the Beacon*, p. 19.
76 Brantlinger, *Rule of Darkness*, p. 12.
77 See for example Charles Rowcroft, *The Perils and Adventures of Mr William Thornley* (Launceston, Tas.: Walch Bros, 1916), based on a publication in London in 1846.
78 Meredith, *My Home in Tasmania*, p. 217.
79 Lloyd, *Thirty-Three Years*, p. 238. The source of this interpretation was probably Robinson himself.
80 Valerie Chancellor, *History for Their Masters: Opinion in the English History Textbook 1800–1914* (London: Adams & Dart, 1970), p. 137. A similar argument is made in Porter, *Absent-Minded Imperialists*, p. 70.
81 Patrick A. Dunae, 'Boys' literature and the idea of empire 1870–1914', *Victorian Studies* xxiv/1 (1980), p. 108.

Notes

82 See for example *Boy's Own Magazine*, November 1855, in which indigenous Australians in general were described as 'utterly unable to progress in any art or towards any comfort'.
83 *Boy's Own Paper*, 18 March 1882.
84 C.R. Low, 'A leaf out of a sailor's log', *Routledge's Every Boy's Annual*, n.d.
85 Quoted in Porter, *Absent-Minded Imperialists*, p. 71.
86 Ibid.
87 Quoted in Patrick Brantlinger, *Dark Vanishings: Discourse on the Extinction of Primitive Races 1800–1930* (Ithaca, NY: Cornell University Press, 2003), p. 6.
88 John West, *The History of Tasmania* (1852; Sydney, NSW: Royal Australian Historical Society, 1971), p. 330.
89 A.G.L. Shaw, 'Introduction', in West, *History* (1971), p. xxi.
90 West, *History* (1971), p. 332.
91 Coral Lansbury, *Arcady in Australia: The Evocation of Australia in Nineteenth-Century English Literature* (Melbourne, Vic.: Melbourne University Press, 1970), pp. 63–72.
92 Charles Dickens, 'The noble savage', *Household Words*, 11 June 1853.'
93 J.H. Davidson, 'Anthony Trollope and the colonies', *Victorian Studies* xii/3 (1969), p. 307.
94 Anthony Trollope, *Australia and New Zealand* (London: Chapman & Hall, 1873), p. 60.
95 Ibid., p. 76.
96 *The Times*, 19 November 1851.
97 Russell McGregor, *Imagined Destinies: Aboriginal Australians and the Doomed Race Theory 1880–1939* (Melbourne, Vic.: Melbourne University Press, 1998), p. 20.
98 *The Times*, 30 December 1864.
99 James Bonwick, *The Last of the Tasmanians, or, The Black War of Van Diemen's Land* (London: Sampson Low, Son & Marston, 1870).
100 Guy Featherstone, 'James Bonwick', *Australian Dictionary of National Biography* (Canberra, ACT: Australian National University, 2012).
101 See for example 'The extermination of Aborigines in Queensland', *Aborigines' Friend and Colonial Intelligencer*, August 1874.
102 Bonwick, *Last of the Tasmanians*, p. 36.
103 Ibid., p. 324.
104 Ibid., p. 31.
105 Ibid., p. 57.
106 *The Times*, 29 July 1869.
107 Brantlinger, *Dark Vanishings*, p. 2.
108 *Daily News*, 18 October 1869.
109 *Morning Post*, 24 December 1869.
110 *Pall Mall Gazette*, 15 May 1884.

111 John Cove, *What the Bones Say: Tasmanian Aborigines, Science and Domination* (Ottawa: Carleton University Press, 1995), p. 8.
112 Helen MacDonald, *Human Remains: Episodes in Human Dissection* (Melbourne, Vic.: Melbourne University Press, 2005), p. 108.
113 Robinson's diary entry, 22 June 1837, in Plomley (ed.), *Weep in Silence*, p. 455.
114 Robinson's diary entry, 26 January 1838, in Plomley (ed.), *Weep in Silence*, p. 530.
115 MacDonald, *Human Remains*, p. 94.
116 See correspondence from December 1861 in TNA: PRO CO 408/44.
117 Duke of Newcastle to J.C. Young, 26 December 1861, TNA: PRO CO 408/44.
118 Lyndall Ryan, *Tasmanian Aborigines: A History Since 1803* (Sydney, NSW: Allen & Unwin, 2012), p. 264.
119 MacDonald, *Human Remains*, pp. 120–3.
120 William Burke and William Hare murdered 16 people in Edinburgh in the 1820s in order to sell their bodies to Knox's Anatomy school. See ibid., p. 23.
121 Robert Knox, *The Races of Men: A Philosophical Enquiry into the Influence of Race over the Destinies of Nations* (London: Henry Renshaw, 1862), p. 229.
122 Ibid., p. v.
123 Charles Darwin, *The Descent of Man and Selection in Relation to Sex* (1871; London: Penguin, 2004), pp. 199–205.
124 On those new racial realities see Andrew Porter, 'Britain and the Empire in the nineteenth century', *The Oxford History of the British Empire: Vol. III: The Nineteenth Century* (Oxford: Oxford University Press, 1999), p. 23.
125 Darwin, *Descent of Man*, p. 212.
126 John George Wood, *The Natural History of Man: Being an Account of the Manners and Customs of the Uncivilised Races of Men* (London: George Routledge & Sons, 1870), p. 68.
127 Darwin, *Descent of Man*, p. 212.
128 John Lubbock, *The Origin of Civilisation and the Primitive Condition of Man* (London: Longmans, Green & Co., 1870), pp. viii, 1.
129 Cressida Fforde, *Collecting the Dead: Archaeology and the Reburial Issue* (London: Duckworth, 2004), p. 69.
130 Quoted in Cove, *What the Bones Say*, p. 61.
131 Quoted in Fforde, *Collecting the Dead*, p. 30.
132 W.J. Sollas, *Ancient Hunters and Their Modern Representatives* (London: Macmillan, 1911), p. 70.
133 Adam Kuper, *The Invention of Primitive Society: Transformations of an Illusion* (London: Routledge, 1988), p. 92.
134 Henry Balfour, 'Introduction', in Augustus Henry Lane-Fox Pitt-Rivers, *The Evolution of Culture and Other Essays*, ed. J.L. Myres (Oxford: Clarendon Press, 1906), p. xvi.

135 Henry Ling Roth, *The Aborigines of Tasmania* (Halifax: F. King & Sons, 1899), p. v.
136 George W. Stocking, *Victorian Anthropology* (New York, NY: The Free Press, 1987), p. 283.
137 Sollas, *Ancient Hunters*, p. 87.
138 Darwin, *Descent of Man*, p. 212.
139 Brantlinger, *Dark Vanishings*, p. 2.
140 James Erskine Calder, 'Some account of the wars of extirpation and habits of the native tribes of Tasmania', *Journal of the Anthropological Institute of Great Britain and Ireland* iii (1873–4), p. 15.
141 See Stefan Petrow, 'The last man: The mutilation of William Lanne in 1869 and its aftermath', *Aboriginal History* xxi (1997), pp. 90–112, on the local political context.
142 There are several accounts of Lanne's dismemberment available. See for example Fforde, *Collecting the Dead*, pp. 45–8.
143 Petrow, 'The last man', p. 96.
144 Fforde, *Collecting the Dead*, p. 47.
145 Ibid.
146 Petrow, 'The last man', p. 100.
147 Bonwick, *Last of the Tasmanians*, pp. 391–400.
148 Calder, 'Some account of the wars', p. 7.
149 MacDonald, *Human Remains*, p. 146.
150 Pitt-Rivers, *Evolution of Culture*, p. xvi.
151 Cove, *What the Bones Say*, p. 50.
152 J.G. Garson, 'Osteology', in Henry Ling Roth, *The Aborigines of Tasmania* (Halifax: F. King & Sons, 1899), p. 191.
153 MacDonald, *Human Remains*, p. 181.
154 There is, for example, a reference, written in 1958, to a 'good collection of Tasmanian skulls including King Billy, in the Anatomy department of Edinburgh University', in the Natural History Museum Archives. See NHM DF PAL/141/99/2.
155 Ling Roth, *The Aborigines of Tasmania*, p. 191.
156 Jane Weeks and Valerie Bott, *Scoping Survey of Historic Human Remains in English Museums Undertaken on Behalf of the Ministerial Working Group on Human Remains* (February 2003), appendix F.
157 See for example *The Times*, 28 July 1899.
158 See the correspondence from 1908 in which the use of Tasmanian skulls in public presentation is discussed between Charles Parker and Arthur Keith, RCS-MUS/5/3/3.
159 William Stearn, *The Natural History Museum at South Kensington* (London: Heinemann, 1981), p. 393.
160 William Henry Flower, *A General Guide to the British Museum (Natural History)* (London: William Clowes, 1887), p. 38.

161 British Museum (Natural History), Department of Zoology, *Guide to the Galleries of Mammalia (Mammalian, Osteological, Cetacean)* (London: Natural History Museum, 1885), p. 68.
162 British Museum (Natural History), Department of Zoology, *Guide to the Specimens Illustrating the Races of Mankind* (London: Natural History Museum, 1908), p. 33.
163 Fforde, *Collecting the Dead*, p. 38.
164 *The Times*, 29 July 1869.

SIX · COMING TO TERMS WITH THE PAST?

1   Richard Price, 'One big thing: Britain, its empire, and their imperial culture', *Journal of British Studies* xlv/3 (2006), p. 604.
2   For a very neat summary of the nature of post-colonial studies see Bill Schwarz, 'Conquerors of truth: Reflections on postcolonial theory', in Bill Schwarz (ed.), *The Expansion of England: Race, Ethnicity and Cultural History* (London: Routledge, 1996), pp. 9–31.
3   See for example George Le Hunte, 'The Aborigines of Australia', in Godfrey Lagden (ed.), *The Native Races of the Empire* (London: W. Collins Sons & Co., 1924), pp. 227–38. This was part of a multi-volume set published to coincide with the Empire Exhibition.
4   H.G. Wells, *The War of the Worlds*, ed. Patrick Parrinder and Andy Sawyer (London: Penguin Classics, 2005), p. 9.
5   Ibid., p. 188, n. 10.
6   John Sutherland, 'Devil take the hindmost', *London Review of Books* xvii/24 (14 December 1995).
7   Douglas Duff, *Palestine Picture* (London: Hodder & Stoughton, 1936), p. 68. I am very grateful for John Docker for drawing my attention to this reference, which he came across on the website *Middle East Reality Check*. Available at http://middleeastrealitycheck.blogspot.co.uk/2012/10/truganini-in-jerusalem.html (accessed 16 September 2013).
8   Sebastian Faulks, *Engleby* (London: Vintage, 2008), p. 205.
9   Ann Curthoys, 'Genocide in Tasmania: The history of an idea', in A. Dirk Moses (ed.), *Empire, Colony, Genocide: Conquest, Occupation, and Subaltern Resistance in World History* (New York, NY: Berghahn, 2008), p. 239.
10 Clive Turnbull, *Black War: The Extermination of the Tasmanian Aborigines* (Melbourne, Vic.: Cheshire-Lansdown, 1948), p. 3.
11 V.G. Kiernan, *The Lords of Human Kind: European Attitudes to the Outside World in the Imperial Age* (London: Penguin, 1972), p. 277.
12 Ibid., p. 276.
13 Jeremy Paxman, *Empire: What Ruling the World Did to the British* (London: Penguin, 2011), p. 165.
14 *Guardian*, 8 December 2000.

15 *Independent*, 18 March 2000.
16 Matthew Kneale, *English Passengers* (London: Penguin, 2000), p. 456.
17 It was broadcast on BBC2 on 23 May 1978. See the *Radio Times*, 20–26 May 1978, p. 39.
18 *Radio Times*, 10–16 June 1978, p. 67 (emphasis added). Many thanks to James Jordan for both *Radio Times* references.
19 *Guardian*, 23 September 1987. For other examples see John Spurling's play *The British Empire*, which was staged in Birmingham in 1980 and broadcast on BBC Radio 3 in 1982. See the review in the *Observer*, 28 November 1982. For a more contemporary newspaper reference to the 'complete genocide of the Aborigines in Tasmania', see *Guardian*, 15 August 1997.
20 Ian Hernon, *Britain's Forgotten Wars: Colonial Campaigns of the 19th Century* (Stroud, Gloucestershire: Sutton Publishing, 2003), p. 296 (emphasis added).
21 See for example the detailed account of the population of the islands of the Furneaux Group in *The Times*, 23 September 1890. This population was still being reported on some half a century later. See *The Times*, 23 April 1946.
22 Henry Ling Roth, *The Aborigines of Tasmania* (Halifax: F. King & Sons, 1899), Appendix G.
23 See for example 'Lord Northcliffe on Tasmania: Ideal holiday place', *The Times*, 22 September 1921.
24 See George Porter, *Wanderings in Tasmania* (London: Selwyn & Blount, 1934), and the review of that publication in the *Guardian*, 25 October 1934.
25 Andrew Markus, 'William Cooper and the 1937 petition to the king', *Aboriginal History* vii (1983), pp. 46–61.
26 *The Times*, 25 November 1937.
27 I have been unable to find definitive evidence of when the skulls were removed from public display. The Natural History Museum speculated in correspondence with me in 2012 that displays were removed in the 1950s.
28 Lyndall Ryan, *Tasmanian Aborigines: A History Since 1803* (Sydney, NSW: Allen & Unwin, 2012), p. 319.
29 For a detailed analysis of regional museums' collections in reference to imperial identity, see Claire Loughney, 'Colonialism and the development of the English provincial museum', PhD thesis, University of Newcastle, 2006.
30 Len Pole, *World Connections: World Cultures Collections in the South West of England* (South West Museums Council, 2000), p. 37.
31 Fragment of a local newspaper, n.d. [21 October 1933], RAMM.
32 From a photograph of the display provided by the Royal Albert Memorial Museum, Exeter.
33 Ryan, *Tasmanian Aborigines*, p. 269.
34 Tasmanian Museum report, cited in John Cove, *What the Bones Say: Tasmanian Aborigines, Science and Domination* (Ottawa: Carleton University Press, 1995), pp. 143–4.

35 Cove, *What the Bones Say*, p. 150.
36 See various correspondence between the Natural History Museum and the Tasmanian Museum and Art Gallery in Hobart, NHM DF PAL/141/99/2.
37 For a discussion of the fate of race science in the aftermath of World War II, see Gavin Schaffer, *Racial Science and British Society, 1930–62* (Basingstoke: Palgrave Macmillan, 2008), pp. 120–32.
38 Quoted in Cressida Fforde, *Collecting the Dead: Archaeology and the Reburial Issue* (London: Duckworth, 2004), p. 97.
39 Jane Hubert, 'Human remains: Objects to study or ancestors to bury' [transcript of debate, 2 May 2003]. Available at www.instituteofideas.com/transcripts/human_remains.pdf (accessed 26 August 2013).
40 Jeanette James, Laurie Lowery and Caroline Spotswood, *Free Exchange or Captive Culture? The Tasmanian Aboriginal Perspective on Museums and Repatriation: Paper Presented at the Museums Association Seminar, Museums and Repatriation, London, 4 November 1997* (Hobart, Tas.: Tasmanian Aboriginal Centre, 1997), p. 4.
41 Mark Cocker, *Rivers of Blood, Rivers of Gold: Europe's Conflict with Tribal Peoples* (London: Pimlico, 1999), p. 184.
42 Fforde, *Collecting the Dead*, pp. 124–5.
43 'Minutes of University Court, 10 December 1990', Special Collections, University of Edinburgh.
44 United Nations, *Declaration on the Rights of Indigenous Peoples* (2 October 2007), UN Doc A/RES/61/295. Available at http://www.un.org/ga/search/view_doc.asp?symbol=A/RES/61/295 (accessed 30 August 2013).
45 See Fforde, *Collecting the Dead*, pp. 90–2.
46 For a review of this policy see Tim Sullivan, Lynda Kelly and Phil Gordon, 'Museums and indigenous people in Australia: A review of *Previous Possessions, New Obligations*: Policies for museums in Australia and Aboriginal and Torres Strait islander peoples', *Curator: The Museum Journal* xlvi/2 (2010), pp. 208–27.
47 James, Lowery and Spotswood, *Free Exchange or Captive Culture?*, p. 8.
48 Fforde, *Collecting the Dead*, pp. 126–7.
49 John Howard, 'Press release: Joint Statement with Tony Blair on Aboriginal remains' (4 July 2000). Previously available at http://www.pm.gov.au/news/media_releases/2000/Aboriginal_4-7.htm (link no longer working).
50 Department for Culture, Media and Sport, *Report of the Working Group on Human Remains* (2003). Available at http://webarchive.nationalarchives.gov.uk/20100113212249/http://www.culture.gov.uk/reference_library/publications/4553.aspx (accessed 29 August 2013).
51 Department for Culture, Media and Sport, *Guidance for the Care of Human Remains in Museums* (2005).
52 See for example: 'Policy on human remains held by the University of Oxford's museums', *Oxford University Gazette* (Supplement to No. 4787, 15 November 2006); Natural History Museum, *Policy on Human Remains* (2010).

Notes

53 Marion Tewkesbury to John Allan (Curator of Antiquities, Royal Albert Memorial Museum), 3 August 1994, RAMM.
54 See N.J.B. Plomley, 'A list of Tasmanian Aboriginal material in collections in Europe', *Records of the Queen Victoria Museum, Launceston*, new ser., 15 (1962), pp. 1–18.
55 John Wells to the directors of the Royal Albert Memorial Museum, 8 June 1994, RAMM.
56 John Allan to John Wells, 21 June 1994, RAMM.
57 John Wells to John Allan, 25 July 1994, RAMM.
58 From 'The repatriation of Truganini's necklace and bracelet' (unpublished manuscript, 2011), a narrative given to the author by Len Pole, former curator at the Royal Albert Memorial Museum in Exeter.
59 Exeter City Council, Leisure Committee, 'Disposal of museum artefacts' (14 March 1995), RAMM.
60 Anonymous to John Allan, 7 June 1994, RAMM.
61 Fforde, *Collecting the Dead*, p. 123.
62 See 'Extract from a paper discussed at a meeting of the University Court on 5 November 1990', Special Collections, University of Edinburgh.
63 See ibid.
64 'Extract from Minute of Court held on 9 July 1990', Special Collections, University of Edinburgh.
65 'Extract from Senatus Minutes, University of Edinburgh, 5 December 1990' (Appendix D1 (2)), Special Collections, University of Edinburgh.
66 DCMS, *Report of the Working Group*, p. 51.
67 Ibid., p. 45.
68 Ibid., p. 35.
69 See for example: 'Bones of contention', *Guardian*, 9 July 2002; 'The long road home', *Observer*, 28 June 2009.
70 G.L. Pullar quoted in Tristram Besterman, 'Returning the ancestors'. Available at http://www.museum.manchester.ac.uk/collection/humanremains/fileuploadmax10mb,120894,en.pdf (accessed 30 August 2013).
71 Quoted in the *Observer*, 28 September 2003.
72 Robert Foley, 'Should human parts in museums be returned to their place of origin? No', *BBC History Magazine*, July 2003, p. 51.
73 See 'Statement of dissent from Neil Chalmers', reproduced in Department for Culture, Media and Sport, *Care of Historic Human Remains: A Consultation of the Working Group on Human Remains* (2004), pp. 62–8.
74 Kenan Malik, 'Who owns knowledge?', *Index on Censorship* (2007). Available at http://www.kenanmalik.com/essays/index_knowledge.html (accessed 26 August 2013) (emphasis added).
75 From a debate held by the Institute of Ideas, 2 May 2003. Available at http://www.instituteofideas.com/transcripts/human_remains.pdf (accessed 25 September 2013).

76 Quoted in the *Observer*, 28 September 2003.
77 Quoted in Fforde, *Collecting the Dead*, p. 159.
78 Cocker, *Rivers of Blood*, p. 184.
79 DCMS, *Report of the Working Group*, p. 33.
80 Ibid., p. 38.
81 Ibid., p. 53.
82 Tasmanian Aboriginal Centre, 'Tasmanian Aboriginal Centre submission to the trustees of the Natural History Museum for the repatriation of Tasmanian Aboriginal human remains' (2006). Sent to the author by the Natural History Museum on request (paper HRAP/0610/4a).
83 Natural History Museum, *Report on NHM Human Remains from Tasmania* (2006) (emphasis added). Sent to the author by the Natural History Museum on request (paper HRAP/0610/4b).
84 'Minutes of the meeting of the trustees of the Natural History Museum, Item 1008' stated that 'the act of return should follow the completion of generation of data that will be of continuing uses in science for generating new knowledge'. Sent to the author by the Natural History Museum on request.
85 *The Times*, 12 May 2007.
86 Len Pole, 'Pacific collections in the Saffron Walden museum' (unpublished manuscript, 1995), p. 12.
87 David Olusoga, *White Slaves: Black War* (Oxford: Oxford University Press, forthcoming).
88 *Independent*, 29 April 1996.
89 William Rees-Mogg, 'We're still waiting for those apologies', *The Times*, 20 April 1998.

CONCLUSION

1 From a leaflet titled *Tombstone Trail: Bath Abbey Cemetery* produced by the Widcombe Association (emphasis added).

BIBLIOGRAPHY

ARCHIVAL AND MANUSCRIPT SOURCES

Archives Office of Tasmania, Hobart

AOT CSO Colonial Secretary's Office Papers.

Mitchell Library, Sydney

ML CY 1025 Sir George Arthur – Papers, 1821–55, vol. 28: Aborigines.
ML CY 2343 William Sorell – Papers, 1817–24.
ML CYA 2164 Sir George Arthur – Papers, 1821–55, vol. 4: Correspondence with James Stephen.
ML FM 4/1564; 4/1567 Van Diemen's Land Company – Records 1824–1954.

National Archives, Public Record Office, London

TNA: PRO CO 280 Colonial Office: Tasmania, Original Correspondence (1825–72).
TNA: PRO CO 408 Colonial Office and Predecessor: Tasmania, Entry Books (1825–72).

Natural History Museum Archives, London

NHM DF PAL/141/99/2 Primate File: Tasmania, 1955–8.

Rhodes House Library, University of Oxford

RHL MSS Brit. Emp. s444 Papers of Sir Thomas Fowell Buxton, 1786–1845.

Royal Albert Memorial Museum Archives, Exeter

[Papers relating to Truganini's necklace.]

Royal College of Surgeons Archive, London

RCS-MUS/5/3/3 Museum Letters 1908.

The Last Man

Saffron Walden Museum

[Papers relating to the Wedge collection.]

Special Collections, University of Edinburgh

[Papers relating to the return of Tasmanian human remains (available on request).]

OFFICIAL PAPERS

Bathurst, Henry, and House of Commons, *Van Diemens Land: Return to an Address of the Honourable House of Commons, Dated 10th May 1825; for Minutes of the Intended Arrangements between Earl Bathurst... and the Proposed Van Diemens Land Company* (1825).

Bigge, John Thomas, *Report of the Commissioner of Inquiry on the State of Agriculture and Trade in the Colony of New South Wales* (1823).

Department for Culture, Media and Sport, *Report of the Working Group on Human Remains* (2003).

—— *Care of Historic Human Remains: A Consultation of the Working Group on Human Remains* (2004).

—— *Guidance for the Care of Human Remains in Museums* (2005).

House of Commons, *Report from the Select Committee on Aborigines (British Settlements) with Minutes of Evidence, Appendix and Index* (1836).

—— *Copy of a Despatch from Colonel Arthur to Lord Glenelg Dated the 29th October 1836* (1837).

—— *Report of the Parliamentary Select Committee on Aboriginal Tribes (British Settlements)* (1837).

—— *Australian Aborigines: Copies or Extracts of Despatches Relative to the Massacre of Various Aborigines, in the Year 1838 and Respecting the Trial of Their Murderers* (1839).

—— *Aborigines (Australian Colonies): Copies or Extracts from the Despatches of the Governors of the Australian Colonies, with the Reports of the Protectors of Aborigines, and Any Other Correspondence to Illustrate the Condition of the Aboriginal Population of the Said Colonies* (1844).

Shaw, A.G.L. (ed.), *Van Diemen's Land: Copies of All Correspondence between Lieutenant Governor Arthur and His Majesty's Secretary of State for the Colonies, on the Subject of the Military Operations Lately Carried Out against the Aboriginal Inhabitants of Van Diemen's Land* (originally published by the House of Commons, 23 September 1831; facs. ed., Hobart, Tas.: Tasmanian Historical Association, 1971).

Bibliography

PUBLISHED BOOKS AND ARTICLES

Aborigines' Protection Society, *The First Annual Report of the Aborigines' Protection Society* (London, 1838).

——— *Seventh Annual Report of the Aborigines' Protection Society* (London: Smith, Elder & Co., 1844).

Arendt, Hannah, *The Origins of Totalitarianism* (New York, NY: Schocken Books, 2004).

Attwood, Bain, *Telling the Truth about Aboriginal History* (Crows Nest, NSW: Allen & Unwin, 2005).

Backhouse, James, *A Narrative of a Visit to the Australian Colonies* (London: Hamilton Adams, 1843).

Barta, Tony, 'Relations of genocide: Land and lives in the colonization of Australia', in Isidor Wallimann and Michael N. Dobkowski (eds), *Genocide and the Modern Age: Etiology and Case Studies of Mass Death* (Westport, CT: Greenwood Press, 1987), pp. 237–51.

——— '"They appear actually to vanish from the face of the earth." Aborigines and the European project in Australia Felix', *Journal of Genocide Research* x/4 (2008), pp. 519–39.

Besterman, Tristram, 'Returning the ancestors'. Available at http://www.museum.manchester.ac.uk/collection/humanremains/fileuploadmax10mb,120894,en.pdf (accessed 30 August 2013).

Bischoff, James, *Sketch of the History of Van Diemen's Land and an Account of the Van Diemen's Land Company* (London: John Richardson, 1832).

——— *A Comprehensive History of the Woollen and Worsted Manufactures and the Natural and Commercial History of Sheep* (London: Smith, Elder & Co., 1842).

Blair, Tony, *A Journey* (London: Hutchinson, 2010).

Bloxham, Donald, *The Great Game of Genocide: Imperialism, Nationalism and the Destruction of the Ottoman Armenians* (Oxford: Oxford University Press, 2005).

Bonwick, James, *The Last of the Tasmanians, or, The Black War of Van Diemen's Land* (London: Sampson Low, Son & Marston, 1870).

Bonyhady, Tim, *Images in Opposition: Australian Landscape Painting 1801–1890* (Melbourne, Vic.: Oxford University Press, 1985).

——— *The Colonial Image: Australian Painting 1800–1880* (Sydney, NSW: Australian National Gallery and Ellsyd Press, 1987).

Boyce, James, *God's Own Country? The Anglican Church and Tasmanian Aborigines* (Hobart, Tas.: Social Action and Research Centre, 2001).

——— *Van Diemen's Land* (Melbourne, Vic.: Black, Inc., 2010).

Brantlinger, Patrick, *Rule of Darkness: British Literature and Imperialism 1830–1914* (Ithaca, NY: Cornell University Press, 1988).

——— *Dark Vanishings: Discourse on the Extinction of Primitive Races 1800–1930* (Ithaca, NY: Cornell University Press, 2003).

Brendon, Piers, *The Decline and Fall of the British Empire* (London: Vintage, 2008).
British Museum (Natural History), Department of Zoology, *Guide to the Galleries of Mammalia (Mammalian, Osteological, Cetacean)* (London: Natural History Museum, 1885).
—— *Guide to the Specimens Illustrating the Races of Mankind* (London: Natural History Museum, 1908).
Burn, David, *A Picture of Van Diemen's Land* (originally published in the *Colonial Magazine*, 1840–1; facs. ed., Hobart, Tas.: Cat and Fiddle Press, 1973).
Butlin, N.G., *Our Original Aggression: Aboriginal Populations of Southeastern Australia 1788–1850* (Sydney, NSW: Allen & Unwin, 1983).
Calder, Graeme, *Levee, Line and Martial Law: A History of the Dispossession of the Mairremmener People of Van Diemen's Land* (Launceston, Tas.: Fullers Bookshop, 2010).
Calder, James Erskine, 'Some account of the wars of extirpation and habits of the native tribes of Tasmania', *Journal of the Anthropological Institute of Great Britain and Ireland* iii (1873–4), pp. 7–28.
Campbell, Alastair H., *John Batman and the Aborigines* (Malmsbury, Vic.: Kibble Books, 1987).
Campbell, Judy, *Invisible Invaders: Smallpox and Other Diseases in Aboriginal Australia 1780–1880* (Melbourne, Vic.: Melbourne University Press, 2002).
Chalk, Frank, and Kurt Jonassohn (eds), *The History and Sociology of Genocide* (New Haven, CT: Yale University Press, 1990).
Chancellor, Valerie, *History for Their Masters: Opinion in the English History Textbook 1800–1914* (London: Adams & Dart, 1970).
Chapman, Peter (ed.), *Historical Records of Australia, Resumed Series III, Despatches and Papers Relating to the History of Tasmania, Volume VII, January to December 1828* (Canberra, ACT: Commonwealth Parliamentary Library, 1997).
Chase, Bob, 'History and poststructuralism: Hayden White and Fredric Jameson', in Bill Schwarz (ed.), *The Expansion of England: Race, Ethnicity and Cultural History* (London: Routledge, 1996), pp. 61–91.
Clendinnen, Inga, *Dancing with Strangers: The True History of the Meeting of the British First Fleet and the Aboriginal Australians, 1788* (London: Canongate, 2005).
Cocker, Mark, *Rivers of Blood, Rivers of Gold: Europe's Conflict with Tribal Peoples* (London: Pimlico, 1999).
Connor, John, *The Australian Frontier Wars 1788–1838* (Sydney, NSW: University of New South Wales Press, 2002).
Cove, John, *What the Bones Say: Tasmanian Aborigines, Science and Domination* (Ottawa: Carleton University Press, 1995).
Cree, Nicholas, *Oyster Cove: Last Home of the Tasmanian Aboriginal* (Latrobe, Vic.: Geneva Press, 1979).

Bibliography

Curr, Edward, *An Account of the Colony of Van Diemen's Land* (London: George Cowie & Co., 1824).

Curthoys, Ann, 'Genocide in Tasmania: The history of an idea', in A. Dirk Moses (ed.), *Empire, Colony, Genocide: Conquest, Occupation, and Subaltern Resistance in World History* (New York, NY: Berghahn, 2008), pp. 229–52.

Darwin, Charles, *The Voyage of the Beagle: A Naturalist's Voyage Around the World* (1839; London: John Murray, 1913).

—— *The Descent of Man and Selection in Relation to Sex* (1871; London: Penguin, 2004).

Davidson, J.H., 'Anthony Trollope and the colonies', *Victorian Studies* xii/3 (1969), pp. 305–30.

Dickens, Charles, 'The noble savage', *Household Words*, 11 June 1853.

Dixon, John, *Condition and Capabilities of Van Diemen's Land as a Place of Emigration: Being the Experience of Nearly Ten Years' Residence in the Colony* (London: Smith, Elder & Co., 1839).

Docker, John, *The Origins of Violence: Religion, History and Genocide* (London: Pluto Press, 2008).

—— 'The "great Australian silence" and the "indelible stain": Genocide denial, historical consciousness, and the honour of nations and empires' (forthcoming).

Dow, Gwyneth and Hume, *Landfall in Van Diemen's Land: The Steels' Quest for Greener Pastures* (Footscray, Vic.: Footprint, 1990).

Duff, Douglas, *Palestine Picture* (London: Hodder & Stoughton, 1936).

Dunae, Patrick A., 'Boys' literature and the idea of empire 1870–1914', *Victorian Studies* xxiv/1 (1980), pp. 105–21.

Edmonds, Penelope, '"Failing in every endeavour to conciliate": Governor Arthur's proclamation boards to the Aborigines, Australian conciliation narratives and their transnational connections', *Journal of Australian Studies* xxxv/2 (2011), pp. 201–18.

Elbourne, Elizabeth, 'The sin of the settler: The 1835–36 select committee on aborigines and debates over virtue and conquest in the early nineteenth-century British white settler empire', *Journal of Colonialism and Colonial History* iv/3 (2003).

Evans, George William, *History and Description of the Present State of Van Diemen's Land, Containing Important Hints to Emigrants* (London: John Souter, 1824).

Faulks, Sebastian, *Engleby* (London: Vintage, 2008).

Featherstone, Guy, 'James Bonwick', *Australian Dictionary of National Biography* (Canberra, ACT: Australian National University, 2012).

Ferguson, Niall, *Empire: How Britain Made the Modern World* (London: Penguin, 2003).

Fforde, Cressida, *Collecting the Dead: Archaeology and the Reburial Issue* (London: Duckworth, 2004).

Finzsch, Norbert, "'...Extirpate or remove that vermine": Genocide, biological warfare, and settler imperialism in the eighteenth and early nineteenth century', *Journal of Genocide Research* x/2 (2008), pp. 215-32.

Fitzmaurice, Andrew, 'The genealogy of *Terra nullius*', *Australian Historical Studies* xxxviii/129 (2007), pp. 1-15.

Flower, William Henry, *A General Guide to the British Museum (Natural History)* (London: William Clowes, 1887).

Foley, Robert, 'Should human parts in museums be returned to their place of origin? No', *BBC History Magazine*, July 2003, p. 51.

Fox Bourne, Henry, *The Aborigines' Protection Society: Chapters in Its History* (London: P.S. King, 1899).

Gammage, Bill, *The Biggest Estate on Earth: How Aborigines Made Australia* (Sydney, NSW: Allen & Unwin, 2011).

Garson, J.G., 'Osteology', in Henry Ling Roth, *The Aborigines of Tasmania* (Halifax: F. King & Sons, 1899), pp. 191-217.

Glover, John, *A Catalogue of Pictures Descriptive of the Scenery and Customs of the Inhabitants of Van Diemen's Land, Together with Views in England and Italy Painted by John Glover Esq.* (London, 1835).

Gray, Stephen, *The Protectors: A Journey through Whitefella Past* (Sydney, NSW: Allen & Unwin, 2011).

Hall, Catherine, *Civilising Subjects: Metropole and Colony in the English Imagination 1830-67* (Cambridge: Polity Press, 2002).

Hansen, David, 'The picturesque and the Palawa: John Glover's *Mount Wellington and Hobart Town from Kangaroo Point*', in Timothy Barringer, Geoff Quilley and Douglas Fordham (eds), *Art and the British Empire* (Manchester: Manchester University Press, 2007), pp. 38-52.

Hansen, David (ed.), *John Glover and the Colonial Picturesque* (Hobart, Tas.: Tasmanian Museum and Art Gallery, 2003).

Heartfield, James, *The Aborigines' Protection Society: Humanitarian Imperialism in Australia, New Zealand, Fiji, Canada, South Africa and the Congo, 1836-1909* (New York, NY: Columbia University Press, 2011).

Heaviside Clark, John, *Field Sports of the Native Inhabitants of New South Wales* (London: Edward Orme, 1813).

Hernon, Ian, *Britain's Forgotten Wars: Colonial Campaigns of the 19th Century* (Stroud, Gloucestershire: Sutton Publishing, 2003).

Hoorn, Jeanette, *Australian Pastoral: The Making of a White Landscape* (Fremantle, WA: Fremantle Press, 2007).

Hughes, Robert, *The Fatal Shore: A History of the Transportation of Convicts to Australia 1787-1868* (London: Vintage, 2003).

Jeanneret, Henry, *The Vindication of a Colonial Magistrate* (London: Hope & Co., 1854).

Jeffreys, Charles, *Van Diemen's Land: Geographical and Descriptive Delineations of the Island* (London: J.M. Richardson, 1820).

Bibliography

Johnston, Anna, 'George Augustus Robinson, the "Great Conciliator": Colonial celebrity and its postcolonial aftermath', *Postcolonial Studies* xii/2 (2009), pp. 153–72.

Kiernan, Ben, *Blood and Soil: A World History of Genocide and Extermination from Sparta to Darfur* (New Haven, CT: Yale University Press, 2009).

Kiernan, V.G., *The Lords of Human Kind: European Attitudes to the Outside World in the Imperial Age* (London: Penguin, 1972).

Knaplund, Paul, *James Stephen and the British Colonial System 1813–1847* (Madison, WI: University of Wisconsin Press, 1953).

Kneale, Matthew, *English Passengers* (London: Penguin, 2000).

Knopwood, Robert, *The Diary of the Reverend Robert Knopwood 1803–1838*, ed. Mary Nicholls (Hobart, Tas.: Tasmanian Historical Research Association, 1977).

Knox, Robert, *The Races of Men: A Philosophical Enquiry into the Influence of Race over the Destinies of Nations* (London: Henry Renshaw, 1862).

Kuper, Adam, *The Invention of Primitive Society: Transformations of an Illusion* (London: Routledge, 1988).

Lagden, Godfrey (ed.), *The Native Races of the Empire* (London: W. Collins Sons & Co., 1924).

Laidlaw, Zoe, '"Aunt Anna's report": The Buxton women and the Aborigines Select Committee, 1835–37', *Journal of Imperial and Commonwealth History* xxxii/1 (2004), pp. 1–28.

Lansbury, Coral, *Arcady in Australia: The Evocation of Australia in Nineteenth-Century English Literature* (Melbourne, Vic.: Melbourne University Press, 1970).

Lawson, Tom, *Debates on the Holocaust* (Manchester: Manchester University Press, 2010).

—— 'Bishop Bell and the trial of German war criminals: A moral history', in Andrew Chandler (ed.), *The Church and Humanity: The Life and Work of George Bell* (London: Ashgate, 2012), pp. 129–48.

Lawson, Tom, and James Jordan (eds), *The Memory of the Holocaust in Australia* (London: Vallentine Mitchell, 2008).

Lester, Alan, 'Humanitarians and white settlers in the nineteenth century', in Norman Etherington (ed.), *Missions and Empire* (Oxford: Oxford University Press, 2005), pp. 64–85.

—— 'George Augustus Robinson and imperial networks', in Anna Johnston and Mitchell Rolls (eds), *Reading Robinson: Companion Essays to Friendly Mission* (Hobart, Tas.: Quintus Publishing, 2008), pp. 27–43.

Levene, Mark, *Genocide in the Age of the Nation State, Vol. II: The Rise of the West and the Coming of Genocide* (London: I.B.Tauris, 2005).

Levi, Neil, '"No sensible comparison"? The place of the Holocaust in Australia's history wars', *History and Memory* xix/1 (2007), pp. 124–56.

Ling Roth, Henry, *The Aborigines of Tasmania* (Halifax: F. King & Sons, 1899).

Lloyd, George Thomas, *Thirty-Three Years in Tasmania and Victoria* (London: Houlston & Wright, 1862).

Lower, Wendy, *Nazi Empire-Building and the Holocaust in the Ukraine* (Chapel Hill, NC: University of North Carolina Press, 2005).

Lubbock, John, *The Origin of Civilisation and the Primitive Condition of Man* (London: Longmans, Green & Co., 1870).

Lycett, Joseph, *Views in Australia or New South Wales and Van Diemen's Land* (London: John Souter, 1824).

MacDonald, Helen, *Human Remains: Episodes in Human Dissection* (Melbourne, Vic.: Melbourne University Press, 2005).

McFarlane, Ian, *Beyond Awakening: The Aboriginal Tribes of North West Tasmania* (Launceston, Tas.: Fullers Bookshop, 2008).

McGregor, Russell, *Imagined Destinies: Aboriginal Australians and the Doomed Race Theory 1880–1939* (Melbourne, Vic.: Melbourne University Press, 1998).

Macintyre, Stuart, and Anna Clark, *The History Wars* (Melbourne, Vic.: Melbourne University Press, 2003).

McLean, Ian, *White Aborigines: Identity Politics in Australian Art* (Melbourne, Vic.: Cambridge University Press, 1998).

—— 'Figuring nature: Painting the indigenous landscape', in David Hansen (ed.), *John Glover and the Colonial Picturesque* (Hobart, Tas.: Tasmanian Museum and Art Gallery, 2003), pp. 122–33.

Madley, Benjamin, 'Patterns of frontier genocide', *Journal of Genocide Research* vi/2 (2004), pp. 167–92.

Malik, Kenan, 'Who owns knowledge?', *Index on Censorship* (2007). Available at http://www.kenanmalik.com/essays/index_knowledge.html (accessed 26 August 2013).

Manne, Robert (ed.), *Whitewash: On Keith Windschuttle's Fabrication of Aboriginal History* (Melbourne, Vic.: Black, Inc., 2003).

Markus, Andrew, 'William Cooper and the 1937 petition to the king', *Aboriginal History* vii (1983), pp. 46–61.

Martin, Robert Montgomery, *History of the Colonies of the British Empire in the West Indies, South America, North America, Asia, Australasia, Africa and Europe* (London: W.H. Allen & Co., 1843).

Meaney, Neville, '"In history's page": Identity and myth', in Deryck M. Schreuder and Stuart Ward (eds), *Australia's Empire* (Oxford: Oxford University Press, 2009), pp. 369–87.

Mear, Craig, 'The origin of the smallpox outbreak in Sydney in 1789', *Journal of the Royal Australian Historical Society* xciv/1 (2008), pp. 1–14.

Melvern, Linda, *A People Betrayed: The Role of the West in Rwanda's Genocide* (London: Zed Books, 2000).

Melville, Henry, *The History of the Island of Van Diemen's Land: From the Year 1824 to 1835* (London: Smith, Elder & Co., 1835).

Bibliography

Meredith, Louisa Anne, *My Home in Tasmania: During a Residence of Nine Years* (London: John Murray, 1852).

—— *Some of My Bush Friends in Tasmania: Native Flowers, Berries and Insects* (London: Day & Son, 1860).

Moncrieff, William Thomas, *Van Diemen's Land: An Operatic Drama in Three Acts* (London: Thomas Richardson, 1831).

Morgan, Sharon, *Land Settlement in Early Tasmania: Creating an Antipodean England* (Cambridge: Cambridge University Press, 1992).

Moses, A. Dirk, 'An Antipodean genocide? The origins of the genocidal moment in the colonization of Australia', *Journal of Genocide Research* ii/1 (2000), pp. 89–106.

—— 'Genocide and Holocaust consciousness in Australia', *History Compass* i/1 (2003), pp. 1–11.

—— 'Empire, colony, genocide: Keywords and the philosophy of history', in A. Dirk Moses (ed.), *Empire, Colony, Genocide: Conquest, Occupation, and Subaltern Resistance in World History* (New York, NY: Berghahn, 2010), pp. 3–54.

Motte, Standish, *Outline of a System of Legislation for Securing Protection to the Aboriginal Inhabitants of All Countries Colonised by Great Britain* (London: John Murray, 1840).

Napier, Charles James, *Colonization, Particularly in Southern Australia, with Some Remarks on Small Farms and Over-Population* (London: T. & W. Boone, 1835).

National Inquiry into the Separation of Aboriginal and Torres Strait Islander Children from Their Families, *Bringing Them Home* (1997).

Natural History Museum, *Report on NHM Human Remains from Tasmania* (2006).

—— *Policy on Human Remains* (2010).

Nixon, Francis R., *The Cruise of the Beacon: A Narrative of a Visit to the Islands in Bass's Straits* (London: Bell & Daldy, 1857).

Olusoga, David, *White Slaves: Black War* (Oxford: Oxford University Press, forthcoming).

Palmer, Alison, *Colonial Genocide* (Adelaide, SA: Crawford House Publishing, 2000).

Paxman, Jeremy, *Empire: What Ruling the World Did to the British* (London: Penguin, 2011).

Pearce, Andy, 'The development of Holocaust consciousness in contemporary Britain, 1979–2001', *Holocaust Studies: A Journal of Culture and History* xiv/2 (2008), pp. 71–94.

Petrow, Stefan, 'The last man: The mutilation of William Lanne in 1869 and its aftermath', *Aboriginal History* xxi (1997), pp. 90–112.

Pink, Kerry, *Winds of Change: A History of Woolnorth* (Timaru, New Zealand: Van Diemen's Land Company, 2003).

Pitt-Rivers, Augustus Henry Lane-Fox, *The Evolution of Culture and Other Essays*, ed. J.L. Myres (Oxford: Clarendon Press, 1906).

Plomley, N.J.B., 'A list of Tasmanian Aboriginal material in collections in Europe', *Records of the Queen Victoria Museum, Launceston*, new ser., 15 (1962), pp. 1–18.

—— *Jorgen Jorgenson and the Aborigines of Van Diemen's Land* (Hobart, Tas.: Blubber Head Press, 1991).

Plomley, N.J.B. (ed.), *Weep in Silence: A History of the Flinders Island Aboriginal Settlement* (Hobart, Tas.: Blubber Head Press, 1987).

—— *Friendly Mission: The Tasmanian Journals and Papers of George Augustus Robinson 1829–1934* (2nd ed., Hobart, Tas.: Queen Victoria Museum and Art Gallery and Quintus Publishing, 2008).

Pole, Len, *World Connections: World Cultures Collections in the South West of England* (South West Museums Council, 2000).

'Policy on human remains held by the University of Oxford's museums', *Oxford University Gazette* (Supplement to No. 4787, 15 November 2006).

Porter, Andrew, 'Britain and the Empire in the nineteenth century', *The Oxford History of the British Empire: Vol. III: The Nineteenth Century* (Oxford: Oxford University Press, 1999).

Porter, Bernard, *The Absent-Minded Imperialists: What the British Really Thought about Empire* (Oxford: Oxford University Press, 2004).

—— 'Further thoughts on imperial absent-mindedness', *Journal of Imperial and Commonwealth History* xxxvi/1 (2008), pp. 101–17.

Porter, George, *Wanderings in Tasmania* (London: Selwyn & Blount, 1934).

Price, Richard, 'One big thing: Britain, its empire, and their imperial culture', *Journal of British Studies* xlv/3 (2006), pp. 602–27.

Prinsep, Mrs Augustus, *The Journal of a Voyage from Calcutta to Van Diemen's Land, Comprising a Description of That Colony During a Six Months' Residence* (London: Smith, Elder & Co., 1833).

Pybus, Cassandra, *Community of Thieves* (Port Melbourne, Vic.: Minerva Australia, 1992).

Rae-Ellis, Vivienne, *Black Robinson: Protector of the Aborigines* (Melbourne, Vic.: Melbourne University Press, 1996).

Reynolds, Henry, *The Law of the Land* (Ringwood, Vic.: Penguin Australia, 1992).

—— *An Indelible Stain? The Question of Genocide in Australia's History* (Ringwood, Vic.: Penguin Australia, 2001).

—— *Fate of a Free People* (Camberwell, Vic.: Penguin Australia, 2004).

—— 'Genocide in Tasmania', in A. Dirk Moses (ed.), *Genocide and Settler Society: Frontier Violence and Stolen Indigenous Children in Australian History* (New York, NY: Berghahn, 2004), pp. 127–49.

—— *A History of Tasmania* (Melbourne, Vic.: Cambridge University Press, 2012).

Richards, Eric, *Britannia's Children: Emigration from England, Scotland, Wales and Ireland since 1600* (London: Hambledon Press, 2004).

Rowcroft, Charles, *The Perils and Adventures of Mr William Thornley* (Launceston, Tas.: Walch Bros, 1916).

Ryan, Lyndall, *The Aboriginal Tasmanians* (Sydney, NSW: Allen & Unwin, 1996).

Bibliography

—— 'Historians, friendly mission and the contest for Robinson and Trukanini', in Anna Johnston and Mitchell Rolls (eds), *Reading Robinson: Companion Essays to Friendly Mission* (Hobart, Tas.: Quintus Publishing, 2008), pp. 147–59.
—— *Tasmanian Aborigines: A History Since 1803* (Sydney, NSW: Allen & Unwin, 2012).
—— 'List of multiple killings of Aborigines in Tasmania: 1804–35', *Online Encyclopedia of Mass Violence*. Available at http://www.massviolence.org/List-of-multiple-killings-of-Aborigines-in-Tasmania-1804?cs=print (accessed 29 August 2013).
Schaffer, Gavin, *Racial Science and British Society, 1930–62* (Basingstoke: Palgrave Macmillan, 2008).
Schreuder, Deryck M., and Stuart Ward (eds), *Australia's Empire* (Oxford: Oxford University Press, 2009).
Schwarz, Bill, 'Conquerors of truth: Reflections on postcolonial theory', in Bill Schwarz (ed.), *The Expansion of England: Race, Ethnicity and Cultural History* (London: Routledge, 1996), pp. 9–31.
Shaw, A.G.L., 'British attitudes to the colonies', *Journal of British Studies* ix/1 (1969), pp. 71–95.
—— 'British policy towards the Australian Aborigines, 1830–1850', *Australian Historical Studies* xxv/99 (1992), pp. 265–85.
Short, Damien, 'Australia: A continuing genocide?', *Journal of Genocide Research* xii/1–2 (2010), pp. 45–68.
Smith, Bernard, *European Vision and the South Pacific 1768–1850: A Study in the History of Art and Ideas* (Oxford: Clarendon Press, 1960).
Sollas, W.J., *Ancient Hunters and Their Modern Representatives* (London: Macmillan, 1911).
Stearn, William, *The Natural History Museum at South Kensington* (London: Heinemann, 1981).
Stephen, Caroline Emilia, *The Right Honourable Sir James Stephen: Letters with Biographical Notes* (London: John Bellows, 1906).
Stocking, George W., *Victorian Anthropology* (New York, NY: The Free Press, 1987).
Stokes, John Lort, *Discoveries in Australia* (London: T. & W. Boone, 1846).
Sullivan, Tim, Lynda Kelly and Phil Gordon, 'Museums and indigenous people in Australia: A review of *Previous Possessions, New Obligations*: Policies for museums in Australia and Aboriginal and Torres Strait islander peoples', *Curator: The Museum Journal* xlvi/2 (2010), pp. 208–27.
Sutherland, John, 'Devil take the hindmost', *London Review of Books* xvii/24 (14 December 1995).
Tatz, Colin, 'Genocide in Australia', *Journal of Genocide Research* i/3 (1999), pp. 315–52.
—— 'Genocide in Australia: By accident or design?', *Indigenous Human Rights and History: Occasional Papers* i/1 (2011).

Taylor, Rebe, *Unearthed: The Aboriginal Tasmanians of Kangaroo Island* (Kent Town, SA: Wakefield Press, 2002).
Thomas, Nicholas, *Possessions: Indigenous Art / Colonial Culture* (London: Thames & Hudson, 1999).
Trollope, Anthony, *Australia and New Zealand* (London: Chapman & Hall, 1873).
Turnbull, Clive, *Black War: The Extermination of the Tasmanian Aborigines* (Melbourne, Vic.: Cheshire-Lansdown, 1948).
Wedge, John Helder, *The Diaries of John Helder Wedge*, eds Justice Crawford, W.F. Ellis and G.H. Stancombe (Hobart, Tas.: Royal Society of Tasmania, 1962).
Weeks, Jane, and Valerie Bott, *Scoping Survey of Historic Human Remains in English Museums Undertaken on Behalf of the Ministerial Working Group on Human Remains* (February 2003).
Wells, H.G., *The War of the Worlds*, ed. Patrick Parrinder and Andy Sawyer (London: Penguin Classics, 2005).
West, John, *The History of Tasmania, Vol. II* (1852; Launceston, Tas.: J.S. Waddell, 1966).
—— *The History of Tasmania* (1852; Sydney, NSW: Royal Australian Historical Society, 1971).
Wood, John George, *The Natural History of Man: Being an Account of the Manners and Customs of the Uncivilised Races of Men* (London: George Routledge & Sons, 1870).

UNPUBLISHED THESES AND OTHER MATERIAL

Howard, John, 'Press release: Joint Statement with Tony Blair on Aboriginal remains' (4 July 2000). Previously available at http://www.pm.gov.au/news/media_releases/2000/Aboriginal_4-7.htm (link no longer working).
Hubert, Jane, 'Human remains: Objects to study or ancestors to bury' [transcript of debate, 2 May 2003]. Available at www.instituteofideas.com/transcripts/human_remains.pdf (accessed 26 August 2013).
James, Jeanette, Laurie Lowery and Caroline Spotswood, *Free Exchange or Captive Culture? The Tasmanian Aboriginal Perspective on Museums and Repatriation: Paper Presented at the Museums Association Seminar, Museums and Repatriation, London, 4 November 1997* (Hobart, Tas.: Tasmanian Aboriginal Centre, 1997).
Loughney, Claire, 'Colonialism and the development of the English provincial museum', PhD thesis, University of Newcastle, 2006.
Pole, Len, 'Pacific collections in the Saffron Walden museum' (unpublished manuscript, 1995).
—— 'The repatriation of Truganini's necklace and bracelet' (unpublished manuscript, 2011).
Sampson, David, 'Strangers in a strange land: The 1868 Aborigines cricket tour

and other indigenous performers in mid-Victorian Britain', PhD thesis, University of Technology, Sydney, 2000.

Tasmanian Aboriginal Centre, 'Tasmanian Aboriginal Centre submission to the trustees of the Natural History Museum for the repatriation of Tasmanian Aboriginal human remains' (2006).

United Nations, *Declaration on the Rights of Indigenous Peoples* (2 October 2007), UN Doc A/RES/61/295. Available at http://www.un.org/ga/search/view_doc.asp?symbol=A/RES/61/295 (accessed 30 August 2013).

INDEX

Abolitionists 43, 72, 91, 93, 94, 95, 96, 161, 176, 205
Aboriginal and Torres Strait Islander Commission 186, 194
'Aboriginality' 122, 179, 186
Aborigines Committee (Hobart) 32, 36–7, 47, 55, 77, 79, 82, 97
Aborigines Protection Society 100–1, 110–11, 115, 121, 146, 155, 160, 176, 197
Allport, Morton 159–60
Arthur, Lieutenant-Governor George xvii, 6, 32–3, 55, 108, 118, 131, 134, 203
and the Black War 42–4, 46, 48–56, 58–60
and conciliation 70–7
and deportation policy 78–84
and economic development of Van Diemen's Land 87–90
and the Goldie Affair 60, 64–7
and the Select Committee on Aborigines 96–8
Arthur, Mary Ann 116, 155
Arthur, Walter George 104–5, 113, 114
and the petition to Queen Victoria 116–18

Backhouse, James 95–6
Barta, Tony 23
Bartholomew, Thomas 79
Bathurst, Lord Henry 44–5, 59, 101
Batman, John 53–4, 63, 138, 147, 201
Bennelong 133–4
Big River People 31, 80–2, 84, 131, 141–2
Bigge, Thomas 39
Bischoff, James 60
Black War 6–8, 44–56
reporting in Britain 129–31
Bonwick, James 8–9, 36, 129, 154–7, 166, 169
Bourke, Governor Richard 101
Bourne, Henry Fox 97
Boyce, James 7, 11, 31, 61, 70, 82, 87–8
Brantlinger, Patrick 109, 143, 149, 164
Briggs, Dolly 37
Bringing them Home, 15, 20–1
British Empire Exhibition 175
Broughton, William 97
Bruny Island 7, 69–73
Burn, David 146
Bushrangers 42, 46, 134
Buxton, Thomas Fowell 91, 94, 96–100, 107, 110

Index

Calder, James-Erskine 164
Cape Barren Island 179–80
Chalmers, Neil, 195
Chesson, Frederick 108
Clark, Bessy 121, 159
Clark, John Heaviside 134
Clendinnen, Inga 16–17, 22
Cochrane-Smith, Fanny 180
Coexistence between settler and indigenous communities 5, 11, 37–8, 105
Colonial Office 12–13, 24, 32, 42, 64, 66, 70
   and Aboriginal policy after 1840 112–20
   and the Black War 44–60
   and the collection of human remains in Tasmania 159
   and ethnic cleansing in Van Diemen's Land 73–87
   and Flinders Island settlement (Wybalenna) 101–11
   and the Select Committee on Aborigines 94–6, 98
   summary of role in genocide 203–6
Cooper, William 180
Cove, John 184
Crowther, William 165, 167–8, 185, 187

Denison, William 118, 120
Dickens, Charles 152, 156
Dillon, Rodney 195
Disease (and role in genocide) 7, 22–3, 75, 86, 104, 164, 205
Docker, John 100
Duff, Douglas 176–7
Duterrau, Benjamin 136

Emigration to Van Diemen's Land 39–41, 64–6
Englishness 41
Exeter 100, 182, 190–2
Exeter City Council 192
Extermination discourse (dying race theory) 23, 41–2, 112–16, 121
Extinction, myth of 9, 179–82

Faulks, Sebastian 177
Fforde, Cressida 168, 194
First contact between British and indigenous Tasmanians 3–5, 30–7
Flinders Island (see also Wybalenna) 2, 7, 17, 20–4, 69, 84, 86, 89, 91–3, 96, 99, 101–9, 112–14, 116–24, 132, 141, 150, 158–9, 205–6, 209
Flower, William Henry 160
Foley, Robert 196–7
Furneaux Islands 179

Genocide xvi–xviii, xx–xxi
   in Australian history 15–28
   and Britain 12–14, 27
   previous accounts of 8–15
Gentleman's Magazine 123
Gipps, Governor George 102, 107, 109, 114
Glenelg, Lord (Charles Grant) 89, 94, 101–3, 105, 107–8, 111
Goderich, Lord (Frederick John Robinson) 64, 67, 78, 83–4, 89, 103
Great Exhibition 121
Grey, Lord Henry 119–21

Index

Hernon, Ian 179
'History wars' xviii, 15–17
Hobart Town Courier 132
Hobart Town Gazette 35
Hobler, George 48
Hodgkin, Thomas 93, 97, 98, 100
Holocaust, the xv, 16, 171–20, 25–6, 173, 177–8, 208
  memory of xvi–xvii, xx
Human Origins (debate on) 129, 157–64
Human Remains
  collection of 32, 158–9, 165–7
  debate on return of 182–200
  display of 168–71
Human Remains Working Group 190, 194, 199
Hunterian Museum (*see also* Royal College of Surgeons) 159, 169
Huskisson, William 50–1

Independent 201

Jeanneret, Henry 116–18
Jeffreys, Charles 40
Jones, Rhys 179
Jorgenson, Jorgen 52, 58

Keating, Paul 14
Kiernan, V.G. 177–8
Kneale, Matthew 178
Knight, Charles 150
Knopwood, Robert 32, 35–7, 58
Kuper, Adam 163

Lanne, William 2, 122, 155, 157, 183, 185, 187, 193
  dismemberment of corpse 165–7

Launceston 37, 47, 138
Lemkin, Raphael 9, 20, 25
Levene, Mark 19
Leverhulme Centre for Human Evolutionary Studies (Cambridge) 195
'The Line' 6, 29, 57–8, 60, 64–5, 69, 75–7, 79, 88, 130–1, 137, 203
  memory of 80
Lloyd, George Thomas 147, 149
Lubbock, John 163
Lycett, Thomas 135, 137–8

Macleod, Donald 39
Macquarie Harbour 85
Malik, Kenan 196, 200
Mannalargenna 80
Mansell, Michael 190
Maulboyheenner 113
Melville, Henry 8, 55, 57, 112
Meredith, Louisa 147, 149
Moncrieff, William Thomas 133–4
Morning Post 38, 145, 157
Mouheneenner Clan 5
Mountgarret, Jacob 32, 37
Murray, Sir George xviii–xix, 33, 51, 64, 75, 83
  approval of use of force 51–4
  and the Goldie Affair 59–60
  and indelible stain dispatch 56–8
Musquito 46
Myall Creek Massacre 101

Natural History Museum (London) 169, 185, 189, 194–5, 199–200

Index

Netley Hospital (Southampton) 168
New South Wales 1–2, 31, 36, 39, 43, 44, 46, 71
New Zealand 146, 152
Nuenonne Clan 73–4

Oyster Bay People 29, 31, 46, 82, 84, 131, 141–2
Oyster Cove 119–22, 155, 159

Paxman, Jeremy 178
Pevay 113–14
Phillips, Thomas 144
Pitt-Rivers Museum, Oxford 159, 169, 190
Plomley, Brian 4
Porter, Bernard 128, 150
Pybus, Cassandra 64

Queensland xix, 18, 19, 110, 155

Radio Times 179
Rees-Mogg, William 202
Reynolds xii, xviii–xix, 9, 11–12, 14–15, 17, 19, 25, 30, 51, 57–60, 64, 76, 81–2, 98, 104, 117–19
Risdon Cove, massacre at 29, 31–3, 38, 41, 96, 147–8, 156, 158, 204
Robinson, George Augustus 7, 33–4, 48, 69, 92, 96, 118, 123–4, 178, 205–6
   and 1831 agreement 78–83
   at Bruny Island 73–4
   and economic development 87–90
   emigration to Hobart 70–1
   and Flinders Island settlement (Wybalenna) 102–9
   grave 209
   and human remains 158–9, 200
   motivation of 71–2
   relationship with John Glover 136, 141
   reporting of in Britain 131–3, 149
   role in 'bringing in' indigenous Tasmanians 75–6
   and the Select Committee on Aborigines 98–9
   and transfer to Port Philip 113–116
   and the use of force 77, 84–6
Robertson, Gilbert 47
Rothberg, Michael 177
Royal Albert Memorial Museum (Exeter) 181–2, 190, 192
Royal College of Surgeons 165, 168, 189–90
Russell, Lord John 109, 111, 114, 119
Ryan, Lyndall 4–6, 11, 14, 49–50, 75, 104, 116, 181

Saffron Walden Museum 65, 146, 181, 201
Select Committee on Aborigines (British Settlements) 94–101
Shaw, A.G.L. 120
Sheep farming (in Van Diemen's Land) 40–3, 60, 88–9
Smith, Bernard 140
Sollas, W.J. 163–4
Sorell, William 5–6, 35, 38, 42
South Australia 99, 103
Spring-Rice, Thomas 94
Stanley, Lord 114–15

Index

Stephen, Alfred 59
Stephen, James 42–4, 94, 111, 114, 118–20
Stocking, George 164
Stokell, George 165
Stokes, John Lort 112, 147
Swan Island 76–7
Swindon 181, 201

Talisker, Donald 39
Tasmanian Aboriginal Centre 168, 182–3, 185–91, 198–200
Tasmanian Museum and Art Gallery (Hobart) 183–5
Tatz, Colin 18, 48
terra nullius 3, 34–5
Tewkesbury, Marion 190
Times, The 123, 153–4, 156, 171, 181, 200, 202
Tongerlongter 158
Trollope, Anthony 24, 152–4, 156
Truganini ix, 2, 7, 73, 93, 104, 113, 116, 122–3, 155, 179–80, 182–7, 190–2, 197
Turnbull, Clive 9, 177

University of Cambridge 189–90, 195, 197
University of Edinburgh 157, 168, 187–93, 197

Van Diemen's Land Company 59–64
Vattel, Emer de 34
Vermillion Accord 188

Wedge, John Helder 40, 65–6, 146, 181, 201
Wells, H.G. 175–6
Wells, John 191
West, John 8, 13, 30, 39, 151–2
Western Australia 110
Widcombe 209
Windschuttle, Keith 16–17
Wood, John George 161
Wood-Jones, Frederic 181–2
Woorraddy 73, 85, 113, 181, 201
World Archaeological Congress 188
Wybalenna (*see also* Flinders Island) 7, 16–17, 23, 69, 86, 103–5, 107, 113, 119

1   Gov. Arthur's Proclamation to the Tasmanian Peoples, 1830

2 *My Harvest Home* by John Glover

3 *A Corrobery of Natives in Mills Plains* by John Glover

4 *Mount Wellington and Hobart Town from Kangaroo Point* by John Glover

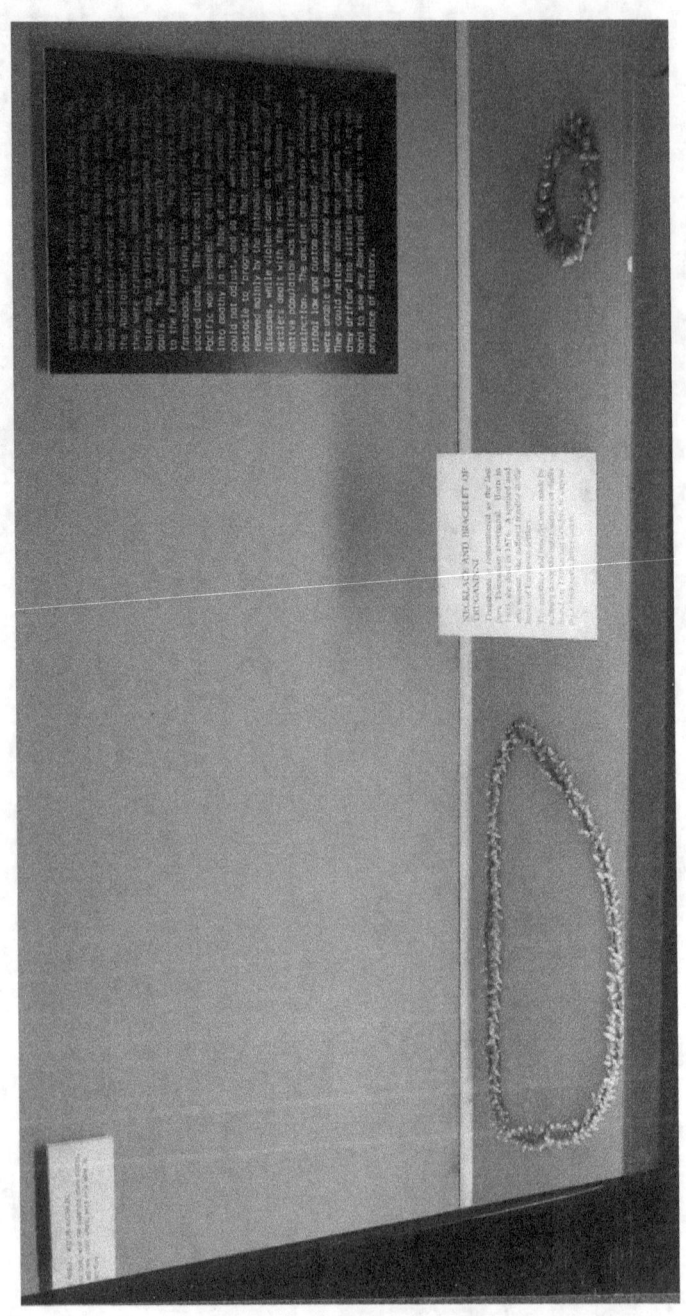

5 Truganini Necklace from Exeter Museum

6 George Augustus Robinson's grave

7   *Natives at a Corrobory,* under the wild woods of the Country [River Jordan below Brighton, Tasmania], ca. 1835

8   *The Conciliation* by Benjamin Duterreau

www.ingramcontent.com/pod-product-compliance
Lightning Source LLC
Chambersburg PA
CBHW060944230426
43665CB00015B/2061